THE
DIETER'S
CALORIE COUNTER

THE
DIETER'S
CALORIE COUNTER

CORINNE T. NETZER

A DELL TRADE PAPERBACK

A DELL TRADE PAPERBACK

Published by
Dell Publishing Co., Inc.
1 Dag Hammarskjold Plaza
New York, New York 10017

Dell ® TM 681510, Dell Publishing Co., Inc.

Printed in the United States of America
First printing—May 1983

LIBRARY OF CONGRESS CATALOGING IN PUBLICATION DATA

Netzer, Corinne T.
The dieter's calorie counter.

1. Food—Caloric content—Tables.   I. Title.
TX551.N4   1983   641.1'042   82-25268
ISBN 0-440-52086-X

INTRODUCTION

The Dieter's Calorie Counter is the most complete book of caloric listings ever published. It is a total compilation of both basic generic foods and brand-name foods, all integrated and alphabetized under one cover.

Because this book is alphabetized, you should have no trouble finding whatever food you want to look up. However, there are instances where you may have to look in more than one place. If you are looking for a specific food and cannot find it immediately, look for it under a category, such as cakes, pies, cookies, soups. Wherever sensible, I have cross-referenced listings, but the pressure of space has made it impossible to do that for every item.

All of the foods included in *The Dieter's Calorie Counter* have been listed in useful household portions. And similar foods are generally listed in uniform measures. However, this was not possible—or even reasonable—in certain cases. All crackers, for example, could have been listed in a standard one-ounce measure, but that would mean you would have to weigh a cracker in order to determine its caloric content. Hence, crackers and various other foods are listed by the piece, as packaged by the manufacturer. This means that although you can determine the calories in an individual cracker, you should *not* compare different varieties of crackers (or other foods listed by the piece) because they may vary a great deal in size.

Since the purpose of this book is to help you lose weight, remember also to compare only foods that are listed in similar measures. Do not compare foods listed in *dis*similar measures. This rule particularly applies to the confusion between measures by capacity and measures by weight. Eight ounces is not necessarily equivalent to eight fluid ounces or one cup. Eight ounces is a measure of how much something weighs; a cup is a measure of how much space it occupies. For example, a cup of lightweight food, such as puffed rice or popcorn, weighs about one ounce, and eight ounces of the same product would fill many cups.

Naturally, you can convert a similar unit of measure into a smaller or larger amount. The following table may be useful in making such conversions.

Equivalents by Capacity
(all measures level)

1 quart	=	4 cups
1 cup	=	8 fluid ounces
	=	½ pint
	=	16 tablespoons
2 tablespoons	=	1 fluid ounce
1 tablespoon	=	3 teaspoons

Equivalents by Weight

1 pound	=	16 ounces
3.57 ounces	=	100 grams
1 ounce	=	28.35 grams

All the material in *The Dieter's Calorie Counter* is based on information from the United States Government and from producers and processors of all brand-name foods. The data contained herein is the most complete and accurate information available as this book goes to press. However, bear in mind that the food industry often changes recipes and sizes, and may discontinue a product or add new ones. In the future I will be revising and updating this book to keep you completely informed.

Good luck and good dieting.

CORINNE T. NETZER

ABBREVIATIONS IN THIS BOOK

cond. .... condensed

diam. .... diameter

fl. .... fluid

″ .... inch

lb. .... pound

oz. .... ounce

pkg. .... package

pt. .... pint

semicond. .... semicondensed

tbsp. .... tablespoon

tsp. .... teaspoon

tr. .... trace

A

*Prepared according to directions on container

Alexander cocktail mix:
  instant (*Holland House*), 1 packet 69
Allspice:
  ground (all brands), 1 tsp. 6
Almond butter:
  (*Hain*), 1 tbsp. 95
Almond extract:
  (*Virginia Dare*), 1 tsp. 7
  pure (*Durkee*), 1 tsp. 13
  pure (*Ehlers*), 1 tsp. 12
Almond meal:
  partially defatted, 1 oz. 116
Almonds:
  dried, in shell, 4 oz. 347
  dried, 10 nuts 60
  dried, shelled, 4 oz. 678
  dried, shelled, chopped, ½ cup 389
  dried, shelled, chopped, 1 tbsp. 48
  dried, shelled, slivered, ½ cup loosely packed 344
  dry roasted (*Planters*), 1 oz. 170
  roasted in oil, 1 oz. 178
Amaranth:
  fresh, whole, 1 lb. 103
  fresh, leaves, 1 lb. 163
Amaretto cocktail mix:
  bottled (*Holland House*), 1 fl. oz. 79
Amaretto liqueur:
  (*Hiram Walker*), 1 fl. oz. 76
  and cognac (*Hiram Walker*), 1 fl. oz. 62
Anchovies:
  canned, 2-oz. can, drained 79
  canned (*Reese*), 2-oz. can 100
  canned, 5 average anchovies 35
Anchovy paste:
  (*Crosse & Blackwell*), 1 tbsp. 20
Angel food cake, see "Cakes, mix"

Anise extract:
  pure (*Ehlers*), 1 tsp. 26
  imitation (*Durkee*), 1 tsp. 16
Anise-licorice liqueur:
  (*DuBouchett Absant*), 1 fl. oz. 84
  (*Pernod*), 1 fl. oz. 79
Anise seed:
  all brands, 1 tbsp. 55
Anisette liqueur:
  red or white (*Bols*), 1 fl. oz. 111
  red or white (*DuBouchett*), 1 fl. oz. .85
  red or white (*Hiram Walker*), 1 fl. oz. 92
  white (*Dolfi*), 1 fl. oz. 102
  white (*Garnier*), 1 fl. oz. 82
  white (*Old Mr. Boston*—60 proof), 1 fl. oz. 90
  white (*Old Mr. Boston* Connoisseur—42 proof), 1 fl. oz. . . .64
Apple butter:
  1 tbsp. 33
  (*Bama*), 1 tbsp. 31
  (*Ma Brown*), 1 tbsp. 32
  (*Musselman's*), 1 tbsp. 33
  cider and spiced (*Smucker's*), 1 tbsp. 37
Apple-cherry drink:
  canned (*Musselman's* Breakfast Cocktail), 6 fl. oz. 83
Apple drink:
  canned, 1 cup 116
  canned (*Bama*), 6 fl. oz. 80
  canned (*Hi-C*), 6 fl. oz. 92
  mix* (*Kool-Aid*), 6 fl. oz. 75
Apple dumpling:
  frozen (*Pepperidge Farm*), 1 piece .280
Apple, escalloped:
  frozen (*Stouffer's*), 4 oz. 140

Prepared according to directions on container

Apple fritters:
frozen (*Hanover*), 2 oz. 150
frozen (*Mrs. Paul's*), 2-oz. fritter 120
Apple fruit roll:
dried, sweetened (*Grocer's Choice*), 1 oz. 90
dried, sweetened (*Sahadi*), 1 oz. 90
Apple-grape drink:
canned or bottled (*Mott's "P.M."*), 6 fl. oz. 90
canned (*Musselman's* Breakfast Cocktail), 6 fl. oz. 83
Apple juice:
bottled (*Hood*), 6 fl. oz. 85
bottled (*Red Cheek*), 6 fl. oz. 80
bottled (*Seneca*), 6 fl. oz. 90
canned (*Heinz*), 6 fl. oz. 90
canned (*Musselman's*), 6 fl. oz. 80
canned (*Tree Top*), 6 fl. oz. 75
canned or bottled, 5½-fl.-oz. can 80
canned or bottled, 1 cup 117
canned or bottled (*Mott's*), 6 fl. oz. 80
frozen* (*Seneca*), 6 fl. oz. 90
frozen* (*Tree Top*), 6 fl. oz. 75
Apple pie, see "Pies, frozen" and "Pies, snack"
Apple pie filling:
canned (*Comstock*), 3½ oz. 110
Apple pie tart:
frozen (*Pepperidge Farm*), 1 piece 280
Apple strudel:
frozen (*Pepperidge Farm*), 3-oz. piece 250
Apple turnover:
frozen (*Pepperidge Farm*), 1 piece 310
refrigerator (*Pillsbury*), 1 piece 170
Apples:
fresh:
with skin, 1 lb. 242

*Prepared according to directions on container

with skin, 1 apple (3″ in diam.; about 2½ per lb.) 96
with skin, quarters or finely chopped, 1 cup 73
with skin, sliced or diced, 1 cup 64
pared, 1 apple (3″ in diam.; about 2½ per lb.) 84
pared, quarters or finely chopped, 1 cup 68
pared, sliced or diced, 1 cup 59
dehydrated:
   uncooked, 8 oz. 801
   uncooked, 1 cup 353
   cooked, sweetened, 1 cup 194
dried:
   uncooked, 8 oz. 625
   uncooked, 1 cup 234
   cooked, sweetened, 1 cup 314
   cooked, unsweetened, 1 cup 199
   evaporated (*Del Monte*), 1 oz. 70
   freeze-dried (*Mountain House*), 1 oz. 100
   frozen, sliced, sweetened, 8 oz. 210
Applesauce, canned or in jars:
unsweetened, 8 oz. 93
unsweetened, 1 cup 100
sweetened, 8 oz. 207
sweetened, 1 cup 232
   (*Del Monte*), ½ cup 85
   (*Mott's*), ½ cup 105
   (*Musselman's*), ½ cup 97
   (*Seneca*), ½ cup 93
   (*Seneca* Cinnamon), ½ cup 90
   (*Seneca* Golden Delicious), ½ cup 93
   (*Seneca* McIntosh), ½ cup 90
   (*Stokely-Van Camp*), ½ cup 90
sugar-free (*Mott's* Natural Style), 4 oz. 45
sugar-free (*Musselman's*), ½ cup 50
sugar-free (*Seneca* 100% Natural), ½ cup 50
Applesauce spice bread, see "Bread, sweet, mix"

Apricot brandy:
  (*Bols*), 1 fl. oz. 100
  (*DuBouchett*), 1 fl. oz. 81
  (*Garnier*), 1 fl. oz. 86
  (*Hiram Walker*), 1 fl. oz. 88
  (*Old Mr. Boston*—70 proof), 1 fl. oz. 100
  (*Old Mr. Boston* Connoisseur—42 proof), 1 fl. oz. 75
Apricot fruit roll:
  dried, sweetened (*Grocer's Choice*), 1 oz. 100
  dried, sweetened (*Sahadi*), 1 oz. 90
Apricot liqueur:
  (*Bols*), 1 fl. oz. 96
  (*Dolfi*), 1 fl. oz. 100
  (*DuBouchett*), 1 fl. oz. 63
  (*Hiram Walker*), 1 fl. oz. 79
Apricot nectar:
  canned (*Del Monte*), 6 fl. oz. 100
  canned (*Heart's Delight*), 6 fl. oz. .100
  canned (*Sunsweet*), 6 fl. oz. 105
Apricot nut bread, see "Bread, sweet, mix"
Apricot-orange juice drink, see "Orange-apricot drink"
Apricot pie filling:
  canned (*Comstock*), ⅓ cup 100
Apricot sour cocktail mix:
  bottled (*Holland House*), 1 fl. oz. 48
Apricots:
  fresh:
    whole, 1 lb. 217
    whole, 3 apricots (about 12 per lb.) 55
    pitted, halves, 1 cup 79
    candied, 1 oz. 96
  canned:
    in water, with liquid, 8 oz. 86
    in water, with liquid, halves, 1 cup 93
    in water, 3 halves and 1¾ tbsp. liquid 32
    in juice, with liquid, 8 oz. 123

in syrup, halves with liquid, unpeeled
(*Del Monte*), ½ cup 100
in syrup, halves with liquid, unpeeled
(*Libby's*), ½ cup 99
in syrup, halves with liquid
(*Stokely-Van Camp*), ½ cup 110
in syrup, whole, peeled, with liquid
(*Del Monte*), ½ cup 100
in heavy syrup, halves, with liquid, 8 oz. 195
in heavy syrup, whole or halves,
with liquid, 1 cup 222
in heavy syrup, 2 whole apricots and 2 tbsp. liquid 78
in heavy syrup, 3 halves and 1¾ tbsp. liquid 73
dehydrated (nugget type):
uncooked, 8 oz. 753
uncooked, 1 cup 332
cooked, sweetened, 1 cup 337
dried:
uncooked, halves, 8 oz. 590
uncooked, halves, 1 cup (about 37 medium halves) 338
uncooked, 10 large halves (1½″ in diam.) 125
uncooked (*Del Monte*), 1 oz. 70
uncooked (*Sunsweet*), ½ cup 224
cooked, unsweetened, with liquid, 1 cup 213
cooked, sweetened, 1 cup 329
frozen, sweetened, 8 oz. 223
frozen, sweetened, 1 cup 256
Aquavit:
(*Leroux*—90 proof), 1 fl. oz. 75
Artichoke hearts:
frozen, 3 average 22
frozen (*Birds Eye*), 3 oz. 30
Artichokes, globe or French:
fresh, raw, whole, 1 lb. 85
fresh, stored, boiled, drained,
1 whole bud (about 13½ oz.) 67

Artichokes, Jerusalem, see "Jerusalem artichokes"
Asparagus:
  fresh:
    raw, whole spears, 1 lb. 66
    raw, cut spears, 1 cup 35
    boiled, drained, 4 medium spears (½″ diam. base) 12
    boiled, drained, cut spears, 1 cup 29
  canned:
    green or white, with liquid, 8 oz. 41
    green or white, with liquid, 1 cup 44
    drained, 1 cup 51
    (*Joan of Arc Pride*), ½ cup 24
    (*Musselman's*), ½ cup 20
    spears (*Le Sueur*), ½ cup 20
    spears (*Stokely-Van Camp*), ½ cup 25
    spears and tips (*Del Monte*), ½ cup 18
    cut spears (*Green Giant*), ½ cup 20
    cut spears (*Kounty Kist/Lindy*), ½ cup 20
    cut spears, drained, 1 cup 49
    cuts (*Stokely-Van Camp*), ½ cup 23
    puree (*Cellu*), ½ cup 25
  frozen:
    boiled, drained, 1 cup 44
    boiled, drained, 4 medium spears (½″ diam. base) 14
    spears (*Stokely-Van Camp*), 4 oz. 30
    spears or cut spears (*Birds Eye*), 3.3 oz. 25
    spears or cut spears (*Seabrook Farms*), 3.3 oz. 25
    cut spears (*Stokely-Van Camp*), 4 oz. 35
    cut spears in butter sauce (*Green Giant*), ½ cup 45
    cuts and tips, boiled, drained, 1 cup 40
Asparagus soufflé:
  frozen (*Stouffer's*), 12-oz. pkg. 345
Asparagus soup, see "Soups"
Asti Spumante wine:
  (*Gancia*), 2 fl. oz. 84

Au jus gravy mix*:
  (*Durkee*), ½ cup 16
  (*French's*), ½ cup 16
  (*McCormick/Schilling*), ½ cup 15
Au jus seasoning mix:
  (*Durkee Roastin' Bag*), 1-oz. packet 64
Avocado dip:
  (*Kraft*), 2 tbsp. 60
Avocados:
  California:
    whole, with peel and pit, 1 lb. 589
    peeled and pitted, average half (3⅛" in diam.) 185
    cubed, 1 cup 257
    mashed, 1 cup 393
  Florida:
    whole, with peel and pit, 1 lb. 389
    peeled and pitted, average half (3⅝" in diam.) 196
    cubed, 1 cup 192
    mashed, 1 cup 294

---

*Prepared according to directions on container

B

imitation (*Durkee*), 1 tsp. 8
imitation (*French's Crumbles*), 1 tsp. 6
imitation (*McCormick/Schilling*), 1 tbsp. 30
Bacon cheese food, see "Cheese food"
Bacon and horseradish dip:
  (*Kraft*), 2 tbsp. 60
  (*Kraft* Ready to Serve), 1 oz. 50
Bagels:
  egg or water, 1 medium (3″ in diam). 165
  frozen:
    plain (*Lender's*), 1 piece 150
    plain, small (*Lender's* Bagelette), 1 piece 70
    egg (*Lender's*), 1 piece 150
    garlic (*Lender's*), 1 piece 160
    onion (*Lender's*), 1 piece 160
    onion, small (*Lender's* Bagelette), 1 piece 70
    pizza, see "Pizza, frozen"
    poppy seed (*Lender's*), 1 piece 150
    pumpernickel (*Lender's*), 1 piece 160
    raisin (*Lender's* Raisin 'n Honey), 1 piece 200
    rye (*Lender's*), 1 piece 150
    sesame seed (*Lender's*), 1 piece 160
Baked beans, see "Beans, baked"
Baking powder:
  SAS, 1 tbsp. 14
  SAS, 1 tsp. 4
  phosphate, 1 tbsp. 15
  phosphate, 1 tsp. 5
  tartate, 1 tbsp. 7
  tartate, 1 tsp. 2
  (*Calumet*), 1 tsp. 2
  (*Davis*), 1 tsp. 5
Bamboo shoots:
  raw, cuts, 1 cup 41
  raw, 8 oz. 61
  canned (*Chun King*), 4¼ oz. 20
  canned (*La Choy*), 4 oz. 12

19

Banana bread, see "Bread, sweet, mix"
Banana chips:
  dried (*Mountain House*), 1 oz. 155
Banana cream pie filling:
  canned (*Comstock*), ⅓ cup 110
Banana daiquiri cocktail mix:
  instant (*Holland House*), 1 packet 66
Banana extract:
  imitation (*Durkee*), 1 tsp. 15
  imitation (*Ehlers*), 1 tsp. 20
Bananas, baking type, see "Plantains"
Bananas, common varieties:
  fresh:
    whole, with skin, 1 lb. 262
    whole, 1 large (9¾" long) 116
    whole, 1 medium (8¾" long) 101
    whole, 1 small (7¾" long) 81
    sliced, 1 cup 136
    mashed, 1 cup 191
  dehydrated:
    flakes, 4 oz. 388
    flakes, 1 oz. 96
    flakes, 1 cup 340
    flakes, 1 tbsp. 21
Bananas, red:
  fresh, whole, with skin, 1 lb. 278
  fresh, whole, 1 average (7¼" long) 118
  fresh, sliced, 1 cup 135
Banquet loaf:
  beef (*Eckrich*), 1 slice 75
  beef (*Eckrich Smorgas Pac*), 1 slice 55
Barbados cherries, see "Acerolas"
Barbecue loaf:
  (*Hormel BBQ*), 1-oz. slice 47
  (*Oscar Mayer Bar-B-Q*), 1-oz. slice 45

Barbecue relish:
  (*Crosse & Blackwell*), 1 tbsp. 22
  (*Heinz*), 1 tbsp. 32
Barbecue sauce, in jars:
  8 oz. 207
  1 cup 228
  (*Cris & Pitt's*), ½ cup 120
  (*French's Cattlemen's*), 2 tbsp. 50
  (*Heinz*), ½ cup 110
  (*Kraft*), 2 tbsp. 45
  (*Open Pit*), 4 oz. 104
  garlic flavor (*Kraft*), 2 tbsp. 35
  hickory smoke flavor (*Heinz*), ½ cup 125
  hickory smoke flavor (*Kraft*), 2 tbsp. 45
  hickory smoke flavor (*Open Pit*), 4 oz. 106
  hot (*Heinz*), ½ cup 125
  hot (*Kraft*), 2 tbsp. 40
  hot hickory smoke flavor (*Kraft*), 2 tbsp. 40
  smoky flavor (*French's Cattlemen's*), 2 tbsp. 50
  sweet and sour (*Kraft*), 2 tbsp. 70
  with mushrooms (*Heinz*), ½ cup 125
  with onions (*Heinz*), ½ cup 125
  with onions (*Kraft*), 2 tbsp. 50
  with onions (*Open Pit*), 4 oz. 109
Barbecue seasoning:
  (*French's*), 1 tsp. 6
Barley, pearled:
  light, uncooked, 8 oz. 792
  light, uncooked, 1 cup 698
  pot or scotch, uncooked, 8 oz. 790
  pot or scotch, uncooked, 1 cup 696
  regular or quick, uncooked
    (*Quaker Scotch Brand*), ¼ cup 172
Barracuda, Pacific:
  raw, meat only, 4 oz. 129
Basella, see "Vine spinach"

Basil leaves:
ground (all brands), 1 tsp. 3
Bass, black sea:
raw, whole, 1 lb. 165
raw, meat only, 4 oz. 106
Bass, smallmouth and largemouth:
raw, whole, 1 lb. 146
raw, meat only, 4 oz. 118
Bass, striped:
raw, whole, 1 lb. 205
raw, meat only, 4 oz. 120
Bay leaves:
ground (all brands), 1 tsp. 5
(*B & B*) liqueur:
1 fl. oz. 94
Bean combination:
frozen (*Hanover* Romano Bean Medley), 3.2 oz. 30
Bean curd, see "Soybean curd"
Bean flour (lima):
8 oz. 779
sifted and spooned, 1 cup 432
Bean salad:
kidney (*Read*), ½ cup 138
three-bean (*Green Giant*), ½ cup 95
three-bean (*Hanover* Old Fashioned), 4 oz. 123
three-bean (*Read*), ½ cup 103
Bean soup, see "Soups"
Bean sprouts:
mung, uncooked, 1 cup 37
mung, boiled, drained, 1 cup 35
soy, uncooked, 1 cup 48
soy, boiled, drained, 1 cup 48
canned (*Chun King*), 4 oz. 20
canned (*La Choy*), ½ cup 12
Beans, baked, canned:
(*Campbell's* Home Style), 8 oz. 300

(*Howard Johnson's*), 1 cup 340
(*Van Camp Beanee Weenee*), 1 cup 340
(*Van Camp* October Beans), 1 cup 230
with bacon (*Hormel*), 7½-oz. can 339
barbecue (*Campbell's*), 8 oz. 280
in brown sugar sauce:
   (*Van Camp*), 1 cup 330
   pea beans (*B & M*), 1 cup 336
   red kidney beans (*B & M*), 1 cup 360
   yellow eye (*B & M*), 1 cup 360
with frankfurters:
   (*Hormel* Beans 'n Wieners), 7½-oz. can 286
   in tomato sauce (*Heinz*), 8¾-oz. can 399
   in tomato sauce and molasses (*Campbell's*), 8 oz. 370
with ham (*Hormel*), 7½-oz. can 367
in molasses sauce:
   (*Heinz*), 1 cup 284
   (*Libby's*), 1 cup 279
   and brown sugar (*Campbell's* Old Fashioned), 8 oz. 290
pea beans (*Homemaker's*), 1 cup 320
with pork:
   (*Hanover*), 8 oz. 273
   (*Van Camp*), 1 cup 250
   in tomato sauce (*Campbell's*), 8 oz. 260
   in tomato sauce (*Heinz*), 1 cup 262
   in tomato sauce (*Joan of Arc*), 1 cup 280
   in tomato sauce (*Libby's*), 1 cup 274
red kidney beans (*Homemaker's*), 1 cup 336
vegetarian:
   (*Hanover*), 8 oz. 270
   (*Van Camp*), 1 cup 260
   in tomato sauce (*Libby's*), 1 cup 266
Beans and beef patties dinner:
frozen (*Swanson TV Brand*), 11-oz. pkg. 500
Beans, black:
dry, uncooked, 8 oz. 768

canned, turtle (*Progresso*), ½ cup 103
Beans, broad, see "Broad beans"
Beans, butter:
canned:
    (*Hanover*), 4 oz. 113
    (*Joan of Arc*), ½ cup 100
    (*Van Camp*), ½ cup 85
    with ham (*Libby's*), ½ cup 114
frozen:
    baby (*Birds Eye*), 3.3 oz. 140
    baby (*Seabrook Farms*), 3.3 oz. 140
    baby (*Stokely-Van Camp*), 3.3 oz. 140
    speckled (*Green Giant*), ½ cup 140
    speckled (*Seabrook Farms*), 3.3 oz. 130
    speckled (*Southland*), 3.3 oz. 110
Beans, cannellini or white kidney:
canned (*Progresso*), ½ cup 95
Beans, chili:
canned (*Joan of Arc*), ½ cup 110
canned (*Van Camp* Mexican Style), ½ cup 120
Beans, fava:
canned (*Progresso*), ½ cup 90
Beans and franks dinner:
frozen (*Banquet*), 10¼-oz. pkg. 591
frozen (*Morton*), 10¾-oz. pkg. 530
frozen (*Swanson TV Brand*), 11¼-oz. pkg. 550
Beans, great northern:
dry, uncooked, 8 oz. 771
dry, uncooked, 1 cup 612
dry, cooked, 8 oz. 268
dry, cooked, 1 cup 212
canned (*Joan of Arc*), ½ cup 95
Beans, green or snap:
fresh:
    raw, whole, 1 lb. 128
    raw, trimmed, 1 lb. 145

raw, cuts, 1 cup 34
boiled, drained, cuts or French, 1 cup 31
canned:
  whole (*Del Monte*), ½ cup 18
  whole (*Libby's* Blue Lake), ½ cup 16
  whole (*Stokely-Van Camp*), ½ cup 15
  whole, tiny (*Del Monte*), ½ cup 20
  whole, cut, or French (*Green Giant*), ½ cup 15
  whole, cut, or French (*Kounty Kist/Lindy*), ½ cup 20
  cut (*Del Monte*), ½ cup 20
  cut (*Hanover*), 4 oz. 20
  cut (*Libby's* Blue Lake), ½ cup 19
  cut (*Stokely-Van Camp*), ½ cup 18
  French, drained, 1 cup 31
  French (*Del Monte*), ½ cup 20
  French (*Hanover*), 4 oz. 19
  French (*Libby's* Blue Lake), ½ cup 18
  sliced (*Stokely-Van Camp*), ½ cup 18
  puree (*Cellu*), ½ cup 35
  seasoned (*Del Monte*), ½ cup 20
  with potatoes, in ham flavor sauce
    (*Hanover*), 4 oz. 33
frozen:
  whole (*Birds Eye*), 3 oz. 25
  whole (*Hanover* Blue Lake), 3.2 oz. 25
  whole (*Seabrook Farms*), 3 oz. 30
  whole (*Southland*), 3.3 oz. 25
  cut (*Birds Eye*), 3 oz. 25
  cut (*Hanover* Blue Lake), 3.2 oz. 28
  cut (*Kounty Kist/Lindy*), ½ cup 15
  cut (*Southland*), 3.2 oz. 28
  cut (*Stokely-Van Camp*), 3 oz. 30
  French, boiled, drained, 8.8 oz.
    (yield from 10-oz. pkg). 65
  French, boiled, drained, 1 cup 34
  French (*Birds Eye*), 3 oz. 25

French (*Hanover* Blue Lake), 3.2 oz. 25
French (*Seabrook Farms*), 3 oz. 30
French (*Southland*), 3.3 oz. 25
French (*Stokely-Van Camp*), 3.3 oz. 30
French, in butter sauce (*Green Giant*), ½ cup 35
French, in cheese sauce (*Birds Eye*), 5 oz. 160
French, with onions and bacon (*Green Giant*), ½ cup 40
French, with sliced mushrooms (*Birds Eye*), 3 oz. 30
French, with toasted almonds (*Birds Eye*), 3 oz. 50
French, and cauliflower and carrots
   (*Birds Eye* Farm Fresh), 3.2 oz. 25
with spaetzle (*Birds Eye* Bavarian Style), 3.3 oz. 50
Beans, green, and mushroom casserole:
frozen (*Stouffer's*), 4¾-oz. pkg. 150
Beans, Italian:
canned (*Del Monte*), ½ cup 30
Beans, kidney:
dry:
   red, uncooked, 8 oz. 778
   red, uncooked, 1 cup 635
   red, cooked, 1 cup 218
canned:
   red (*Progresso*), ½ cup 93
   red (*Van Camp* New Orleans Style), ½ cup 100
   red, dark (*Hanover*), 4 oz. .123
   red, dark (*Joan of Arc*), ½ cup 115
   red, dark (*Van Camp*), ½ cup 100
   red, light (*Hanover*), 4 oz. .122
   red, light (*Joan of Arc*), ½ cup 110
   red, light (*Van Camp*), ½ cup 105
   white, see "Beans, cannellini"
Beans, kidney, salad, see "Bean salad"
Beans, lima, immature seeds:
fresh:
   in pods, raw, 1 lb. 223
   shelled, raw, 8 oz. 279

shelled, raw, 1 cup 191
boiled, drained, 8 oz. 252
boiled, drained, 1 cup 189
canned:
(*Del Monte*), ½ cup 75
(*Libby's*), ½ cup 87
(*Stokely-Van Camp*), ½ cup 80
seasoned (*Del Monte*), ½ cup 80
frozen:
baby (*Birds Eye*), 3.3 oz. 130
baby (*Green Giant*), ½ cup 75
baby (*Hanover*), 3.2 oz. 115
baby (*Kounty Kist/Lindy*), ½ cup 95
baby (*Seabrook Farms*), 3.3 oz. 130
baby (*Stokely-Van Camp*), 3.3 oz. 120
baby, in butter sauce (*Green Giant*), ½ cup 110
Fordhook (*Birds Eye*), 3.3 oz. 100
Fordhook (*Hanover*), 3.2 oz. 100
Fordhook (*Seabrook Farms*), 3.3 oz. 100
Fordhook (*Stokely-Van Camp*), 3.3 oz. 100
Beans, lima, mature seeds:
dry, uncooked, 8 oz. 783
dry, uncooked, baby, 1 cup 656
dry, uncooked, Fordhook, 1 cup 621
dry, cooked, 8 oz. 313
dry, cooked, 1 cup 262
Beans, mung:
dry, uncooked, 8 oz. 771
dry, uncooked, 1 cup 714
Beans, pea or navy:
dry, uncooked, 8 oz. 771
dry, uncooked, 1 cup 697
dry, cooked, 1 cup 224
Beans, pink:
canned (*Hanover*), 4 oz. 115

Beans, pinto or red Mexican:
canned (*Hanover*), 4 oz. 100
canned (*Joan of Arc*), ½ cup 110
canned (*Progresso*), ½ cup 83
canned, red (*Joan of Arc*), ½ cup 115
canned, red (*Van Camp*), ½ cup 110
Beans, refried:
canned, Mexican style (*Gebhardt*), 4 oz. 114
Beans, Roman:
canned (*Progresso*), ½ cup 105
Beans, shellie:
canned (*Stokely-Van Camp*), ½ cup 40
Beans, wax or yellow:
fresh:
  raw, 1 lb. 122
  raw, cuts, 1 cup 30
  boiled, drained, whole or cuts, 8 oz. 50
  boiled, drained, cuts, 1 cup 28
canned:
  whole (*Stokely-Van Camp*), ½ cup 20
  cut, drained, 1 cup 32
  cut (*Del Monte*), ½ cup 18
  cut (*Libby's*), ½ cup 22
  cut (*Stokely-Van Camp*), ½ cup 20
  French (*Del Monte*), ½ cup 18
  sliced (*Stokely-Van Camp*), ½ cup 18
frozen:
  cut (*Birds Eye*), 3 oz. 25
Beans, white:
dry, uncooked, 8 oz. 771
dry, cooked, 1 cup 224
Beaujolais wine:
imported (*Crus & Fils Frères*), 4 fl. oz. 96
Beaver:
roasted, 8 oz. 563

Beechnuts:
in shell, 4 oz. 393
shelled, 4 oz. 644
Beef, fresh, choice-grade, retail trim:
chuck, arm, roast or steak, boneless, lean with fat:
braised, drained, 10.7 oz. (yield from 1 lb. raw) 879
braised, drained, 4 oz. 328
braised, drained, chopped or diced, 1 cup 405
chuck, arm, roast or steak, boneless, lean only (fat trimmed):
braised, drained, 9.1 oz.
(yield from 1 lb. raw with fat) 498
braised, drained, 4 oz. 219
braised, drained, chopped or diced, 1 cup 270
chuck, rib, roast or steak, boneless, lean with fat:
braised, drained, 10.7 oz.
(yield from 1 lb. raw) 1,298
braised, drained, 4 oz. 484
braised, drained, chopped or diced, 1 cup 598
chuck, rib, roast or steak, boneless, lean only (fat trimmed):
braised, drained, 7.4 oz.
(yield from 1 lb. raw with fat) 523
braised, drained, 4 oz. 282
braised, drained, chopped or diced, 1 cup 349
chuck, stewing, boneless, lean with fat:
stewed, drained, 10.7 oz. (yield from 1 lb. raw) 994
stewed, drained, 4 oz. 371
stewed, drained, chopped or diced, 1 cup 458
chuck, stewing, boneless, lean only (fat trimmed):
stewed, drained, 10.7 oz. (yield from 1 lb. raw) 651
stewed, drained, 4 oz. 243
stewed, drained, chopped or diced, 1 cup 300
club steak, with 16% bone, lean with fat:
broiled, 9.8 oz. (yield from 1 lb. raw) 1,262
broiled, 4 oz. without bone 515
club steak, with 16% bone, lean only (fat trimmed):
broiled, 5.7 oz. (yield from 1 lb. raw with fat) 393
broiled, 4 oz. without bone 277

flank steak, boneless, all lean:
   braised, drained, 10.7 oz. (yield from 1 lb. raw) 596
   braised, drained, 4 oz. 222
   braised, drained, 1 piece (2½″ × 2½″ × ¾″) 167
ground, lean with 10% fat:
   broiled, well-done, 12 oz. (yield from 1 lb. raw) 745
   broiled, well-done, 3-oz. patty (yield from 4 oz. raw) 186
ground, lean with 21% fat:
   broiled, rare to medium, 11.5 oz.
     (yield from 1 lb. raw) 932
   broiled, rare to medium, 2.9-oz. patty
     (yield from 4 oz. raw) 235
plate, boneless, lean with fat:
   simmered, drained, 10.7 oz. (yield from 1 lb. raw). ...1,313
   simmered, drained, 4 oz. 490
plate, boneless, lean only (fat trimmed):
   simmered, drained, 6.5 oz.
     (yield from 1 lb. raw with fat) 368
   simmered, drained, 4 oz. 226
porterhouse steak, with 9% bone, lean with fat:
   broiled, 10.6 oz. (yield from 1 lb. raw) 1,400
   broiled, 4. oz. without bone 527
porterhouse steak, with 9% bone, lean only (fat trimmed):
   broiled, 6.1 oz. (yield from 1 lb. raw with fat) 385
   broiled, 4 oz. without bone 254
rib roast, boneless, lean with fat:
   roasted, 11.7 oz. (yield from 1 lb. raw) 1,456
   roasted, 4 oz. 499
   roasted, chopped or diced, 1 cup 616
rib roast, boneless, lean only (fat trimmed):
   roasted, 7.5 oz. (yield from 1 lb. raw with fat) 511
   roasted, 4 oz. 273
   roasted, chopped or diced, 1 cup 337
round steak, boneless, lean with fat:
   braised or broiled, 11.1 oz. (yield from 1 lb. raw) 820
   braised or broiled, 4 oz. 296

round steak, boneless, lean only (fat trimmed):
braised or broiled, 9.5 oz.
    (yield from 1 lb. raw with fat) 507
braised or broiled, 4 oz. 214
rump roast, boneless, lean with fat:
roasted, 11.7 oz. (yield from 1 lb. raw) 1,149
roasted, 4 oz. 394
roasted, chopped or diced, 1 cup 486
rump roast, boneless, lean only (fat trimmed):
roasted, 8.8 oz. (yield from 1 lb. raw with fat) 516
roasted, 4 oz. 236
roasted, chopped or diced, 1 cup 291
sirloin steak, double bone, 18% bone, lean with fat:
broiled, 9.6 oz. (yield from 1 lb. raw) 1,110
broiled, 4 oz. without bone 463
sirloin steak, double bone, 18% bone, lean only (fat trimmed):
broiled, 6.3 oz. (yield from 1 lb. raw with fat) 387
broiled, 4 oz. without bone 245
sirloin steak, hipbone, 15% bone, lean with fat:
broiled, 9.9 oz. (yield from 1 lb. raw). 1,368
broiled, 4 oz. without bone 552
sirloin steak, hipbone, 15% bone, lean only (fat trimmed):
broiled, 5.5 oz. (yield from 1 lb. raw with fat) 372
broiled, 4 oz. without bone 272
sirloin steak, round bone, 7% bone, lean with fat:
broiled, 10.9 oz. (yield from 1 lb. raw) 1,192
broiled, 4 oz. without bone 439
sirloin steak, round bone, 7% bone, lean only (fat trimmed):
broiled, 7.2 oz. (yield from 1 lb. raw with fat) 420
broiled, 4 oz. without bone 235
T-bone steak, 11% bone, lean with fat:
broiled, 10.4 oz. (yield from 1 lb. raw) 1,395
broiled, 4 oz. without bone 537
T-bone steak, 11% bone, lean only (fat trimmed):
broiled, 5.8 oz. (yield from 1 lb. raw with fat) 368
broiled, 4 oz. without bone 253

Beef bacon, see "Bacon"
Beef, breaded:
  frozen, with American cheese food
    (*Pierre Golddiggers*), 3½ oz. 310
Beef burgundy crepe:
  frozen (*Stouffer's*), 6¼-oz. pkg. 335
Beef, chipped, see "Beef, dried"
Beef chop suey, see "Chop suey"
Beef, chopped:
  canned (*Armour Star*), 12-oz. can 1,190
Beef, chopped, dinner, see "Beef dinners, frozen"
Beef chow mein, see "Chow mein"
Beef, corned:
  cooked, 10.7 oz. (yield from 1 lb. raw) 1,131
  cooked, 4 oz. 422
  canned, 12-oz. can 734
  canned, 4 oz. 245
  canned, 1 slice (3″ × 2″ × ⅜″) 86
  (*Danola* Thin Sliced), 1 oz. 35
  (*Eckrich* Slender Sliced), 1 slice 40
  (*Hormel* Loaf), .8-oz. slice 37
  brisket (*Vienna*), 3½ oz. 305
  brisket (*Wilson Certified Tender Made*), 8 oz. 361
  flats (*Vienna*), 3½ oz. 171
  jellied loaf (*Oscar Mayer*), 1-oz. slice 45
Beef, corned, hash:
  canned, 15½-oz. can 795
  canned, 8 oz. 410
  canned, 1 cup 398
  canned (*Armour Star*), 8 oz. 435
  canned (*Mary Kitchen*), 7½ oz. 398
  canned (*Mary Kitchen* Short Order), 7½-oz. can 366
Beef, corned spread:
  (*Underwood*), 1 tbsp. 27
Beef dinners, frozen:
  (*Banquet*), 11-oz. pkg. 312

(*Morton*), 10-oz. pkg. 260
(*Swanson*), 15-oz. pkg. 490
(*Swanson TV Brand*), 11½-oz. pkg. 370
chopped (*Banquet*), 11-oz. pkg. 443
chopped, beefsteak (*Swanson Hungry-Man*),
   18-oz. pkg. 730
chopped sirloin (*Morton Steak House*), 9½-oz. pkg. 760
chopped sirloin (*Swanson TV Brand*), 10-oz. pkg. 460
rib eye (*Morton Steak House*), 9-oz. pkg. 820
sirloin strip (*Morton Steak House*), 9½-oz. pkg. 760
sliced (*Morton Country Table*), 15-oz. pkg. 510
sliced (*Swanson Hungry-Man*), 17-oz. pkg. 540
tenderloin (*Morton Steak House*), 9½-oz. pkg. 890
Beef, dried (chipped):
   uncooked, 2½-oz. jar 144
   uncooked, 5-oz. jar 288
   (*Armour Star*), 5-oz. jar 234
   (*Swift Premium*), 3-oz. pkg. 140
   canned, creamed (*Hormel* Short Order), 7½-oz. can 157
   frozen, creamed (*Banquet Cookin' Bag*), 5-oz. pkg. 124
   frozen, creamed (*Morton* Boil-in-Bag), 5-oz. pkg. 160
   frozen, creamed (*Stouffer's*), 11-oz. pkg. 470
Beef enchilada, see "Enchilada, beef"
Beef flavor mix*:
   (*Lipton Lite-Lunch*), 7 fl. oz. 140
Beef goulash:
   canned (*Heinz*), 7½-oz. can 253
   canned (*Hormel* Short Order), 7½-oz. can 229
Beef gravy:
   canned (*Franco-American*), 4 oz. 60
   brown, canned (*Howard Johnson's*), ½ cup 51
Beef heart, see "Heart"
Beef kidney, see "Kidney"
Beef liver, see "Liver"

**Prepared according to directions on container*

Beef luncheon meat (see also specific listings):
(*Danola* Thin Sliced), 1 oz. 35
(*Eckrich* Slender Sliced), 1 slice 40
(*Kahn's*), 1 oz. 90
jellied loaf (*Hormel*), 1.2-oz. slice 32
peppered (*Vienna*), 3½ oz. 176
Beef noodle mix:
dry (*Hamburger Helper*), ⅕ pkg. .140
with meat* (*Hamburger Helper*), ⅕ pkg. 320
Beef patties, frozen:
(*Morton* Boil-in-Bag), 5 oz. 200
and mushroom gravy (*Morton*), 8 oz. 300
and onion gravy (*Morton*), 8 oz. 300
Beef pot pie, frozen:
8-oz. pie 436
(*Banquet*), 8-oz. pie 449
(*Morton*), 8-oz. pie 320
(*Stouffer's*), 10-oz. pie 550
(*Swanson*), 8-oz. pie 430
(*Swanson Hungry-Man*), 16-oz. pie 770
sirloin burger (*Swanson Hungry-Man*), 16-oz. pie 800
Beef, potted:
canned, 5½-oz. can 387
canned, 1 oz. 70
canned, 1 cup 558
canned, 1 tbsp. 32
Beef puff pastry:
frozen (*Durkee*), 1 piece 47
Beef, roast (see also "Beef, rib roast or rump roast"):
canned or refrigerated:
8 oz. 508
(*Wilson Certified Tender Made*), 8 oz. 267
with gravy (*Armour Star*), 8 oz. .290

Prepared according to directions on container

Beef, roast, hash:
    canned (*Mary Kitchen*), 7½ oz. 395
    canned (*Mary Kitchen* Short Order), 7½-oz. can 366
    frozen (*Stouffer's*), 11½-oz. pkg. 530
Beef Romanoff mix:
    dry (*Hamburger Helper*), ⅕ pkg. 160
    with meat* (*Hamburger Helper*), ⅕ pkg. 304
Beef sauce mix:
    hearty (*Durkee* Simmer Sauce), 2-oz. pkg. 168
Beef seasoning and roasting mix, dry:
    ground (*Durkee*), 1⅛-oz. packet 91
    ground, with onion (*Durkee*), 1⅛-oz. packet 102
    ground, with onion (*French's*), 1⅛-oz. packet 100
    ground, with onion (*McCormick/Schilling*),
      1-oz. packet 86
    hamburger, see "Hamburger and meat loaf seasoning mix"
    stew (*Durkee*), 1¾-oz. packet 99
    stew (*French's*), 1⅞-oz. packet 150
    stew (*McCormick/Schilling*), 1½-oz. packet 90
    Stroganoff, see "Beef Stroganoff seasoning mix"
Beef short ribs:
    frozen, with vegetable gravy (*Stouffer's*),
      11½-oz. pkg. 700
Beef, sliced:
    canned, with gravy (*Morton House* Heat 'n Serve),
      6¼-oz. 190
    frozen:
      (*Morton* Boil-in-Bag), 5 oz. 120
      (*Swanson Hungry-Man* Entree), 12¼-oz. pkg. 330
      with barbecue sauce (*Banquet Cookin' Bag*),
        5-oz. pkg. 126
      with gravy (*Banquet Buffet Suppers*), 32-oz. pkg. 782
      with gravy (*Banquet Cookin' Bag*), 5-oz. pkg. 116
      with gravy (*Green Giant Toast Toppers*),
        5-oz. pkg. 130

Prepared according to directions on container

with gravy (*Morton*), 8 oz. 210
with gravy and potatoes
    (*Swanson TV Brand* Entree), 8-oz. pkg. 190
Beef, smoked:
  (*Oscar Mayer* Thin Sliced), 3-oz. pkg. 118
Beef soup, see "Soups"
Beef steaks:
  frozen, breaded (*Hormel*), 4 oz. 373
Beef stew:
  canned:
    (*Armour Star*), 8 oz. 200
    (*Dinty Moore*), 7½ oz. 183
    (*Dinty Moore* Short Order), 7½-oz. can 173
    (*Heinz*), 7½-oz. can 200
    (*Libby's*), 8 oz. 206
    (*Morton House*), 8 oz. 240
    (*Swanson*), 7½ oz. 190
  frozen:
    (*Banquet Buffet Suppers*), 32-oz. pkg. 700
    (*Green Giant* Entree), 9-oz. pkg. 160
    (*Morton*), 8 oz. 190
    (*Morton* Boil-in-Bag), 5-oz. pkg. 210
    (*Stouffer's*), 10-oz. pkg. 310
    and biscuits (*Green Giant* Baked Entree),
      7-oz. pkg. 190
Beef stew seasoning, see "Beef seasoning and roasting mix"
Beef Stroganoff:
  frozen, with parsley noodles (*Stouffer's*),
    9¾-oz. pkg. 390
Beef Stroganoff seasoning mix, dry:
  (*Durkee*), 1¼-oz. packet 90
  (*French's*), 1½-oz. packet 55
  (*McCormick/Schilling*), 1½-oz. packet 113
Beef tongue, see "Tongue"
Beer:
  (*Blatz*), 12 fl. oz. 150

(Brauhaus), 12 fl. oz. 150
(Budweiser), 12 fl. oz. 157
(Busch Bavarian), 12 fl. oz. 157
(Carling Black Label), 12 fl. oz. 162
(Carlsberg Light de Luxe), 12 fl. oz. 153
(Falstaff), 12 fl. oz. 150
(Grand Union), 12 fl. oz. 150
(Heidelberg), 12 fl. oz. 147
(Heidelberg Light Pilsner), 12 fl. oz. 130
(Heileman Grain Belt), 12 fl. oz. 150
(Heileman National Bohemian), 12 fl. oz. 150
(Heileman National Premium), 12 fl. oz. 170
(Heileman Old Style), 12 fl. oz. 150
(Heileman Special Export), 12 fl. oz. 170
(Michelob), 12 fl. oz. 160
(Old Dutch), 12 fl. oz. 150
(Old Ranger), 12 fl. oz. 150
(Pabst), 12 fl. oz. 150
(Pearl), 12 fl. oz. 147
(Pilsner's Original), 12 fl. oz. 150
(Rainier), 12 fl. oz. 150
(Rupert-Knickerbocker), 12 fl. oz. 158
(Schaefer), 12 fl. oz. 160
(Schlitz), 12 fl. oz. 153
(Schmidt), 12 fl. oz. 150
(Schmidt Extra Special), 12 fl. oz. 190
(Stag), 12 fl. oz. 150
(Sterling), 12 fl. oz. 150
(Tudor), 12 fl. oz. 150
(Wiedemann), 12 fl. oz. 150
light *(Blatz)*, 12 fl. oz. 96
light *(Heileman)*, 12 fl. oz. 96
light *(Rainier)*, 12 fl. oz. 96
Beer, near:
(Kingsbury), 12 fl. oz. 60
(Maltcrest), 12 fl. oz. 70

(*Metbrew*), 12 fl. oz. 70
(*Schmidt Select*), 12 fl. oz. 60
(*Zing*), 12 fl. oz. 60
Beet greens:
  fresh, raw, trimmed, 1 lb. 61
  fresh, boiled, drained, 8 oz. 41
  fresh, boiled, drained, 1 cup 26
Beets:
  fresh:
    raw, trimmed, 1 lb. 137
    raw, whole, 1 medium beet (2″ in diam.) 21
    raw, diced, 1 cup 58
    boiled, drained, whole, 2 medium beets
      (2″ in diam.) 32
    boiled, drained, diced, 1 cup 58
    boiled, drained, sliced, 1 cup 66
  canned:
    whole (*Stokely-Van Camp*), ½ cup 40
    whole, cut, or sliced (*Comstock*), ½ cup 25
    whole, cut, or sliced (*Del Monte*), ½ cup 35
    cut (*Stokely-Van Camp*), ½ cup 40
    diced (*Stokely-Van Camp*), ½ cup 35
    shoestring (*Libby's*), ½ cup 25
    sliced (*Libby's*—canned), ½ cup 35
    sliced (*Libby's*—in jars), ½ cup 37
    sliced (*Stokely-Van Camp*), ½ cup 40
    Harvard (*Comstock*), ½ cup 55
    Harvard (*Stokely-Van Camp*), ½ cup 80
    Harvard, diced (*Libby's*—canned), ½ cup 84
    Harvard, diced (*Libby's*—in jars), ½ cup 86
    pickled, whole, tiny (*Libby's*), ½ cup 84
    pickled, whole, (*Stokely-Van Camp*), ½ cup 100
    pickled, crinkle-cut (*Del Monte*), ½ cup 75
    pickled, sliced (*Comstock*), ½ cup 45
    pickled, sliced (*Libby's*), ½ cup 78
    pickled, sliced (*Stokely-Van Camp*), ½ cup 95

pickled, with onions (*Comstock*), ½ cup 45
puree (*Cellu*), ½ cup 50
Benai liqueur:
(*DuBouchett*), 1 fl. oz. 110
and brandy (*DuBouchett*), 1 fl. oz. 89
(*Benedictine*) **liqueur:**
1 fl. oz. 112
(*Bennett's Special Sauce*):
1 tbsp. 50
Berry drink:
wild, canned (*Hi-C*), 6 fl. oz. 88
Beverages, see individual listings
Biscuit dough:
canned, chilled, 4 oz. 318
canned, frozen, 4 oz. 263
Biscuit mix*:
made with milk, 1-oz. biscuit (2″ in diam., 1¼″ high) 91
(*Bisquick*), 2 oz. or ½ cup 240
Biscuits:
(*Wonder*), 1 piece 105
refrigerated:
(*Ballard* Oven Ready), 1 piece 50
(*Big Country* Good 'N Buttery), 1 piece 100
(*1869 Brand* Baking Powder), 1 piece 100
(*1869 Brand* Baking Powder—prebaked), 1 piece 100
(*1869 Brand Butter Tastin'*), 1 piece 100
(*1869 Brand* Heat 'N Eat), 1 piece 100
(*Hungry Jack Butter Tastin'*), 1 piece 95
(*Hungry Jack* Flaky), 1 piece 90
(*Pillsbury Big Country*), 1 piece 95
(*Pillsbury* Country Style), 1 piece 50
(*Pillsbury* Prize), 1 piece 65
(*Tenderflake* Baking Powder Dinner Biscuits), 1 piece . . . 55
buttermilk (*Ballard* Oven Ready), 1 piece 50

*Prepared according to directions on container

39

buttermilk (*1869 Brand*), 1 piece 100
buttermilk (*1869 Brand*—prebaked), 1 piece 100
buttermilk (*Hungry Jack* Extra Rich), 1 piece 65
buttermilk (*Hungry Jack* Flaky), 1 piece 80
buttermilk (*Hungry Jack* Fluffy), 1 piece 100
buttermilk (*Pillsbury*), 1 piece 50
buttermilk (*Pillsbury Big Country*), 1 piece 90
buttermilk (*Pillsbury* Extra Lights), 1 piece 60
buttermilk (*Tenderflake* Dinner Biscuits), 1 piece 55

Bitters:
(*Angostura*), ¼ tsp. 4

Black cherry dessert topping, see "Cherry, black, dessert topping"

Black Russian cocktail mix:
bottled (*Holland House*), 1 fl. oz. 92

Black walnut flavoring, see "Walnut, black, flavoring"

Blackberries:
fresh, 1 lb. 250
fresh, 1 cup 84
canned:
in water, with liquid, 8 oz. 91
in water, with liquid, 1 cup 98
in heavy syrup, with liquid, 8 oz. 207
in heavy syrup, with liquid, 1 cup 233
frozen, see "Boysenberries"

Blackberry brandy:
(*Bols*), 1 fl. oz. 100
(*DuBouchett*), 1 fl. oz. 88
(*Garnier*), 1 fl. oz. 86
(*Hiram Walker*), 1 fl. oz. 88
(*Old Mr. Boston*—70 proof), 1 fl. oz. 100
(*Old Mr. Boston* Connoisseur—42 proof), 1 fl. oz. 75

Blackberry juice:
canned, unsweetened, 1 cup 91

Blackberry liqueur:
(*Bols*), 1 fl. oz. 96

(*Dolfi*), 1 fl. oz. 93
(*DuBouchett*), 1 fl. oz. 70
(*Hiram Walker*), 1 fl. oz. 93
Blackberry sour cocktail mix:
   bottled (*Holland House*), 1 fl. oz. 50
Black-eyed peas, see "Cowpeas"
Blackfish, see "Tautog"
Blood sausage, see "Sausages"
Bloody Mary cocktail mix:
   bottled (*Holland House*), 1 fl. oz. 10
   canned (*Sacramento*), 5½ fl. oz. 45
   extra tangy, bottled (*Holland House*), 1 fl. oz. 10
   smooth and spicy, bottled (*Holland House*), 1 fl. oz. 6
   instant (*Holland House*), 1 packet 56
Blue cheese dip:
   (*Kraft* Ready to serve), 1 oz. 50
Blueberries:
   fresh, 1 lb. 259
   fresh, 1 cup 90
   canned:
      in water, with liquid, 8 oz. 89
      in heavy syrup, with liquid, 8 oz. 230
      in heavy syrup, with liquid, 1 cup 253
   freeze-dried (*Mountain House*), 1 oz. 134
   frozen:
      unsweetened, 10-oz. pkg. 156
      unsweetened, 1 cup 91
      sweetened, 10-oz. pkg. 298
      sweetened, 1 cup 242
Blueberry nut bread, see "Bread, sweet, mix"
Blueberry pie, see "Pies, frozen" and "Pies, snack"
Blueberry pie filling:
   canned (*Comstock*), ⅓ cup 100
Blueberry pie tart:
   frozen (*Pepperidge Farm*), 1 piece 280

Blueberry turnover:
    frozen (*Pepperidge Farm*), 1 piece 320
    refrigerator (*Pillsbury*), 1 piece 170
Bluefish fillets:
    raw, meat only, 1 lb. 531
    broiled with butter, 12⅞ oz. (yield from 1 lb. raw) 580
    broiled with butter, 4 oz. 180
Bockwurst:
    1 lb., about 7 links 1,198
    1 link, about 2.3 oz. 172
Bologna:
    without binders:
        chub, 1 slice (3″ in diam., ⅛″ thick) 36
        ring, 12-oz. ring (15″ long, 1⅜″ in diam.) 942
        sliced, 8-oz. pkg. 629
        sliced, 6-oz. pkg. 471
        sliced, 1-oz. slice 79
    with cereal:
        chub, 1 slice (3″ in diam., ⅛″ thick) 34
        ring, 12-oz. ring (15″ long, 1⅜″ in diam.) 891
        sliced, 8-oz. pkg. 595
        sliced, 6-oz. pkg. 445
        sliced, 1-oz. slice 74
        (*Armour Star*), 1 oz. 90
        (*Eckrich*), 1 slice 95
        (*Eckrich* Thick Sliced—12-oz. pkg.), 1 slice 160
        (*Eckrich* Thick Sliced—1 lb. pkg.), 1 slice 170
        (*Eckrich Smorgas Pac*), 1 slice 90
        (*Kahn's* Jumbo), 1 oz. 87
        (*Oscar Mayer*), .8-oz. slice 75
        (*Swift Premium*), 1-oz. slice 95
        (*Wilson Certified*), 1 slice 90
        (*Wilson Corn King*), 1 slice 90
    beef:
        (*Eckrich*), 1-oz. slice 95
        (*Eckrich Smorgas Pac*), 1 slice 70

(*Hormel*), 1-oz. slice 82
(*Kahn's*), 1-oz. slice 88
(*Oscar Mayer Lebanon*), .8-oz. slice 75
(*Vienna*), 3½ oz. 296
(*Wilson Certified*), 1 slice 90
(*Wilson Corn King*), 1 slice 90
beef-garlic (*Oscar Mayer*), .8-oz. slice 75
garlic (*Eckrich*), 1 slice 95
meat:
   (*Hormel*), 1-oz. slice 84
   (*Wilson Certified*), 1 oz. 87
   (*Wilson Corn King*), 1 oz. 87
ring:
   (*Eckrich*), 1 oz. 100
   (*Hormel*—coarse ground), 1 oz. 76
   (*Hormel*—fine ground), 1 oz. 82
   (*Oscar Mayer Wisconsin*—coarse ground), 1 oz. 82
   (*Oscar Mayer Wisconsin*—fine ground), 1 oz. 88
   garlic (*Eckrich*), 1 oz. 95
turkey, see "Turkey bologna"
and cheese (*Oscar Mayer*), .8-oz. slice 73
Bonito:
raw, meat only, 4 oz. 192
Bordeaux wine:
red:
   (*Château La Garde*), 4 fl. oz. 108
   (*Château Olivier*), 4 fl. oz. 108
   (*Château Pontet-Canet, Cruse & Fils Frères*),
     4 fl. oz. 96
   Bordeaux rouge (*Chanson Père & Fils*), 4 fl. oz. 108
   Bordeaux rouge (*Cruse & Fils Frères*), 4 fl. oz. 84
   Margaux (*B & G*), 4 fl. oz. 84
   Medoc (*Cruse & Fils Frères*), 4 fl. oz. 96
   St. Emilion (*B & G*), 4 fl. oz. 84
   St. Emilion (*Crus & Fils Frères*), 4 fl. oz. 92
   St. Julien (*Crus & Fils Frères*), 4 fl. oz. 92

white, Graves (*Château Olivier*), 4 fl. oz. 108
white, Graves (*Crus & Fils Frères*), 4 fl. oz. 92
Borscht, see "Soups"
Boston cream pie, see "Pies, frozen"
Bouillon (see also "Soups"):
    dry form, cubes ½″ cube 5
    powder, 1 packet 6
    powder, 1 tsp. 2
    beef (*Herb-Ox*), 1 cube 7
    beef (*Maggi*), 1 cube 6
    beef (*Steero*), 1 cube or 1 tsp. 10
    beef (*Wyler's*), 1 cube or 1 tsp. 6
    chicken (*Herb-Ox*), 1 cube 7
    chicken (*Steero*), 1 cube or 1 tsp. 10
    chicken (*Wyler's*), 1 cube or 1 tsp. 8
    vegetable (*Herb-Ox*), 1 cube 7
    vegetable (*Steero*), 1 cube or 1 tsp. 10
Boysenberries:
    fresh, see "Blackberries"
    canned, in water, with liquid, 8 oz. 82
    canned, in water, with liquid, 1 cup 88
    frozen:
        unsweetened, 10-oz. pkg. 136
        unsweetened, 1 cup 60
        sweetened, 10-oz. pkg. 272
        sweetened, 1 cup 137
Brains:
    fresh, all types, raw, 8 oz. 284
Bran, wheat, see "Wheat bran"
Bran flakes, see "Cereals, ready-to-eat"
Brandy extract:
    imitation (*Durkee*), 1 tsp. 15
Brandy flavoring:
    pure (*Ehlers*), 1 tsp. 16
Bratwurst:
    (*Kahn's*), 2-oz. link 180

(*Kahn's Lauderdale* Jumbo), 1 link 178
cured (*Oscar Mayer*), 3-oz. link 277
Braunschweiger (smoked liverwurst):
rolls, 8-oz. roll (5½" long, 2" in diam.) 724
rolls, 1 slice (2" in diam., ¼" thick) 32
slices, 6-oz. pkg. (6 slices) 542
slices, 1 slice (3⅛" in diam., ¼" thick) 90
(*Oscar Mayer*—sliced), 1-oz. slice 103
(*Oscar Mayer*—tube), 1 oz. 95
(*Wilson Certified*), 8-oz. pkg. 716
spread (*Oscar Mayer*), ½ oz. 50
Brazil nuts:
in shell, 1 lb. 1,424
in shell, 1 cup 383
in shell, 3 large or 3½ medium nuts (1 oz.) 89
shelled, 4 oz. 741
shelled, 1 cup 916
shelled, 6 large or 8 medium nuts (1 oz.) 185
Bread:
bran and high fiber:
(*Arnold Bran'nola*), 1 slice 90
(*Brownberry* Whole Bran), 1 slice 75
(*Monk's* Hi-Fibre), 1 slice 50
(*Oroweat Bran'nola*), 1 slice 93
(*Pepperidge Farm* Honey Bran), 1 slice 58
Boston brown, 1 slice (3" × ¾") 101
brown, canned (*B & M*), ½" slice 78
brown, with raisins, canned (*B & M*), ½ " slice 78
corn, see "Cornbread"
corn and molasses (*Pepperidge Farm*), 1 slice 70
cracked wheat:
(*Northridge*), 1 slice 70
(*Pepperidge Farm*), 1 slice 70
(*Taystee*), 1 slice 80
(*Wonder*), 1 slice 75
date nut (*Thomas'*), 1 slice 90

French:

    (*Francisco*—long, sliced), 1 slice 60

    (*Francisco*—mini loaves), ⅓ of loaf 200

    (*Francisco*—round, sliced), 1 slice 85

    (*Francisco*—square, sliced), 1 slice 110

    (*Pepperidge Farm* Brown & Serve), 1-oz. slice 75

    (*Wonder*), 1 slice 75

gluten (*Oroweat*), 1 slice 70

gluten (*Thomas' Glutogen*), 1 slice 30

(*Hillbilly*), 1 slice 70

(*Hollywood*—dark), 1 slice 70

(*Hollywood*—light), 1 slice 70

(*Home Pride* 7 Grain), 1 slice 70

Italian (*Pepperidge Farm* Brown & Serve),

    1-oz. slice 75

oatmeal:

    (*Brownberry*), 1 slice 80

    (*Northridge*), 1 slice 70

    (*Pepperidge Farm*), 1 slice 65

(*Profile*—dark), 1 slice 75

(*Profile*—light), 1 slice 75

protein (*Thomas' Protogen*—fresh), 1 slice 45

protein (*Thomas' Protogen*—frozen), 1 slice 55

pumpernickel:

    (*Arnold*), 1 slice 75

    (*Brownberry* Sandwich Dark Bread), 1 slice 75

    (*Oroweat* Bavarian Pumpernickel), 1 slice 69

    (*Oroweat* Bohemian Pumpernickel), 1 slice 100

    (*Pepperidge Farm* Family), 1 slice 75

    (*Pepperidge Farm* Party Pumpernickel), 2 small slices 45

raisin:

    (*Arnold* Raisin Tea Loaf), 1 slice 70

    (*Brownberry* Raisin Cinnamon), 1 slice 85

    (*Brownberry* Raisin Nut), 1 slice 95

    (*Monk's*), 1 slice 90

(*Northridge* Royal Raisin Nut), 1 slice 85
(*Oroweat* Raisin Nugget), 1 slice 85
(*Pepperidge Farm*), 1 slice 75
(*Thomas'* Cinnamon Raisin Loaf), 1 slice 60
(*Roman Meal*), 1 slice 70
rye:
    (*Arnold*), 1 slice 75
    (*Arnold* Seeded Rye), 1 slice 75
    (*Arnold* Soft Rye), 1 slice 75
    (*Brownberry* Extra Thin), 1 slice 65
    (*Grossinger's*), 1 slice 70
    (*Oroweat* Buffet Rye), 2 small slices 50
    (*Oroweat* Dark Rye), 1 slice 65
    (*Oroweat* Dill Rye), 1 slice 70
    (*Oroweat* Hearth Rye), 1 slice 61
    (*Oroweat* Russian Rye), 1 slice 70
    (*Oroweat* Swedish Rye), 1 slice 51
    (*Pepperidge Farm* Family Rye), 1 slice 80
    (*Pepperidge Farm* Jewish Rye), 1 slice 65
    (*Pepperidge Farm* Party Rye), 2 small slices 35
    (*Pepperidge Farm* Seedless Rye), 1 slice 80
    (*Wonder*), 1 slice 75
sourdough (*Di Carlo*), 1 slice 70
sweet, see "Bread, sweet, mix"
Vienna (*Francisco*—long, sliced), 1 slice 34
wheat:
    (*Arnold* American Granary), 1 slice 70
    (*Arnold* Brick Oven Wheat—1-lb. loaf), 1 slice 60
    (*Arnold* Brick Oven Wheat—2-lb. loaf), 1 slice 80
    (*Arnold* Honey Wheat Berry), 1 slice 90
    (*Arnold* Melba Wheat), 1 slice 40
    (*Arnold* Natural Wheat), 1 slice 65
    (*Arnold* Small Family Wheat), 1 slice 60
    bran, see "bran and high fiber," above
    (*Brownberry* Health Nut), 1 slice 85
    (*Brownberry* Natural Wheat), 1 slice 85

(*Brownberry* Great Grains), 1 slice .70
cracked, see "cracked wheat," above
(*Fresh Horizons*), 1 slice 50
(*Fresh & Natural*), 1 slice 70
(*Home Pride* Butter Top), 1 slice 75
(*Home Pride* Honey Wheat Berry), 1 slice 70
(*Home Pride* Honey Wheat), 1 slice 70
(*Home Pride* Wheatberry), 1 slice 70
(*Northridge*), 1 slice 70
(*Northridge* Thin Sliced), 1 slice 45
(*Oroweat* American Granary), 1 slice 70
(*Oroweat* Honey Wheat Berry), 1 slice 85
(*Oroweat* Soya), 1 slice 67
(*Oroweat* Sprouted Wheat), 1 slice 65
(*Oroweat* Thin Sliced), 1 slice .45
(*Oroweat* Wheat Nuggets), 1 slice 79
(*Pepperidge Farm* Honey Wheatberry), 1 slice 60
(*Pepperidge Farm* Sprouted Wheat), 1 slice 65
(*Pepperidge Farm* Wheat—1½-lb. loaf), 1 slice 90
(*Pepperidge Farm* Wheat Germ), 1 slice 60
(*Taystee*), 1 slice 80
(*Wonder*), 1 slice 75
wheat, whole:
(*Arnold* Stoneground 100%), 1 slice 55
(*Home Pride* 100%), 1 slice 70
(*Monk's* Stone Ground), 1 slice .80
(*Oroweat* 100%), 1 slice 94
(*Northridge* 100%), 1 slice 70
(*Pepperidge Farm*), 1 slice 70
(*Pepperidge Farm* Very Thin), 1 slice 40
(*Thomas'*), 1 slice 50
(*Wonder* 100%), 1 slice 70
white:
(*Arnold* Brick Oven White—1-lb. loaf), 1 slice 65
(*Arnold* Brick Oven White—2-lb. loaf), 1 slice 85
(*Arnold* Country White), 1 slice .95

(*Arnold* Hearthstone Country White—1-lb. loaf),
  1 slice 70
(*Arnold* Hearthstone White—2-lb. loaf), 1 slice 85
(*Arnold* Melba White), 1 slice 40
(*Arnold* Small Family White), 1 slice 65
(*Brownberry* Extra Thin), 1 slice 70
(*Brownberry* Sandwich), 1 slice 75
(*D'Agostino*), 1 slice 75
(*Fresh Horizons*), 1 slice 50
(*Home Pride* Butter Top), 1 slice 75
(*Monk's*), 1 slice 70
(*Northridge*), 1 slice 70
(*Northridge* Honey Egg), 1 slice 70
(*Northridge* Soya Nut), 1 slice 67
(*Northridge* Thin), 1 slice 45
(*Oroweat* Old Style), 1 slice 75
(*Pepperidge Farm* Family White), 1 slice 75
(*Pepperidge Farm* Sandwich), 1 slice 65
(*Pepperidge Farm* Thin Sliced), 1 slice 75
(*Pepperidge Farm* Toasting), 1 slice 85
(*Pepperidge Farm* Unsliced), 1-oz. slice 85
(*Pepperidge Farm* Very Thin), 1 slice 40
(*Taystee*), 1 slice 75
(*Wonder*), 1 slice 70
  with buttermilk (*Wonder*), 1 slice 75

Bread, sweet, mix*:
  applesauce spice (*Pillsbury*), $\frac{1}{12}$ of loaf 150
  apricot nut (*Pillsbury*), $\frac{1}{12}$ of loaf 160
  banana (*Pillsbury*), $\frac{1}{12}$ of loaf 150
  blueberry nut (*Pillsbury*), $\frac{1}{12}$ of loaf 150
  cherry nut (*Pillsbury*), $\frac{1}{12}$ of loaf 170
  cranberry (*Pillsbury*), $\frac{1}{12}$ of loaf 160
  date (*Pillsbury*), $\frac{1}{12}$ of loaf 160
  nut (*Pillsbury*), $\frac{1}{12}$ of loaf 170

*Prepared according to directions on container

Bread crumbs:

dry, grated, 1 oz. 111
dry, grated, 1 cup 392
soft, 1 cup 122
(*Colonna*), 2 tbsp. 29
(*Wonder*), 1 oz. 108
Italian style (*Old London*), 1 oz. 105
seasoned (*Contadina*), 2 tbsp. 50
toasted (*Old London*), 1 oz. 105

Breadfruit:

fresh, raw, untrimmed, 1 lb. 360
fresh, raw, trimmed, peeled, 4 oz. 117

Breadsticks:

plain, 1 oz. 109
plain, 1 stick (4½″ long, ½″ in diam.) 38
plain (*Stella D'Oro*), 1 piece 41
cheese, see "Cheese straws"
lightly salted (*Pepperidge Farm* Snack Sticks), ½ oz. 60
onion (*Stella D'Oro*), 1 piece 39
pumpernickel (*Pepperidge Farm* Snack Sticks), ½ oz. 55
sesame (*Flavor Tree*), ½ oz. 79
sesame (*Pepperidge Farm* Snack Sticks), ½ oz. 60
sesame (*Stella D'Oro*), 1 piece 53
sesame-bran (*Flavor Tree*), ½ oz. 82
sour cream and onion sesame (*Flavor Tree*), ½ oz. 75
Vienna, 1 oz. 86
Vienna, 1 stick (6½ ″ long, 1¼″ in diam.) 106
whole wheat (*Pepperidge Farm* Snack Sticks), ½ oz. 55

Bread stuffing:

dry:
    coarse crumbs, 1 cup 260
    cornbread (*Pepperidge Farm*), 1 oz. 110
    cubes, 1 cup 111
    cubes (*Pepperidge Farm*), 1 oz. 110
    herb (*Pepperidge Farm*), 1 oz. 110
    chicken and herb, pan style (*Pepperidge Farm*), 1 oz. 110

seasoned, pan style (*Pepperidge Farm*), 1 oz. 110

mix*:

(*Bell's*—6-oz. pkg.), ½ cup 220

(*Bell's*—16-oz. pkg.), ½ cup 233

chicken (*Stove Top*), ½ cup 170

chicken (*Uncle Ben's*), ½ cup 177

cornbread (*Stove Top*), ½ cup 170

cornbread (*Uncle Ben's*), ½ cup 176

herb seasoned (*Croutettes*), ½ cup 130

pork (*Stove Top*), ½ cup 170

(*Stove Top* Americana New England), ½ cup 180

(*Stove Top* Americana San Francisco), ½ cup 170

traditional sage (*Uncle Ben's*), ½ cup 177

with rice (*Stove Top*), ½ cup 180

Breakfast bars:

(*Nature Valley* Breakfast Squares), 2 bars 380

almond (*Nature Valley* Granola Bars), 1 bar 110

almond (*Nature Valley* Granola Cluster), 1 roll 140

almond crunch (*Carnation* Breakfast Bar),

1.44-oz. bar 200

caramel (*Nature Valley* Granola Cluster), 1 roll 140

chocolate chip (*Carnation* Breakfast Bar), 1.49-oz. bar 200

chocolate crunch (*Carnation* Breakfast Bar),

1.49-oz. bar 200

cinnamon (*Nature Valley* Granola Bar), 1 bar 110

coconut (*Nature Valley* Granola Bar), 1 bar 120

oats and honey (*Nature Valley* Granola Bar), 1 bar 110

peanut (*Nature Valley* Granola Bar), 1 bar 120

peanut butter and chocolate chip (*Crunchola*), 1 bar 160

peanut butter crunch (*Carnation* Breakfast Bar),

1.51-oz. bar 210

raisin (*Nature Valley* Granola Cluster), 1 roll 140

yogurt and granola, orange (*Crunchola*), 1 bar 140

yogurt and granola, strawberry (*Crunchola*), 1 bar 140

*Prepared according to directions on container

Breakfast drinks see "Milk beverages, flavored"
Breakfast sausage, see "Sausages"
(*Brighton Punch*):
  1 fl. oz. . . . . :89
Broad beans:
  raw, immature seeds, 8 oz. 238
  raw, mature seeds, 8 oz. 767
Broccoli:
  fresh:
    raw, 1 lb. 89
    raw, trimmed, 1 lb. 145
    boiled, drained, 8 oz. 59
    boiled, drained, 1 medium spear 47
    boiled, drained, cuts, 1 cup 40
  frozen:
    florets (*Birds Eye*), 3.3 oz. 25
    florets (*Hanover*), 3.2 oz. 35
    spears (*Birds Eye*), 3.3 oz. 25
    spears (*Seabrook Farms*), 3.3 oz. 30
    spears (*Stokely-Van Camp*), 3.3 oz. 30
    spears, baby (*Birds Eye*), 3.3 oz. 30
    cut (*Birds Eye*), 3.3 oz. 25
    cut (*Green Giant*), ½ cup 15
    cut (*Hanover*), 3.2 oz. 25
    cut (*Kounty Kist/Lindy*), ½ cup 15
    cut (*Stokely-Van Camp*), 3 oz. .25
    chopped (*Birds Eye*), 3.3 oz. 25
    chopped (*Seabrook Farms*), 3.3 oz. 25
    chopped (*Stokely-Van Camp*), 3.3 oz. 25
    au gratin (*Stouffer's*), 5 oz. 170
    with butter sauce (*Green Giant*), ½ cup 45
    in cheddar cheese sauce (*Stouffer's*), 9-oz. pkg. 260
    in cheese sauce (*Birds Eye*), 5 oz. 170
    in cheese sauce (*Green Giant*), ½ cup 65
    in cheese sauce (*Green Giant* Bake 'n Serve),
      ½ cup 130

florentine (*Stokely-Van Camp*), 3.3 oz. 30
in hollandaise sauce (*Birds Eye*), 3.3 oz. 100
light batter-fried, and cheese (*Mrs. Paul's*), 2½ oz. 150
light batter-fried, and cheese (*Mrs. Paul's*),
    7½-oz. pkg. 450
and carrots, and pasta twists (*Birds Eye* Blue Ribbon),
    3.3 oz. 90
and cauliflower (*Hanover*), 3.2 oz. 15
and cauliflower and carrots (*Birds Eye* Farm Fresh),
    3.2 oz. 25
and cauliflower and carrots
    (*Kounty Kist* California Blend), ½ cup 15
and cauliflower and carrots with cheese sauce
    (*Birds Eye*), 5 oz. 130
and cauliflower and carrots with cheese sauce
    (*Green Giant*), ½ cup 70
and cauliflower and red peppers (*Birds Eye*), 3.3 oz. 25
and corn and red peppers (*Birds Eye* Farm Fresh),
    3.2 oz. 50
and green beans, onions, and red peppers
    (*Birds Eye* Farm Fresh), 3.2 oz. 25
Brown and serve sausages, see "Sausages"
Brown gravy:
in jars (*Heinz*), ½ cup 60
mix*:
    (*Durkee*), ½ cup 30
    (*Ehlers*), ½ cup 44
    (*French's*), ½ cup 40
    (*McCormick/Schilling*), ½ cup 59
    (*McCormick/Schilling Lite*), ½ cup 20
    (*Pillsbury*), ½ cup 30
    (*Spatini*), ½ cup 32
    with mushrooms (*Durkee*), ½ cup 30
    with onion (*Durkee*), ½ cup 33

*Prepared according to directions on container

with mushroom broth, canned (*Dawn Fresh*), 4 oz. 40
with onion, canned (*Franco-American*), 4 oz. 50
sauce (*La Choy*), 1 tsp. 19
Brownies:
(*Hostess*), 1¼-oz. piece 150
(*Hostess*), 2-oz. piece 240
frozen:
    chocolate (*Sara Lee*), 1.62-oz. piece 200
    with nuts, iced, 1 oz. 119
mix*:
    (*Betty Crocker* Fudge), 1/16 of pkg. 150
    (*Betty Crocker* Fudge Family Size), 1/24 of pkg. 130
    (*Betty Crocker* German Chocolate), 1/16 of pkg. 150
    (*Betty Crocker* Supreme Fudge), 1/24 of pkg. 120
    (*Duncan Hines* Double Fudge—Cake or Chewy),
      1 piece 140
    (*Pillsbury*), 1½" square 65
    (*Pillsbury* Family Size), 1½" square 75
    chocolate chip butterscotch (*Betty Crocker*),
      1/16 of pkg. 130
    with walnuts (*Betty Crocker*), 1/16 of pkg. 160
    with walnuts (*Betty Crocker* Family Size),
      ½ of pkg. 130
    with walnuts (*Pillsbury*), 1½" square 75
    with walnuts (*Pillsbury* Family Size) 1½" square 80
refrigerator:
    (*Pillsbury* Slice 'N Bake Fudge), 1 piece 250
Browning sauce, microwave:
beef (*Holland House*), ½ oz. 28
chicken (*Holland House*), ½ oz. 31
pork (*Holland House*), ½ oz. 33
Brussels sprouts:
fresh:
    raw, whole, 1 lb. 204

*Prepared according to directions on container

54

boiled, drained, 8 oz. 82
boiled, drained, 1 cup 56
boiled, drained, 4 medium sprouts 30
frozen:
boiled, drained, 10 oz. (yield from 10-oz. pkg.) 94
boiled, drained, 1 cup 51
(*Birds Eye*), 3.3. oz. 35
(*Green Giant*), ½ cup 25
(*Hanover*), 3.2 oz. 38
(*Kounty Kist*), ½ cup 25
(*Stokely-Van Camp*), 3.3 oz. 40
with butter sauce (*Green Giant*), ½ cup 55
baby (*Birds Eye*), 3.3 oz. 40
baby with cheese sauce (*Birds Eye*), 4.5 oz. 150
halves, with cheese sauce (*Green Giant*), ½ cup 85
au gratin (*Stouffer's*), 5⁷⁄₁₆ oz. 180
and cauliflower and carrots (*Birds Eye* Farm Fresh),
  3.2 oz. 30
Buckwheat flour, see "Flour"
Buffet loaf:
(*Hormel*), 1-oz. slice 52
Bulgur (parboiled wheat):
club wheat, dry, 8 oz. 814
club wheat, dry, 1 cup 628
hard red winter wheat, dry, 8 oz. 802
hard red winter wheat, dry, 1 cup 603
white wheat, dry, 8 oz. 810
white wheat, dry, 1 cup 553
canned, hard red winter wheat, unseasoned, 8 oz. 382
canned, hard red winter wheat, unseasoned, 1 cup 227
canned, hard red winter wheat, seasoned, 8 oz. 412
canned, hard red winter wheat, seasoned, 1 cup 246
Buns, see "Rolls and buns"
Burger sauce:
in jars (*Hellman's Big H*), 1 tbsp. 70

Burgundy wine:
red:
    domestic (*Gold Seal*), 4 fl. oz. 109
    domestic (*Italian Swiss Colony*), 4 fl. oz. 86
    domestic (*Taylor*), 4 fl. oz. 96
    imported, Beaujolais (*Crus & Fils Frères*), 4 fl. oz. 96
    imported, Beaune (*Chanson Père & Fils* St. Vincent),
        4 fl. oz. 108
    imported, Gevrey-Chambertin (*Crus & Fils Frères*),
        4 fl. oz. 96
    imported, Nuits St. George (*B & G*), 4 fl. oz. 92
    imported, Pommard (*Chanson Père & Fils* St. Vincent),
        4 fl. oz. 108
    imported, Pommard (*Crus & Fils Frères*), 4 fl. oz. 96
    sparkling, domestic (*Gold Seal*), 4 fl. oz. 116
    sparkling, domestic (*Taylor*), 4 fl. oz. 104
white, see "Chablis"

Burrito:
beef, frozen (*Hormel*), 1 burrito 220

Butter:
regular:
    8 oz., or 1 cup 1,625
    4 oz., or 1 stick 812
    1 tbsp. 102
    1 tsp. 34
    1 pat (1″ × ⅓″; 90 pats per lb.) 36
whipped:
    8-oz. container 1,625
    1 cup 1,081
    ½ cup, or 1 stick 541
    1 tbsp. 67
    1 tsp. 23
    1 pat (1¼″ × ⅓″) 27

Butter flavor salt:
imitation (*French's*), 1 tsp. 8
imitation (*McCormick/Schilling*), 1 tsp. 2

Butter flavoring:
  imitation (*Durkee*), 1 tsp. 3
  imitation (*Ehlers*), 1 tsp. 8
Butterfish:
  raw, gulf, meat only, 4 oz. 108
  raw, northern, meat only, 4 oz. 192
Buttermilk, see "Milk"
Butternuts:
  in shell, 4 oz. 100
  shelled, 4 oz. 713
  4–5 nuts 94
Butter oil:
  1 tbsp. 123
Butterscotch candy, see "Candy"
Butterscotch dessert topping:
  (*Kraft*), 1 tbsp. 60
  (*Smucker's*), 1 tbsp. 70
Butterscotch morsels, see "Candy"
Butterscotch pie filling:
  canned (*Comstock*), ⅓ cup 110

C

Cabbage, savoy, fresh:
raw, whole, 1 lb. 98
raw, trimmed, 1 lb. 109
raw, sliced or coarsely shredded, 1 cup 17
Cabbage, spoon, fresh:
raw, whole, 1 lb. 73
raw, trimmed, 1 lb. 69
raw, cuts, 1 cup 11
boiled, drained, cuts, 1 cup 24
Cabbage pierogies:
frozen (*Mrs. Paul's*), 5 oz. 330
Cabbage salad, see "Coleslaw"
Cabbage, stuffed:
canned (*Joan of Arc*), ½ cup 98
frozen, rolls, in tomato sauce
  (*Green Giant* Baked Entree), 7-oz. pkg. 220
Cake icing, see "Icing, cake, mix" and "Icing, cake, ready-to-spread"
Cakes, frozen:
apple walnut (*Sara Lee*), ⅛ of 12¼-oz. cake 166
banana:
  (*Pepperidge Farm* Cake Supreme),
    ¼ of 11½-oz. cake 280
  (*Sara Lee*), ⅛ of 13¾-oz. cake 175
  nut layer (*Sara Lee*), ⅛ of 20-oz. cake 233
Black Forest (*Sara Lee*), ⅛ of 21-oz. cake 203
Boston cream (*Pepperidge Farm* Cake Supreme),
  ¼ of 11½-oz. cake 270
Boston cream pie, see "Pies, frozen" and "Pies, mix"
carrot (*Sara Lee*), ⅛ of 24¼-oz. cake 153
cheesecake, see "Pies, mix"
chocolate:
  (*Pepperidge Farm* Cake Supreme),
    ¼ of 12-oz. cake 310
  (*Sara Lee*), ⅛ of 13¼-oz. cake 185

cream layer (*Sara Lee*), ⅛ of 18-oz. cake 209
double chocolate layer (*Sara Lee*),
  ⅛ of 18-oz. cake 214
fudge (*Pepperidge Farm*), ⅛ of 17-oz. cake 225
fudge (*Pepperidge Farm* Half Cake),
  ¼ of 8½-oz. cake 225
German (*Pepperidge Farm*), ⅛ of 17-oz. cake 200
German (*Sara Lee*), ⅛ of 12¼-oz. cake 172
roll (*Rich's*), ⅛ of 14-oz. cake 150
coconut:
  (*Pepperidge Farm*), ⅛ of 17-oz. cake 225
  (*Pepperidge Farm* Half Cake), ¼ of 8½-oz. cake 225
  (*Sara Lee*), ⅛ of 10-oz. cake 144
coffee cake:
  almond (*Sara Lee* Coffee Ring),
    ⅛ of 11¾-oz. cake 169
  almond (*Sara Lee* Light Coffee Round),
    ⅛ of 8-oz. cake 120
  blueberry (*Sara Lee* Coffee Ring),
    ⅛ of 9¾-oz. cake 133
  blueberry (*Sara Lee* Light Coffee Round),
    ⅛ of 8-oz. cake 115
  butter streusel (*Sara Lee*), ⅛ of 11½-oz. cake 160
  cinnamon streusel (*Sara Lee*), ⅛ of 10⅞-oz. cake 154
  maple (*Sara Lee* Light Coffee Round),
    ⅛ of 8-oz. cake 121
  maple crunch (*Sara Lee* Coffee Ring),
    ⅛ of 9¾-oz. cake 138
  pecan (*Sara Lee*), ⅛ of 11¼-oz. cake 165
  pecan (*Sara Lee*), ¼ of 6½-oz. cake 191
  raspberry (*Sara Lee* Coffee Ring),
    ⅛ of 9¾-oz. cake 140
  raspberry (*Sara Lee* Light Coffee Round),
    ⅛ of 8-oz. cake 115
devil's food (*Pepperidge Farm*), ⅛ of 17-oz. cake 225

golden layer (*Pepperidge Farm*), ⅛ of 17-oz. cake 225
golden layer (*Pepperidge Farm* Half Cake),
　¼ of 8½-oz. cake 225
lemon-coconut (*Pepperidge Farm* Cake Supreme),
　¼ of 12-oz. cake 280
lemon cream roll (*Rich's*), ⅛ of 14-oz. cake 150
orange (*Sara Lee*), ⅛ of 13¾-oz. cake 175
pound cake:
　plain (*Sara Lee*), ⅒ of 10¾-oz. cake 124
　plain (*Sara Lee* Homestyle), ⅒ of 9½-oz. cake 109
　plain (*Sara Lee* Family Size), ⅟₁₅ of 16½-oz. cake 127
　apple nut (*Pepperidge Farm*), ⅒ of 14-oz. cake 130
　banana nut (*Sara Lee*), ⅒ of 11-oz. cake 117
　butter (*Pepperidge Farm*), ⅒ of 10½-oz. cake 130
　carrot (*Pepperidge Farm*), ⅒ of 14-oz. cake 160
　chocolate (*Pepperidge Farm*), ⅒ of 10½-oz. cake 130
　chocolate (*Sara Lee*), ⅒ of 10¾-oz. cake 122
　chocolate swirl (*Sara Lee*), ⅒ of 11¾-oz. cake 130
　raisin (*Sara Lee*), ⅒ of 12.9-oz. cake 128
strawberry:
　cheesecake, see "Pies, frozen"
　cream layer (*Sara Lee*), ⅛ of 20½-oz. cake 213
　shortcake (*Mrs. Smith's*), ⅛ of 20-oz. cake 235
　shortcake (*Sara Lee*), ⅛ of 21-oz. cake 193
　roll (*Rich's*), ⅛ of 14-oz. cake 130
vanilla (*Pepperidge Farm*), ⅛ of 17-oz. cake 237
walnut layer (*Sara Lee*), ⅛ of 18-oz. cake 211
Cakes, mix*:
angel food:
　(*Betty Crocker* One-Step), ⅟₁₂ of cake 140
　(*Betty Crocker* Traditional), ⅟₁₂ of cake 130
　(*Duncan Hines*), ⅟₁₂ of cake 140
　(*Pillsbury*), ⅟₁₂ of cake 140

---

*Prepared according to directions on container

(*Swans Down*), 1/12 of cake 133
chocolate (*Betty Crocker*), 1/12 of cake 140
confetti (*Betty Crocker*), 1/12 of cake 150
lemon custard (*Betty Crocker*), 1/12 of cake 140
raspberry (*Pillsbury*), 1/12 of cake 140
strawberry (*Betty Crocker*), 1/12 of cake 150
applesauce spice (*Pillsbury Plus*), 1/12 of cake 250
banana:
    (*Betty Crocker Supermoist*), 1/12 of cake 270
    (*Pillsbury Plus*), 1/12 of cake 260
    (*Pillsbury Streusel Swirl*), 1/16 of cake 260
    supreme (*Duncan Hines* Layer), 1/12 of cake 200
butter:
    (*Betty Crocker Supermoist Butter Brickle*),
        1/12 of cake 260
    fudge (*Duncan Hines* Layer), 1/12 of cake 270
    golden (*Duncan Hines* Layer), 1/12 of cake 270
    rich (*Pillsbury Streusel Swirl*), 1/16 of cake 260
    yellow (*Betty Crocker Supermoist*), 1/12 of cake 240
    yellow (*Pillsbury Plus*), 1/12 of cake 240
butter pecan (*Betty Crocker Supermoist*), 1/12 of cake 260
carrot and spice (*Pillsbury Plus*), 1/12 of cake 260
cheesecake, see "Pies, mix"
cherry chip (*Betty Crocker Supermoist*), 1/12 of cake 210
cherry supreme (*Duncan Hines* Layer), 1/12 of cake 190
chocolate:
    dark (*Pillsbury Plus*), 1/12 of cake 260
    deep (*Duncan Hines* Layer), 1/12 of cake 200
    fudge (*Betty Crocker Supermoist*), 1/12 of cake 270
    German (*Betty Crocker Supermoist*), 1/12 of cake 270
    German (*Duncan Hines* Pudding Recipe), 1/12 of cake ... 250
    German (*Pillsbury Plus*), 1/12 of cake 250
    German (*Pillsbury Streusel Swirl*), 1/16 of cake 260
    German (*Swans Down*), 1/12 of cake 188
    macaroon (*Pillsbury Bundt*), 1/16 of cake 250

milk (*Betty Crocker Supermoist*), 1/12 of cake 260
mint (*Pillsbury Plus*), 1/12 of cake 250
Swiss (*Duncan Hines* Layer), 1/12 of cake 200
cinnamon (*Pillsbury Streusel Swirl*), 1/16 of cake 260
devil's food:
   (*Betty Crocker Supermoist*), 1/12 of cake 270
   (*Duncan Hines* Layer), 1/12 of cake 200
   (*Duncan Hines* Pudding Recipe), 1/12 of cake 250
   (*Pillsbury Plus*), 1/12 of cake 250
   (*Pillsbury Streusel Swirl*), 1/16 of cake 260
   (*Swans Down*), 1/12 of cake 187
fudge:
   marble (*Duncan Hines* Layer), 1/12 of cake 200
   marble (*Pillsbury Plus*), 1/12 of cake 270
   marble (*Pillsbury Streusel Swirl*), 1/16 of cake 260
   nut crown (*Pillsbury Bundt*), 1/16 of cake 220
   triple (*Pillsbury Bundt*), 1/16 of cake 210
   tunnel of (*Pillsbury Bundt*), 1/16 of cake 270
golden vanilla (*Duncan Hines* Pudding Recipe),
   1/12 of cake 250
lemon:
   (*Betty Crocker Supermoist*), 1/12 of cake 270
   (*Duncan Hines* Pudding Recipe), 1/12 of cake 250
   (*Pillsbury Plus*), 1/12 of cake 260
   (*Pillsbury Streusel Swirl*), 1/16 of cake 260
   chiffon (*Betty Crocker*), 1/12 of cake 190
   supreme (*Duncan Hines* Layer), 1/12 of cake 200
   tunnel of (*Pillsbury Bundt*), 1/16 of cake 270
lemon-blueberry (*Pillsbury Bundt*), 1/16 of cake 200
marble (*Betty Crocker Supermoist*), 1/12 of cake 290
marble fudge, see "fudge" above
marble supreme (*Pillsbury Bundt*), 1/16 of cake 250
orange (*Betty Crocker Supermoist*), 1/12 of cake 270
orange supreme (*Duncan Hines* Layer), 1/12 of cake 200
pineapple supreme (*Duncan Hines* Layer), 1/12 of cake 200
pound (*Pillsbury Bundt*), 1/16 of cake 230

pound, golden (*Betty Crocker*), 1/12 of cake 190
sour cream:
    chocolate (*Betty Crocker Supermoist*), 1/12 of cake 270
    chocolate (*Duncan Hines* Layer), 1/12 of cake 200
    white (*Betty Crocker Supermoist*), 1/12 of cake 200
spice (*Betty Crocker Supermoist*), 1/12 of cake 270
spice (*Duncan Hines* Layer), 1/12 of cake 200
strawberry:
    (*Betty Crocker Supermoist*), 1/12 of cake 270
    (*Pillsbury Plus*), 1/12 of cake 260
    supreme (*Duncan Hines* Layer), 1/12 of cake 200
white:
    (*Betty Crocker Supermoist*), 1/12 of cake 190
    (*Duncan Hines* Layer), 1/12 of cake 190
    (*Duncan Hines* Pudding Recipe), 1/12 of cake 240
    (*Pillsbury Plus*), 1/12 of cake 240
    (*Swans Down*), 1/12 of cake 178
yellow:
    (*Betty Crocker Supermoist*), 1/12 of cake 270
    (*Duncan Hines* Layer), 1/12 of cake 200
    (*Duncan Hines* Pudding Recipe), 1/12 of cake 250
    (*Pillsbury Plus*), 1/12 of cake 260
    (*Swans Down*), 1/12 of cake 188
Cakes, snack (see also "Brownies," "Cupcakes," "Doughnuts," etc):
apricot cake (*El Molino*), 2-oz. piece 250
banana (*Hostess Suzy Q's*), 2¼-oz. piece 240
butterscotch (*Tastykake* Krimpets), 1¾-oz. pkg. 192
chocolate or devil's food:
    (*Drake's Devil Dogs*), 1 cake 170
    (*Drake's Funny Bones*), 1 cake 160
    (*Drake's Ring Ding Jr.*), 1¼-oz. piece 165
    (*Drake's Swiss Roll*), ½ cake 180
    (*Drake's Yodels*), 1 cake 120
    (*Hostess Big Wheels*), 1⅓-oz. piece 170
    (*Hostess Choco-Dile*), 2.2-oz. piece 250

    (*Hostess Ding Dongs*), 1⅓-oz. piece 170
    (*Hostess Ho Ho's*), 1-oz. piece 120
    (*Hostess Suzy Q's*), 2¼-oz. piece 240
    (*Tastykake* Chocolate Cream Tempty), 2-oz. pkg. 197
    (*Tastykake* Chocolate Creamies), 2⅓-oz. pkg. 257
    (*Tastykake* Chocolate Juniors), 2¾-oz. pkg. 307
    (*Tastykake* Chocolate Tasty Klairs), 4-oz. pkg. 435
    (*Tastykake* Kandy Kake), 1⅓-oz. pkg. 181
cinnamon crumb cake (*El Molino*), 2-oz. piece 250
coconut (*Tastykake* Coconut Juniors), 2¾-oz. pkg. 330
coconut patties (*Frito-Lay's Choc-o-Roon*),
    2-oz. pkg. 290
coffee cake:
    (*Drake* Junior), 1.1-oz. piece 125
    (*Hostess* Crumb Cakes), 1¼-oz. piece 130
    (*Tastykake* Koffee Kake), 2-oz. pkg. 247
    (*Tastykake* Koffee Kake Juniors), 2½-oz. pkg. 313
creme fingers (*Drake's*), 1 cake 140
date cake (*El Molino*), 2-oz. piece 240
fruit and spice cake (*El Molino*), 2-oz. piece 230
granola cake (*El Molino*), 2-oz. piece 220
honey and bran cake (*El Molino*), 1½-oz. piece 160
honeybun (*Hostess*), 4¾-oz. piece 580
(*Hostess Twinkies*), 1½-oz. piece 140
(*Hostess Sno Ball*), 1½-oz. piece 140
(*Hostess Tiger Tail*), 2.2-oz. piece 215
jelly (*Tastykake* Jelly Krimpets), 1¾-oz. pkg. 168
lemon (*Tastykake* Lemon Juniors), 2¾-oz. pkg. 297
oatmeal, creme filled (*Frito-Lay's*), 2-oz. pkg. 260
oatmeal raisin bar (*Tastykake*), 1¾-oz. pkg. 267
pound cake, butter (*Drake's*), 1-oz. piece 100
pound cake, butter marble (*Drake's*), 1-oz. piece 100
raspberry crumb cake (*El Molino*), 2-oz. piece 260
spice cake (*Tastykake* Spice Creamie), 2¾-oz. pkg. 272
strawberry filled cake (*El Molino*), 2-oz. piece 240

Cakes, snack, frozen (see also ''Brownies,'' ''Cupcakes,''
''Doughnuts,'' etc.):
  buns, see ''Rolls and buns''
  cheesecake, see ''Pies, frozen''
  crumb cake, blueberry (*Sara Lee*), 1¾-oz. piece 155
  crumb cake, French (*Sara Lee*), 1.7-oz. piece 172
  danish, see ''Danish pastry''
  pies, see ''Pies, snack''
  puffs, vanilla (*Rich's*), 2.17-oz. piece 167
  turnovers, see individual listings
Cakes, snack, mix*:
  apple raisin, spicy (*Duncan Hines* Moist & Easy)
    ⅑ cake 180
  applesauce raisin (*Betty Crocker Snackin' Cake*),
    ⅑ pkg. 200
  banana nut (*Duncan Hines* Moist & Easy), ⅑ cake 200
  banana walnut (*Betty Crocker Snackin' Cake*), ⅑ pkg. 200
  brownies, see ''Brownies''
  cheesecake, see ''Pies, mix''
  chocolate:
    (*Betty Crocker* Pudding Cake), ⅙ pkg. 230
    chip, double (*Duncan Hines* Moist & Easy),
      ⅑ cake 180
    chip, fudge (*Betty Crocker Snackin' Cake*), ⅑ pkg. 220
    chip, golden (*Betty Crocker Snackin' Cake*), ⅑ pkg. 220
    devil's food, chocolate icing
      (*Betty Crocker Stir 'n Frost*), ⅙ pkg. 280
    fudge, vanilla icing (*Betty Crocker Stir 'n Frost*),
      ⅙ pkg. 290
  chocolate almond (*Betty Crocker Snackin' Cake*),
    ⅑ pkg. 210
  coconut pecan (*Betty Crocker Snackin' Cake*), ⅑ pkg. 220
  coffee cake:
    (*Aunt Jemima* Easy Mix), ⅛ cake 170

**Prepared according to directions on container*

apple cinnamon (*Pillsbury*), ⅛ cake 240
butter pecan (*Pillsbury*), ⅛ cake 310
cinnamon streusel (*Pillsbury*), ⅛ cake 250
sour cream (*Pillsbury*), ⅛ cake 270
date nut (*Betty Crocker Snackin' Cake*), ⅑ pkg. 210
devil's food, see "chocolate," above
lemon (*Betty Crocker* Pudding Cake), ⅙ cake 230
lemon, with lemon icing (*Betty Crocker Stir 'n Frost*),
  ⅙ pkg. 230
pineapple upside-down, with topping (*Betty Crocker*),
  ⅑ cake 270
spice, with vanilla icing (*Betty Crocker Stir 'n Frost*),
  ⅙ pkg. 270
spice raisin (*Betty Crocker Snackin' Cake*), ⅑ pkg. 200
white, with milk chocolate icing
  (*Betty Crocker Stir 'n Frost*), ⅙ pkg. 230
yellow, with chocolate icing (*Betty Crocker Stir 'n Frost*),
  ⅙ pkg. 230
Calves' liver, see "Liver"
(*Campari*):
45 proof, 1 fl. oz. 66
Candied fruit, see individual listings
Candy:
(*Baby Ruth*), 1.8-oz. bar 260
(*Black Cow* Sucker), 1 oz. 103
bridge mix (*Nabisco*), 1 oz. 125
bridge mix (*Nabisco*), 1 piece 9
(*Butterfinger*), 1.6-oz. bar 220
(*Butternut*), 1.75-oz. bar 230
(*Butternut*), 1.5-oz. bar 194
butterscotch:
  1 oz. 112
  (*Nestlé* Morsels), 1 oz. 150
  (*Rothchild's*), 1 piece 19
  drops (*Nabisco* Skimmers), 1 oz. 116
  drops (*Nabisco* Skimmers), 1 piece 25

67

candy corn, 1 oz. 103
candy corn (*Heide*), 1 piece 4
(*CaraCoa* Nuggets), 1 oz. 140
caramel:
    plain or chocolate, 1 oz. 113
    plain or chocolate, with nuts, 1 oz. 121
    (*CaraCoa*), 1 oz. 110
    (*Kraft*), 1 piece 35
    (*Pearson* Caramel Nip), 1 oz. 125
    (*Whirligigs*), .22-oz. piece 26
    chocolate-flavored roll, 1 oz. 112
    chocolate (*Sugar Daddy* Junior), .45-oz. piece 51
    chocolate center (*Tootsie Pops/Pop Drops*), 1 oz. 113
    chocolate covered (*Milk Duds*), 1 oz. 111
    chocolate covered (*Pom Poms*), 1 oz. 126
    chocolate covered (*Pom Poms*), 1 piece 14
    chocolate covered (*Rolo*), 1 oz. or 5 pieces 140
    vanilla (*Sugar Babies*), 1 oz. 117
    vanilla (*Sugar Babies*), .05-oz. piece 6
    vanilla (*Sugar Daddy*), 1.07-oz. piece 121
    vanilla (*Sugar Daddy* Giant), 1-lb. piece 1,806
    vanilla (*Sugar Daddy* Junior), .45-oz. piece 50
    vanilla (*Sugar Daddy* Nuggets), .43-oz. piece 48
    vanilla (*Sugar Mama*), .84-oz. piece 101
carob-coated bars:
    (*CaraCoa* Milk Free), 1-oz. bar 145
    (*CaraCoa* Natural), 1-oz. bar 160
    (*Tiger's Milk*), 2-oz. bar 250
    crunchy (*CaraCoa*), ⅞-oz. bar 140
    fruit and nut (*CaraCoa*), 1-oz. bar 155
    mint (*CaraCoa*), 1-oz. bar 160
    orange (*CaraCoa*), 1-oz. bar 160
    peanut (*CaraCoa*), 1-oz. bar 160
    peanut butter (*Tiger's Milk*), 1.7-oz. bar 210
    peanut butter and honey (*Tiger's Milk*),
        1.7-oz. bar 210

peanut butter and jelly (*Tiger's Milk*), 1.7-oz. bar 210
cherries:
   dark chocolate covered (*Nabisco/Welch's*), 1 oz. 113
   dark chocolate covered (*Nabisco/Welch's*), 1 piece 67
   milk chocolate covered (*Nabisco/Welch's*), 1 oz. 112
   milk chocolate covered (*Nabisco/Welch's*), 1 piece 66
chocolate:
   baking type, see "Chocolate, baking type"
   candy-coated (*M & M's*), 1.5-oz. pkg. 215
   candy-coated (*M & M's*), 1-oz. pkg. 138
   candy-coated (*M & M's* Fun Size), .63-oz. pkg. 88
   milk (*Cadbury*), 1 oz. 151
   milk (*Ghirardelli* Bars), 1 oz. 150
   milk (*Ghirardelli* Block), 1 oz. 149
   milk (*Hershey*), 1.2-oz. bar 180
   milk (*Hershey* Chips), 1.5-oz., or ¼ cup 220
   milk (*Hershey* Kisses), 1 oz., or 6 pieces 150
   milk (*Nabisco* Stars), 1 oz., or 10 pieces 152
   milk (*Nestlé*), 1 oz. 150
   mint (*Ghirardelli*), 1 oz. 150
   semisweet (*Eagle*), 1 oz. 149
   semisweet (*Ghirardelli* Chips), 1 oz. 150
   semisweet (*Hershey* Chips), 1.5 oz., or ¼ cup 220
   semisweet (*Hershey* Mini Chips), 1.5 oz., or ¼ cup 220
   semisweet (*Hershey Special Dark*), 1.2-oz. bar 180
   semisweet (*Lindt Excellence*), 1 oz. 162
   semisweet (*Nestlé* Morsels), 1 oz. 150
   semisweet, with vanilla (*Lindt*), 1 oz. 163
chocolate with caramel (*Cadbury Caramello*), 1 oz. 144
chocolate-coated candy, see specific kinds ("coconut,"
   "fudge," etc.)
chocolate with crisps:
   (*Ghirardelli*), 1 oz. 150
   (*Krackel*), 1.2-oz. bar 180
   (*Nestlé Crunch*), 1 oz. 150

chocolate with fruit and/or nuts:
  with almonds (*Cadbury*), 1 oz. .155
  with almonds (*Ghirardelli*), 1 oz. 152
  with almonds (*Hershey*), 1.15-oz. bar 180
  with almonds (*Nestlé*), 1 oz. 150
  with almonds, toasted (*Hershey Golden Almond*),
    1 oz. 160
  with brazil nuts (*Cadbury*), 1 oz. 156
  with fruit and nuts (*Cadbury*), 1 oz. 152
  with fruit and nuts (*Chunky*), 1 oz. 135
  with hazel nuts (*Cadbury*), 1 oz. 155
  with peanuts (*Mr. Goodbar*), 1.5-oz. bar 230
  with raisins (*Ghirardelli*), 1 oz. 142
coconut, chocolate covered:
  (*Mounds*), 1 oz. 147
  (*Nabisco* Coconut Squares), .54-oz. piece 64
  (*Welch's*), 1.07-oz. bar 132
  with almonds (*Almond Joy*), 1 oz. 151
coffee (*Pearson* Coffee Nip), 1 oz. 125
cough drops (*Halls*—Square and Oval), 1 piece 15
crisps, chocolate covered, with caramel (*Caravelle*),
  1 oz. 137
crisps, chocolate covered, with caramel (*$100,000*),
  1.5-oz. 200
dates, carob coated (*CaraCoa*), 1 oz. 125
fondant, uncoated, 1 oz. 103
fondant, chocolate covered, 1 oz. .116
(*Forever Yours*), 1.37-oz. bar 175
fruit chews (*Starburst*), 1.68-oz. pkg. 186
fruit chews (*Starburst*), 1-oz. pkg. 113
fruit roll, see individual listings
fudge:
  chocolate (*Kraft*), 1 piece 35
  chocolate, with nuts, 1 oz. 121
  chocolate, chocolate covered (*Welch's*),
    1.07-oz. bar 144

chocolate, chocolate covered, 1 oz. 122
chocolate, chocolate-coated, with nuts, 1 oz. 128
vanilla, 1 oz. 113
vanilla, with nuts, 1 oz. 120
chocolate-coated, with caramel and nuts, 1 oz. 123
chocolate-coated, with nuts and caramel, 1 oz. 130
(*Nabisco Home Style*), .7-oz. bar 90
with nuts (*Nabisco*), .54-oz. bar 70
with nuts (*Nabisco* Squares), 1 oz. 132
with nuts (*Nabisco* Squares), 1 piece 70
(*Good & Fruity*), 1.5-oz. pkg. 136
gum candy, see ''jellied and gum candy,'' below
hard candy (see also specific flavors):
all flavors (*Bonomo*), 1 oz. 110
all flavors (*Jolly Rancher Stix* Bars), 1 oz. 102
all flavors (*Jolly Rancher Stix* Kisses), 1 oz. 110
all flavors (*Reed's*), 1 oz. 110
(*Heide Chocolate Babies*), 1 piece 9
(*Heide Red Hot Dollars*), 1 piece 15
(*Heide Witchcraft*), 1 piece 5
(*Heide Wet'm 'n Wear'm*), 1 piece 15
honey nougat (*Bit-O-Honey*), 1 oz. 116
jellied and gum candy:
(*Chuckles Ju-Jubes*), 1 oz. 103
(*Chuckles* Variety Pack), 2-oz. pkg. 205
(*Heide Jujubes*), 1 piece 3
(*Just Born*), 1.25 oz. 117
(*Mason Dots*), 1 oz. 95
(*Mason Crows*), 1 oz. 95
beans (*Heide*), 1 piece 9
eggs (*Chuckles*), 1 oz. 109
eggs (*Chuckles*), 1 piece 10
fruit flavor (*Jujyfruits*), 1 piece 9
gum drops, 1 oz. 98
jellybeans, 1 oz. 104
jellybeans, ½ cup 404

licorice, see "licorice," below
nougat center (*Chuckles*), 1 oz. 109
nougat center (*Chuckles*), 1 piece 17
orange flavor slices (*Chuckles*), 1 oz. 97
orange flavor slices (*Chuckles*), 1 piece 29
rings (*Chuckles*), 1 oz. 95
rings (*Chuckles*), 1 piece 37
spearmint flavor leaves (*Chuckles*), 1 oz. 96
spearmint flavor leaves (*Chuckles*), 1 piece 27
spice flavor (*Chuckles*), 1 oz. 98
spice flavor sticks or drops (*Chuckles*), 1 piece 14
spice flavor strings (*Chuckles*), 1 piece 18
(*KitKat*), 1.25-oz. bar 180
licorice:
(*Pearson* Licorice Nip), 1 oz. 125
(*Switzer*), 1 oz. 101
candy-coated (*Good & Plenty*) 1.5-oz. pkg. 136
drops (*Diamond*), 1 piece 14
jellies (*Chuckles*), 1 oz. 95
jellies (*Chuckles*), 1 piece 36
red (*Switzer*), 1 oz. 101
(*Marathon*), 1.37-oz. bar 179
(*Marathon* Fun Size), .44-oz. bar 58
(*Mars*), 1.25-oz. bar 170
marshmallow:
(*Campfire*), 1 oz. 100
(*Just Born*), 1.1-oz. pkg. 94
(*Kraft*), 1 piece 25
eggs (*Chuckles*), 1 oz. 111
eggs (*Chuckles*), 1 piece 38
miniature (*Kraft*), 10 pieces 25
(*Mary Jane*), 1 oz. 74
(*Mary Jane* Bite Size), ¼-oz. piece 18
(*Milky Way*), 2.25-oz. bar 286
(*Milky Way*), 1.81-oz. bar 232
(*Milky Way* Fun Size), .84-oz. bar 106

mints:
    (*Certs* Clear), 1 piece 8
    (*Certs* Pressed), 1 piece 6
    (*Clorets*), 1 piece 6
    (*Delson Merri-Mints*), 1 piece 25
    (*Delson* Thin Mints), 1 piece 52
    (*Jamaica Mints*), 1 oz. 113
    (*Jamaica Mints*), 1 piece 24
    (*Kraft* Party Mints), 1 piece 8
    (*Nabisco* Liberty Mints), 1 oz. 113
    (*Nabisco* Liberty Mints), 1 piece 24
    (*Pearson* Mint Parfait), 1 oz. 136
    (*Rolaids*), 1 piece 4
    (*Tic Tac*), 1 piece 2
    (*Trident*), 1 piece 8
    butter (*Kraft*), 1 piece 8
    butter (*Richardson*), 1 oz. 109
    chocolate covered (*Junior*), 1 oz. 118
    chocolate covered (*Junior*), 1 piece 10
    chocolate covered (*Nabisco* Mint Wafers), 1 oz. 166
    chocolate covered (*Nabisco* Mint Wafers), 1 piece 10
    chocolate covered (*Nabisco* Peppermint Patties),
      1 oz. 122
    chocolate covered (*Nabisco* Peppermint Patties),
      1 piece 63
    chocolate covered (*Nabisco Thin Mints*), 1 oz. 119
    chocolate covered (*Nabisco Thin Mints*), 1 piece 42
    chocolate covered (*York* Peppermint Patties), 1 oz. 124
    jelly center (*Richardson*), 1 oz. 104
    midget (*Richardson*), 1 oz. 109
    striped (*Richardson*), 1 oz. 109
    (*Nabisco* Coco-Mello), 7-oz. bar 91
    (*Nabisco* Crispy Clusters), 1 oz. 114
    (*Nabisco* Crispy Clusters), 1 piece 65
    (*Nabsico* Malted Milk Crunch), 1 oz. 152
    (*Nabisco* Malted Milk Crunch), 1 piece 8

(*Nabisco* Nutty Crunch), .54-oz. bar 71

(*Nestlé Choco Lite*), 1 oz. 150

party mix, carob-coated (*CaraCoa*), 1 oz. 145

(*Payday*), 1.75-oz. bar 239

(*Payday*), 1.5-oz. bar 200

peanut bar, 1 oz. 146

peanut bar (*Munch*), 1.5-oz. bar 229

peanut brittle, 1 oz. 119

peanut brittle (*Kraft*), 1 oz. 140

peanut brittle (*Planter's* Peanut Block), 1 oz. 140

peanut brittle (*Stuckey's*), 1 oz. 122

peanut butter, chocolate covered:

    (*Peter Paul*), 1 oz. 157

    (*Reese's Peanut Butter Cups*), 1.4 oz.

       or 2 pieces 210

    (*Reese's Peanut Butter Flavor Chips*), 1 oz. 150

peanut cluster, chocolate covered (*Royal Cluster*),

    1 oz. 137

peanut cluster, chocolate covered (*Royal Cluster*),

    1 piece 78

peanuts, carob-coated (*CaraCoa*), 1 oz. 160

peanuts, chocolate covered:

    (*Goober's*), 1 oz. 153

    (*Nabisco*), 1 oz. 168

    (*Nabisco*), 1 piece 24

peanuts, chocolate covered, candy coated:

    (*M & M's*), 1.5-oz. pkg. 215

    (*M & M's*), 1-oz. pkg. 143

    (*M & M's* Fun Size), .82-oz. pkg. 117

(*Pearson* Chocolate Parfait), 1 oz. 136

(*Pearson Coffioca*), 1 oz. 136

pecan roll (*Stuckey's* Log), 1 oz. 135

peppermint, see "mints," above

popcorn, see "Popcorn"

popcorn, caramel coated (*Bachman*), 1 oz. 130

popcorn, caramel coated, with nuts (*Cracker Jack*),

    1 oz. 120

(*Power House*), 1 oz. 126
praline, coconut (*Stuckey's*), 1 oz. 125
praline, maple (*Stuckey's*), 1 oz. 125
raisins, carob-coated (*CaraCoa*), 1 oz. 130
raisins, chocolate covered:
   (*Nabisco*), 1 oz. 130
   (*Nabisco*), 1 piece 4
   (*Raisinets*), 1 oz. 90
(*Rally*), 1 oz. 125
(*Reggie*), 2-oz. bar 290
sesame crunch (*Sahadi*—bar), ¾-oz. bar 120
sesame crunch (*Sahadi*—in jars), 20 pieces 180
(*Snickers*), 2.25-oz. bar 286
(*Snickers*), 1.81-oz. bar 232
(*Snickers* Fun Size), .8-oz. bar 110
soynuts, carob-coated (*CaraCoa*), 1 oz. 145
(*Snowcaps*), 1 oz. 124
(*Summit*), 1.37-oz. twin bar 197
taffy, all flavors, except chocolate (*Bonomo*), 1 oz. 108
taffy, chocolate (*Bonomo*), 1 oz. 107
(*3 Musketeers*), 2.62-oz. bar 318
(*3 Musketeers*), 2.06-oz. bar 250
(*3 Musketeers* Fun Size), .8-oz. bar 99
toffee (*Kraft*), 1 piece 30
toffee, chocolate or creamy (*Rothchild's*), 1 piece 22
(*Tootsie Pops/Squares* Chocolate), 1 oz. 110
(*Tootsie Pops/Squares* Flavored), 1 oz. 111
(*Tootsie Roll* Chocolate), 1 oz. 114
(*Tootsie Roll/Squares* Flavored), 1 oz. 117
(*Twix*), 1.75-oz. twin bar 245
vanilla creams, chocolate-coated, 1 oz. 123
(*Welch's* Frappe), 1.07-oz. bar 132
(*Zero*), 1.75-oz. bar 218
(*Zero*), 1.5-oz. bar 183
Cantaloupe:
fresh, ½ melon (5″ in diam.) 58
fresh, cubed or diced, 1 cup 48

Cantonese style vegetables:
  frozen (*Birds Eye* Stir-Fry), 3.3 oz. 50
Cape gooseberries, see "Ground cherries"
Capers:
  (*Crosse & Blackwell*), 1 tbsp. 6
Capicola:
  4½-oz. pkg. (about 6 slices) 639
  1 oz. 141
  1 slice (4¼″ × 4¼″ × ¹⁄₁₆″) 105
Carambolas:
  fresh, raw, whole, 1 lb. 149
  fresh, raw, peeled and seeded, 4 oz. 40
Caramel dessert topping:
  (*Kraft*), 1 tbsp. 60
  (*Smucker's*), 1 tbsp. 70
Caramels, see "Candy"
Caraway seeds:
  all brands, 1 tsp. 8
Cardamom seeds:
  all brands, 1 tsp. 6
Carissas (natal plums):
  fresh, raw, whole, 1 lb. 273
  fresh, raw, peeled and seeded, 4 oz. 79
  fresh, raw, sliced, 1 cup 105
Carob flavor drink mix:
  (*CaraCoa*), 4 heaping tsp. 45
Carob flour, see "Flour"
Carp, see "Sucker, carp"
Carrots:
  fresh:
    raw, whole, with tops, 1 lb. 112
    raw, whole, packaged, without tops, 1 lb. 156
    raw, whole, trimmed and scraped, 8 oz. 95
    raw, whole, 1 medium (5½″ × 1″) 21
    raw, chunks, 1 cup 58
    raw, diced, 1 cup 60

raw, grated or shredded, 1 cup 46
raw, slices, 1 cup 53
raw, strips, 6 strips (¼" × 3") 12
boiled, drained, chunks, 1 cup 51
boiled, drained, diced, 1 cup 43
boiled, drained, slices, 1 cup 47
canned:
   diced (*Del Monte*), ½ cup 30
   diced (*Libby's*), ½ cup 18
   diced (*Stokely-Van Camp*), ½ cup 25
   sliced (*Del Monte*), ½ cup 30
   sliced (*Libby's*), ½ cup 23
   sliced (*Stokely-Van Camp*), ½ cup 23
   puree (*Cellu*), ½ cup 35
dehydrated, 1 oz. 97
frozen:
   whole (*Seabrook Farms*), 3.3 oz. 40
   cut (*Stokely-Van Camp*), 3.3 oz. 35
   sliced (*Hanover*), 3.2 oz. 35
   with brown sugar glaze (*Birds Eye*), 3.3 oz. 80
   nuggets, with butter sauce (*Green Giant*), ½ cup 50
Casaba melon:
whole, with rind, 1 lb. 61
cubed or diced, 1 cup 46
wedge (7¾" × 2") 22
Cashew butter:
(*Hain*), 1 tbsp. 95
Cashew nuts:
roasted in oil, 4 oz. 639
roasted in oil, 1 cup 785
roasted in oil, 1 oz. 159
dry-roasted, 1 oz. 173
dry-roasted (*Flavor House*), 1 oz. 170
dry-roasted (*Planters*), 1 oz. 160
unsalted (*Planters*), 1 oz. 160
(*Frito-Lay's*), ⅝-oz. pkg. 110
(*Planters*), 1 oz. 170

Catawba wine:
   (*Gold Seal*), 4 fl. oz. 167
Catfish:
   freshwater, raw, fillets, 4 oz. 117
   frozen, breaded (*Taste O' Sea*), 1 portion 90
   frozen, fillets (*Taste O' Sea*), 16-oz. pkg. 400
Catsup, tomato, canned or bottled:
   (*Del Monte*), 1 tbsp. 15
   (*Heinz*), 1 tbsp. 16
   (*Hunt's*), 1 tbsp 18
   (*Smucker's*), 1 tbsp. 19
   hot (*Heinz*), 1 tbsp. 21
   imitation (*Hain* Natural), 1 tbsp. 16
Cauliflower:
   fresh:
      raw, whole, 1 lb. 48
      raw, flowerets, 1 lb. 122
      raw, flowerets, whole, 1 cup 27
      raw, flowerets, chopped, 1 cup 31
      raw, flowerets, sliced, 1 cup 23
      boiled, drained, flowerets, 1 cup 28
   frozen:
      (*Birds Eye*), 3.3 oz. 25
      (*Green Giant*), ½ cup 13
      (*Kounty Kist/Lindy*), ½ cup 13
      (*Seabrook Farms*), 3.3 oz. 25
      (*Stokely-Van Camp*), 3.3 oz. 25
      flowerets (*Birds Eye*), 3.3 oz. 25
      flowerets or cut (*Hanover*), 3.2 oz. 20
      au gratin (*Stouffer's*), 5 oz. 155
      and cheese, light batter-fried (*Mrs. Paul's*),
         2.6 oz. 120
      and cheese, light batter-fried (*Mrs. Paul's*),
         7.8-oz. pkg. 360
      with cheddar cheese (*Stouffer's*), 9-oz. pkg. 220
      with cheese sauce (*Birds Eye*), 5 oz. 160

78

    with cheese sauce (*Green Giant*), ½ cup 65
    with cheese sauce (*Green Giant* Bake 'n Serve),
      ½ cup 110
Cauliflower relish:
    sweet (*Heinz*), 1 bud 9
Caviar:
    black sturgeon (*Northland Queen*), 1 oz. 74
    black sturgeon (*Romanoff Iranian*), 1 oz. 74
    red salmon (*Romanoff*), 1 oz. 68
    red salmon (*Romar Brand*), 1 oz. 68
    sturgeon, granular, 1 tbsp. 42
    sturgeon, pressed, 1 tbsp. 54
Celeriac root, fresh:
    whole, with skin, 1 lb. 156
    pared, 4 oz. 45
    pared, 4–6 roots 40
Celery, fresh:
    raw, untrimmed, with leaves, 1 lb. 58
    raw, packaged, trimmed, 1 lb. 61
    raw, 1 large outer stalk (8″ long) 7
    raw, 3 small inner stalks (5″ long) 9
    raw, chopped or diced, 1 cup 20
    raw, sliced, 1 cup 18
    boiled, drained, diced, 1 cup 21
    boiled, drained, sliced, 1 cup 24
Celery cabbage, see "Cabbage, Chinese"
Celery salt:
    (*French's*), 1 tsp. 2
Celery seed:
    all brands, 1 tsp. 11
Cereal beverage, mix*:
    (*Postum* Instant Grain Beverage), 6 fl. oz. 12
    (*Postum* Instant Coffee Flavor Grain Beverage),
      6 fl. oz. 12

*Prepared according to directions on container

Cereals, cooked:

  barley, pearled, quick (*Quaker Scotch Brand*),
    ¾ cup 172
  barley, pearled, regular (*Quaker Scotch Brand*),
    ¾ cup 129
  farina:
    (*Cream of Wheat*), ¾ cup 100
    (*Cream of Wheat* Instant or Quick), ¾ cup 100
    (*Cream of Wheat* Mix 'n Eat), ¾ cup 140
    (*Quaker* Hot 'n Creamy), 1 cup 101
    prepared with milk (*Pillsbury*), ⅔ cup 200
    prepared with water (*Pillsbury*), ⅔ cup 80
    with baked apple flavor and cinnamon
      (*Cream of Wheat* Mix 'n Eat), ¾ cup 170
    with banana flavor and spice
      (*Cream of Wheat* Mix 'n Eat), ¾ cup 170
    with maple flavor and brown sugar
      (*Cream of Wheat* Mix 'n Eat), ¾ cup 170
  oatmeal and oats:
    instant (*H-O*—box), ¾ cup 130
    instant (*H-O*—packet), ¾ cup 110
    instant (*H-O* Sweet & Mellow), ¾ cup 150
    instant (*Quaker*), ¾ cup 105
    old-fashioned (*H-O*), ¾ cup 140
    quick (*H-O*), ¾ cup 130
    quick or old fashioned (*Quaker*), ⅔ cup 109
    with apple and brown sugar (*H-O* Instant), ¾ cup 120
    with apple and cinnamon (*Quaker* Instant), ¾ cup 134
    with bran and raisins (*Quaker* Instant), ¾ cup 153
    with bran and spice (*H-O* Instant), ¾ cup 150
    with cinnamon and spice (*H-O* Instant), ¾ cup 170
    with cinnamon and spice (*Quaker* Instant), ¾ cup 176
    with maple and brown sugar (*H-O* Instant),
      ¾ cup 160
    with maple and brown sugar (*Quaker* Instant),
      ¾ cup 163

    with raisins and spice (*Quaker* Instant), ¾ cup 159
    wheat, whole (*Quaker Pettijohns*), ⅔ cup 106
Cereals, cooking type, dry:
    corn grits or hominy, see "Corn"
    corn meal, see "Corn meal"
    cracked wheat (*Elam's*), 1 oz. 102
    farina:
      (*Cream of Wheat*), 1 oz. 100
      (*Cream of Wheat* Instant), 1 oz. 100
      (*Cream of Wheat* Mix 'n Eat), 1-oz. packet 100
      (*Cream of Wheat* Quick), 1 oz. 100
      (*H-O*), ⅙ cup 108
      (*Malt-O-Meal*), 1 oz., or 3 tbsp. 100
      (*Quaker* Hot 'n Creamy), ⅙ cup 101
      with baked apple and cinnamon
        (*Cream of Wheat* Mix 'n Eat), 1¼-oz. pkt. 130
      with banana flavor and spice
        (*Cream of Wheat* Mix 'n Eat), 1¼-oz. pkt. 130
      with cocoa and toasted malt
        (*Malt-O-Meal*), 1 oz., or 3 tbsp. 100
      with maple flavor and brown sugar
        (*Cream of Wheat* Mix 'n Eat), 1¼-oz. packet 130
      with toasted malt
        (*Malt-O-Meal*), 1 oz., or 3 tbsp. 100
    oatmeal or oats:
      (*Elam's* Scotch Style), 1 oz. 108
      (*Elam's* Steel Cut), 1 oz. 109
      instant (*H-O*—box), ⅓ cup 85
      instant (*H-O*—packet), 1 packet 105
      instant (*H-O* Sweet & Mellow), 1 packet 150
      instant (*Quaker*), 1 packet 105
      instant (*3-Minute Brand*), 1 packet 110
      instant and regular (*Ralston*), ¼ cup 90
      old-fashioned (*H-O*), ⅓ cup 92
      quick (*H-O*), ⅓ cup 89
      quick or old fashioned (*Harvest Brand*), ⅓ cup 110

quick or old fashioned (*Quaker*), ⅓ cup 109
quick or old fashioned (*Ralston*), ⅓ cup 110
quick or old fashioned (*3-Minute Brand*), ⅓ cup 110
with apple and brown sugar (*H-O* Instant),
  1 packet 120
with apple and brown sugar (*3-Minute Brand* Instant),
  1 packet 120
with apple and cinnamon (*Quaker* Instant),
  1 packet 134
with bran and raisins (*Quaker* Instant), 1 packet 153
with bran and spice (*H-O* Instant), 1 packet 145
with cinnamon and spice (*H-O* Instant), 1 packet 170
with cinnamon and spice (*Quaker* Instant),
  1 packet 176
with honey and graham (*Quaker* Instant), 1 packet 136
with maple and brown sugar (*H-O* Instant),
  1 packet 163
with maple and brown sugar (*Quaker* Instant),
  1 packet 163
with raisins and spice (*Quaker* Instant), 1 packet 159
masa harina (*Quaker*), ⅓ cup 137
masa trigo (*Quaker*), ⅓ cup 149
wheat, toasted (*Wheatena*), ¼ cup 120
wheat, whole (*Quaker Pettijohns*), ⅓ cup 106
wheat, whole (*Ralston* Instant and Regular), ¼ cup 110
Cereals, ready-to-eat:
barley (*Nutri•Grain*—barley), 1 oz., or ⅔ cup 110
bran and high fiber:
  (*All-Bran*), 1 oz., or ⅓ cup 70
  (*Bran Buds*), 1 oz., or ⅓ cup 70
  (*Bran Chex*), 1 oz., or ⅔ cup 90
  (*Corn Bran*), 1 oz., or ⅔ cup 109
  (*Cracklin' Bran*), 1 oz., or ½ cup 110
  (*Elam's* Miller's Bran), 1 oz. 87
  (*Honey Bran*), 1 oz., or ⅞ cup 100
  (*Kellogg's* 40% Bran Flakes), 1 oz., or ¾ cup 90

(*Most*), 1 oz., or ¾ cup 110
(*Nabisco* 100% Bran), 1 oz., or ½ cup 70
(*Post* 40% Bran Flakes), 1 oz., or ⅔ cup 90
(*Ralston* 40% Bran Flakes), 1 oz., or ¾ cup 100
(*Van Brode* 40% Bran), 1 oz., or ⅝ cup 100
with raisins (*Kellogg's* Raisin Bran),
   1.3 oz., or ¾ cup. 110
with raisins (*Post* Raisin Bran), 1 oz., or ½ cup 90
with raisins (*Ralston* Raisin Bran),
   1⅓ oz., or ¾ cup 120
with raisins (*Van Brode* Raisin Bran),
   1 oz., or ¾ cup 120
(*Cocoa Pebbles*), 1 oz. 190
corn:
(*Cocoa Puffs*), 1 oz., or 1 cup 110
(*Corn Chex*), 1 oz., or 1 cup 110
(*Corn Total*), 1 oz., or 1 cup 110
(*Country Corn Flakes*), 1 oz., or 1 cup 110
(*Kellogg's* Banana Frosted Flakes), 1 oz.,
   or ⅔ cup 110
(*Kellogg's Corn Flakes*), 1 oz., or 1¼ cup 110
(*Kellogg's* Honey & Nut Corn Flakes), 1 oz.,
   or ¾ cup 120
(*Kellogg's* Sugar Frosted Flakes), 1 oz., or ¾ cup 110
(*Kix*), 1 oz., or 1½ cup 110
(*Nutri•Grain*—corn), 1 oz., or ½ cup 110
(*Pops*), 1 oz., or 1 cup 110
(*Post* Honeycomb), 1 oz., or 1⅓ cup 110
(*Post Toasties* Corn Flakes), 1 oz., or 1¼ cup 110
(*Ralston* Corn Flakes), 1 oz., or 1 cup 110
(*Ralston* Sugar Frosted Flakes), 1 oz., or ¾ cup 110
(*Sugar Corn Pops*), 1 oz., or 1 cup 110
(*Trix*), 1 oz., or 1 cup 110
(*Van Brode* Corn Flakes), 1 oz., or 1¼ cup 110
(*Van Brode* Sugar Toasted Corn Flakes),
   1 oz., or ⅝ cup 110

brown sugar and honey flavor (*Body Buddies*),
  1 oz., or 1 cup 110
chocolate flavor (*Crazy Cow*), 1 oz., or 1 cup 110
chocolate chip flavor (*Cookie Crisp*),
  1 oz., or 1 cup 110
fruit flavor, natural (*Body Buddies*),
  1 oz., or ¾ cup 110
oatmeal flavor (*Cookie Crisp*), 1 oz., or 1 cup 120
strawberry flavor (*Crazy Cow*), 1 oz., or 1 cup 110
vanilla wafer flavor (*Cookie Crisp*),
  1 oz., or 1 cup 110
corn bran, see "bran and high fiber" above
(*Fruit & Fibre*—Apples & Cinnamon), 1 oz. 160
(*Fruit & Fibre*—Dates, Raisins, Walnuts), 1 oz. 160
(*Fruity Pebbles*), 1 oz. 190
(*Graham Cracko's*), 1 oz., or ¾ cup 110
granola and "natural" cereals:
  (*Country Morning*), 1 oz., or ⅓ cup 130
  (*C.W. Post* Hearty), 1 oz., or ¼ cup 130
  (*Heartland*), 1 oz., or ¼ cup 120
  (*Quaker* 100% Natural), 1 oz., or ¼ cup 138
  with almonds (*Sun Country*), 1 oz., or ¼ cup 125
  with apple and cinnamon
    (*Quaker* 100% Natural), 1 oz., or ¼ cup 135
  with cinnamon and raisins (*Nature Valley*),
    1 oz., or ⅓ cup 130
  with coconut (*Heartland*), 1 oz., or ¼ cup 130
  with coconut and honey (*Nature Valley*),
    1 oz., or ⅓ cup 150
  with fruit and nuts (*Nature Valley*),
    1 oz., or ⅓ cup 130
  with raisins (*C.W. Post* Hearty), 1 oz., or ¼ cup 130
  with raisins (*Heartland*), 1 oz., or ¼ cup 120
  with raisins (*Sun Country*), 1 oz., or ¼ cup 125
  with raisins and dates (*Country Morning*),
    1 oz., or ⅓ cup 120

84

with raisins and dates (*Quaker* 100% Natural),
　　1 oz., or ¼ cup 134
toasted oat mixture (*Nature Valley*),
　　1 oz., or ⅓ cup 130
oats:
　　(*Alpha-Bits*), 1 oz., or 1 cup 110
　　(*Cheerios*), 1 oz., or 1¼ cup 110
　　(Cinnamon *Life*), 1 oz., or ⅔ cup 105
　　(*Froot Loops*), 1 oz., or 1 cup 110
　　(*Frosty O's*), 1 oz., or 1 cup 110
　　(*Honey-Nut Cheerios*), 1 oz., or ¾ cup 110
　　(*Life*), 1 oz., or ⅔ cup 105
　　(*Lucky Charms*), 1 oz., or 1 cup 110
　　(*Post* Fortified Oat Flakes), 1 oz., or ⅔ cup 100
　　(*Tasteeos*), 1 oz., or 1¼ cup 110
　　(*Toasty O's*), 1 oz., or 1¼ cup 110
rice:
　　(*Cocoa Krispies*), 1 oz., or ¾ cup 110
　　(*Kellogg's* Frosted Rice), 1 oz., or ¾ cup 110
　　(*Malt-O-Meal* Puffed Rice), 1 oz. or 2 cups 100
　　(*Quaker* Puffed Rice), 1 oz., or 2 cups 110
　　(*Ralston* Crispy Rice), 1 oz., or 1 cup 110
　　(*Rice Chex*), 1 oz., or 1⅛ cup 110
　　(*Rice Krinkles*), 1 oz., or ⅞ cup 110
　　(*Rice Krispies*), 1 oz., or 1 cup 110
　　(*Van Brode* Cocoa Rice), 1 oz., or ¾ cup 110
　　(*Van Brode* Crisp Rice), 1 oz., or 1 cup 110
　　(*Van Brode* Sugar Frosted Rice), 1 oz., or ¾ cup 110
rye (*Nutri•Grain*—rye), 1 oz., or ⅔ cup 110
wheat:
　　(*Buc Wheats*), 1 oz., or ¾ cup 110
　　(*Crispy Wheats 'N Raisins*), 1 oz., or ⅞ cup 100
　　(*Frosted Mini Wheats* with brown sugar and cinnamon),
　　1 oz., or 4 biscuits 110
　　(*Frosted Mini Wheats* with sugar),
　　1 oz., or 4 biscuits 110

(*Malt-O-Meal* Puffed Wheat), 1 oz., or 2 cups 100
(*Most*), 1 oz., or ½ cup 100
(*Nabisco* Shredded Wheat), ⅞-oz. biscuit 90
(*Nabisco* Shredded Wheat—single service),
   ¾-oz. biscuit 80
(*Nabisco Spoon Size* Shredded Wheat), 1 oz.,
   or ⅔ cup 110
(*Nutri•Grain*—wheat), 1 oz., or ⅔ cup 110
(*Pep*), 1 oz., or ¾ cup 110
(*Quaker* Puffed Wheat), 1 oz., or 2 cups 108
(*Quaker* Shredded Wheat), 1.3 oz., or 2 biscuits 104
(*Sugar Smacks*), 1 oz., or ¾ cup 110
(*Sunshine* Shredded Wheat), 1 biscuit 85
(Super *Sugar Crisp* Wheat Puffs),
   1 oz., or ⅞ cup 110
(*Toasted Mini-Wheats*), 1 oz., or 5 biscuits 110
(*Total*), 1 oz., or 1 cup. 110
(*Van Brode* Wheat Flakes), 1 oz., or ¾ cup 110
(*Wheat Chex*), 1 oz., or ⅔ cup 100
(Wheat & Raisin *Chex*), 1⅓ oz., or ¾ cup 120
(*Wheaties*), 1 oz., or 1 cup 110
wheat bran, see "bran and high fiber," above
wheat germ (*Kretschmer*), 1 oz., or ¼ cup 110
wheat germ, with sugar and honey
   (*Kretschmer*), 1 oz., or ¼ cup 107
miscellaneous mixed grains:
(*Apple Jacks*), 1 oz., or 1 cup 110
(*Cap'n Crunch*), 1 oz., or ¾ cup 121
(*Cap'n Crunch* Crunchberries), 1 oz., or ¾ cup 120
(*Cap'n Crunch* Peanut Butter), 1 oz., or ¾ cup 127
(*Concentrate*), 1 oz., or ⅓ cup 110
(*Cookie-Crisp*—vanilla or chocolate),
   1 oz., or 1 cup 110
(*Count Chocula*), 1 oz., or 1 cup 110
(*Frankenberry*), 1 oz., or 1 cup 110
(*Froot Loops*), 1 oz., or 1 cup 110

(*Grape-Nuts*), 1 oz., or ¼ cup 100
(*Grape-Nuts* Flakes), 1 oz., or ⅞ cup 100
(*King Vitaman*), 1 oz., or 1¼ cup 113
(*Product 19*), 1 oz., or ¾ cup 110
(*Quisp*), 1 oz., or 1⅙ cup 121
(*Raisins, Rice & Rye*), 1.3 oz., or ¾ cup 140
(*Special K*), 1 oz., or 1 cup 110
(*Team Flakes*), 1 oz., or 1 cup 110
(*Waffelo's*), 1 oz., or 1 cup 110

Cervelat, dry:
5⅓-oz. roll 677
1 oz. 128
4 slices (1½″ in diam., ⅛″ thick) 54

Cervelat, soft, see "Summer sausage"

Chablis wine:
domestic (*Gold Seal*), 4 fl. oz. 108
domestic (*Italian Swiss Colony*), 4 fl. oz. 86
imported (*Chanson Père & Fils* St. Vincent),
    4 fl. oz. 108
imported (*Crus & Fils Frères*), 4 fl. oz. 88

Champagne:
domestic:
(*Charles Fournier* New York State Brut),
    4 fl. oz. 110
(*Gold Seal* New York State Brut), 4 fl. oz. 113
(*Korbel* California Brut), 4 fl. oz. 104
(*Lejon*), 4 fl. oz. 94
(*Taylor* Dry Royal Quality New York State),
    4 fl. oz. 104
(*Taylor* New York State Brut), 4 fl. oz. 100
pink (*Gold Seal* New York State Extra Dry),
    4 fl. oz. 116
pink (*Taylor* New York State), 4 fl. oz. 108
imported:
(*Bollinger* Extra Dry), 4 fl. oz. 114
(*Mumm's* Cordon Rouge Brut), 4 fl. oz. 88

   (*Mumm's* Extra Dry), 4 fl. oz. 108
   (*Veuve Clicquot* Brut), 4 fl. oz. .104
Chard, Swiss:
   raw, whole, 1 lb. 113
   raw, trimmed, 1 lb. (weighed whole) 104
   boiled, drained, leaves and stalks, 1 cup 26
   boiled, drained, leaves only, 1 cup 32
   Cheddar chips: (*Flavor Tree*), 1 oz. 160
Châteauneuf-du-Pape wine:
   (*B & G*), 4 fl. oz. 92
   (*Crus & Fils Frères*), 4 fl. oz. 96
Cheese:
   American:
      (*Borden*), 1 oz. 110
      (*Dorman's*), 1 oz. 106
      (*Harvest Moon*), 1 oz. 70
      (*Hood*), 1 oz. 110
      (*Kraft*), 1 oz. 110
      (*Kraft Old English*), 1 oz. 110
      (*Land O Lakes*), 1 oz. 110
      (*Light N'Lively*), 1 oz. 70
      (*Pauly*), 1 oz. 106
      (*Saffola*—loaf), 1 oz. 93
      (*Saffola*—slices), 1 oz. 96
      (*Vera Sharp*), 1 oz. 104
   asiago (*Frigo*), 1 oz. 113
   blue:
      (*Borden Blufort*), 1 oz. 100
      (*Borden* Danish), 1 oz. 105
      (*Borden Flora Danica*), 1 oz. 105
      (*Dorman's* Danish), 1 oz. 100
      (*Frigo*), 1 oz. 99
      (*Kraft*), 1 oz. 100
      (*Pauly* Danish), 1 oz. 100
   (*Bonbel*—round), 1 oz. 94
   (*Bonbel*—wedge), 1 oz. 90

brick:
    (*Borden*), 1 oz. 110
    (*Dorman's*), 1 oz. 105
    (*Kraft*—natural), 1 oz. 110
    (*Kraft*—processed), 1 oz. 102
    (*Kraft Lagerkase*), 1 oz. 108
    (*Pauly*), 1 oz. 105
    (*Sargento*), 1 oz. 100
Camembert:
    (*Borden*), 1 oz. 86
    (*Kraft*), 1 oz. 85
caraway:
    (*Dorman's*), 1 oz. 107
    (*Kraft*), 1 oz. 100
    (*Pauly*), 1 oz. 107
(*Chantelle*), 1 oz. 91
cheddar:
    (*Borden*), 1 oz. 110
    (*Borden Country Store*), 1 oz. 110
    (*Cellu*), 1 oz. 110
    (*Cooper*), 1 oz. 110
    (*Dorman's*), 1 oz. 112
    (*Hood*), 1 oz. 110
    (*Kraft*), 1 oz. 110
    (*Pauly*), 1 oz. 112
    (*Sargento*), 1 oz. 100
    (*Sargento* New York Sharp), 1 oz. 110
    bites, mild (*Borden Kisses*), 1 oz. 107
    bites, sharp (*Borden Kisses*), 1 oz. 107
    curds (*Sargento*), 1 oz. 100
colby:
    (*Borden*), 1 oz. 110
    (*Cellu*), 1 oz. 110
    (*Dorman's*), 1 oz. 112
    (*Kraft*), 1 oz. 110
    (*Sargento*), 1 oz. 100

cottage:
   creamed, large curd, 1 cup loosely packed 239
   creamed, small curd, 1 cup loosely packed 223
   creamed (*Borden*), 4 oz. 120
   creamed, large or small curd (*Foremost*), ½ cup 120
   creamed (*Friendship* California Style), 4 oz. 120
   creamed (*Hood*), 4 oz. 120
   creamed (*Hood* Country Style), 4 oz. 120
   creamed (*Kraft*), ½ cup 107
   creamed (*Meadow Gold*), ½ cup 117
   creamed (*Sealtest*), 4 oz. 120
   creamed, with chives (*Foremost*), ½ cup 120
   creamed, with chives (*Hood* Chivier), 4 oz. 110
   creamed, with fruit harvest salad (*Foremost*),
     ½ cup 140
   creamed, with peach-pineapple (*Sealtest*), ½ cup 115
   creamed, with pineapple (*Foremost*), ½ cup 130
   creamed, with pineapple (*Friendship*), 4 oz. 140
   partially creamed (*Foremost So-Lo*), ½ cup 100
   partially creamed (*Meadow Gold*), ½ cup 102
   partially creamed (*Sealtest Light 'n Lively*), ½ cup 77
   uncreamed, 1 cup loosely packed 125
   uncreamed, 1 cup packed 172
   uncreamed, or low-fat (*Foremost Profile* Lowfat),
     ½ cup 90
   uncreamed, or low-fat (*Friendship* Low Fat), 4 oz. 90
   uncreamed, or low-fat (*Friendship* Pot Style),
     4 oz. 100
   uncreamed, or low-fat (*Hood Nuform*), 4 oz. 90
   uncreamed, or low-fat (*Kraft*), 4 oz. 103
   uncreamed, or low-fat (*Sealtest*), 4 oz. 90
cream:
   (*Philadelphia Brand*), 1 oz. 100
   with chives (*Philadelphia Brand*), 1 oz. 100
   with pimentos (*Philadelphia Brand*), 1 oz. 100
   whipped (*Philadelphia Brand*), 1 oz. 100

whipped (*TempTee*), 1 oz. 100
whipped, with bacon and horseradish
   (*Philadelphia Brand*), 1 oz. 90
whipped, with blue cheese (*Philadelphia Brand*),
   1 oz. 100
whipped, with chives (*Philadelphia Brand*), 1 oz. 90
whipped, with onions (*Philadelphia Brand*), 1 oz. 90
whipped, with pimentos (*Philadelphia Brand*), 1 oz. 90
whipped, with smoked salmon (*Philadelphia Brand*),
   1 oz. 100
imitation (*King Smoothee*), 1 oz. 65
Edam:
   (*Dorman's*), 1 oz. 101
   (*House of Gold*), 1 oz. 105
   (*Kraft*), 1 oz. 100
   (*Pauly*), 1 oz. 101
farmer (*Friendship*), 1 oz. 40
farmer (*Wispride*), 1 oz. 100
fontina:
   (*Dorman's*), 1 oz. 110
   (*Pauly* Danish), 1 oz. 110
Frankenmuth (*Kraft*), 1 oz. 113
gjetost (*Kraft*), 1 oz. 134
Gorgonzola, 1 oz. 112
Gouda:
   (*Borden Dutch Maid*), 1 oz. 86
   (*Dorman's*), 1 oz. 101
   (*Kraft*), 1 oz. 100
   (*Pauly*), 1 oz. 101
Gruyère:
   (*Borden*), 1 wedge 90
   (*Dorman's*), 1 oz. 117
   (*Kraft*), 1 oz. 110
   (*Pauly*), 1 oz. 117
   (*Swiss Knight*), 1 oz. 101
jack—dry (*Kraft*), 1 oz. 101

jack—fresh (*Kraft*), 1 oz. 95
Jarlsberg (*Dorman's*), 1 oz. 107
Jarlsberg (*Pauly*), 1 oz. 107
Leyden (*Kraft*), 1 oz. 80
(*Liederkranz Brand*), 1 oz. 86
Limburger (*Kraft*), 1 oz. 98
Monterey Jack:
   (*Borden*), 1 oz. 110
   (*Dorman's*), 1 oz. 106
   (*Frigo*), 1 oz. 103
   (*Kraft*), 1 oz. 100
   (*Pauly*), 1 oz. 100
   (*Sargento*), 1 oz. 100
mozzarella:
   (*Borden*), 1 oz. 90
   (*Dorman's*—part skim), 1 oz. 72
   (*Frigo*), 1 oz. 79
   (*Kraft*), 1 oz. 80
   (*Pauly*—part skim), 1 oz. 80
   (*Sargento*), 1 oz. 90
Muenster:
   (*Borden*), 1 oz. 110
   (*Dorman's*), 1 oz. 104
   (*Kraft*), 1 oz. 100
   (*Pauly*), 1 oz. 104
   (*Sargento*), 1 oz. 100
Neufchâtel:
   plain (*Borden*), 1 oz. 73
   plain (*Kraft*), 1 oz. 80
   flavored, see "Cheese spreads"
nuworld (*Kraft*), 1 oz. 104
Parmesan:
   (*Borden*), 1 oz. 110
   (*Dorman's*), 1 oz. 111
   (*Frigo*), 1 oz. 107
   (*Kraft*), 1 oz. 110

(*Pauly*), 1 oz. 111
grated (*Borden*), 1 oz. 130
grated (*Colonna*), ½ oz. 52
grated (*Frigo*), ½ oz. 65
grated (*Kraft*), ½ oz. 65
and Romano, grated (*Borden*), 1 oz. 140
(*Pauly Slim Line*), 1 oz. 60
pepato (*Frigo*), 1 oz. 110
pimento American, processed, 1″ cube 65
pimento American (*Borden*), 1 oz. 110
pimento American (*Kraft*), 1 oz. 110
pizza:
  (*Borden*), 1 oz. 85
  (*Frigo*), 1 oz. 73
  (*Kraft*), 1 oz. 73
Port du Salut:
  (*Dorman's*), 1 oz. 100
  (*Kraft*), 1 oz. 100
  (*Pauly*), 1 oz. 100
provolone:
  (*Borden*), 1 oz. 90
  (*Dorman's*), 1 oz. 100
  (*Frigo*), 1 oz. 99
  (*Kraft*), 1 oz. 90
  (*Pauly*), 1 oz. 100
ricotta:
  (*Brunetto*—whole milk), 1 oz. 48
  (*Frigo*—part skim), 1 oz. 45
  (*Polly-O*—whole milk), 1 oz. 50
Romano:
  (*Borden*), 1 oz. 100
  (*Dorman's*), 1 oz. 110
  (*Frigo*), 1 oz. 110
  (*Kraft*), 1 oz. 100
  (*Pauly*), 1 oz. 110
  grated (*Kraft*), ½ oz. 65

Roquefort:
 (*Borden Napoleon Brand*), 1 oz. 107
 (*Dorman's*), 1 oz. 105
 (*Kraft*), 1 oz. 105
 (*Pauly*), 1 oz. 105
sap sago (*Kraft*), 1 oz. 76
Sardo Romano (*Kraft*), 1 oz. 110
Scamorze (*Frigo*), 1 oz. 79
Scamorze (*Kraft*), 1 oz. 100
Skandor (*Dorman's* Swedish), 1 oz. 100
Skandor (*Pauly* Swedish), 1 oz. 100
Swiss:
 (*Borden*), 1 oz. 100
 (*Dorman's*—natural), 1 oz. 107
 (*Dorman's*—processed), 1 oz. 95
 (*Kraft*—natural), 1 oz. 100
 (*Kraft Deluxe*—processed), 1 oz. 90
 (*Pauly*—natural), 1 oz. 107
 (*Pauly*—processed), 1 oz. 95
 (*Pauly* Iceland Baby Swiss), 1 oz. 100
 (*Sargento*), 1 oz. 100
Swiss-American (*Borden*), 1 oz. 110
Tilsiter (*Dorman's* Danish), 1 oz. 96
Tilsiter (*Pauly*), 1 oz. 96
washed curd (*Kraft*), 1 oz. 108
Cheese crepes:
frozen, with mustard sauce (*Stouffer's*), 8⅜-oz. pkg. 570
Cheese food, processed:
American:
 (*Borden*), 1 oz. 90
 (*Clearfield*), 1 oz. 90
 (*Kraft*), 1 oz. 90
 (*Pauly*), 1 oz. 90
 grated (*Borden*), 1 oz. 130
 grated (*Kraft*), 1 oz. 130
bacon (*Cheez 'n Bacon*), 1 oz. 100

bacon (*Kraft*), 1 oz. 100
blue cheese (*Wispride*), 1 oz. 100
cheddar:
    (*Borden Country Store*), 1 oz. 100
    (*Wispride*), 1 oz. 90
    sharp (*Kraft*), 1 oz. 90
    smoke flavor (*Kraft*), 1 oz. 100
garlic (*Kraft*), 1 oz. 90
hickory smoke flavor (*Smokelle*), 1 oz. 100
jalapeño pepper (*Kraft*), 1 oz. 90
Monterey Jack (*Kraft*), 1 oz. 90
Muenster (*Kraft*), 1 oz. 90
(*Pauly Sweet Munchee*), 1 oz. 100
pimento:
    (*Borden*), 1 oz. 90
    (*Kraft*), 1 oz. 90
    (*Pauly*), 1 oz. 90
pizza (*Kraft Pizzalone*), 1 oz. 90
port wine (*Wispride*), 1 oz. 100
salami (*Kraft*), 1 oz. 94
sharp (*Kraft*), 1 oz. 100
smoked (*Wispride*), 1 oz. 90
Swiss:
    (*Borden*), 1 oz. 100
    (*Kraft*), 1 oz. 90
    (*Pauly*), 1 oz. 90
    (*Wispride*), 1 oz. 100
Cheese puff pastry:
  frozen (*Durkee*), 1 piece 59
Cheese puffs, see "Corn crisps and puffs"
Cheese sandwich snack:
  (*Cheez-Waffies*), 1 oz. 140
Cheese sauce, mix*:
  (*Durkee*), ½ cup 169

*Prepared according to directions on container

(*French's*), ½ cup 160
(*McCormick/Schilling*), ½ cup 154
Cheese soufflé:
 frozen (*Stouffer's*), 12-oz. pkg. 710
Cheese spreads, processed:
 American:
  (*Borden*), 1 oz. 90
  (*Hood*), 1 oz. 80
  (*Kraft*), 1 oz. 80
  (*Snack Mate*), 4 tsp. 60
 bacon (*Kraft*), 1 oz. 80
 bacon (*Squeez-a-Snak*), 1 oz. 90
 blue (*Roka*), 1 oz. 80
 cheddar (*Snack Mate*), 4 tsp. 60
 cheddar, sharp (*Wispride*), 1 oz. 80
 cheese and bacon (*Snack Mate*), 4 tsp. 60
 (*Cheez Whiz*), 1 oz. 80
 chive and green onion (*Snack Mate*), 4 tsp. 60
 garlic (*Kraft*), 1 oz. 80
 garlic (*Squeez-a-Snak*), 1 oz. 90
 Gruyère (*Dorman's*), 1 oz. 90
 Gruyère (*Pauly*), 1 oz. 90
 hickory smoke flavor (*Kraft Smokelle*), 1 oz. 90
 hickory smoke flavor (*Squeez-a-Snak*), 1 oz. 90
 jalapeño pepper (*Kraft*), 1 oz. 80
 jalapeño pepper (*Squeez-a-Snak*), 1 oz. 80
 (*Land O Lakes Golden Velvet*), 1 oz. 80
 (*Laughing Cow*), 1 oz. 74
 Limburger (*Mohawk Valley*), 1 oz. 70
 Neufchâtel cheese:
  with bacon and horseradish (*Kraft Party Snack*),
   1 oz. 74
  with chipped beef (*Kraft Party Snack*), 1 oz. 67
  with chives (*Kraft Party Snack*), 1 oz. 69
  with clams (*Kraft Party Snack*), 1 oz. 67
  with jalapeño pepper (*Kraft*), 1 oz. 70

96

with olive and pimento (*Kraft*), 1 oz. 70
with onion (*Kraft Party Snack*), 1 oz. 66
with pimento (*Kraft*), 1 oz. 70
with pineapple (*Kraft*), 1 oz. 70
with relish (*Kraft Party Snack*), 1 oz. 70
pimento:
   (*Cheez Whiz*), 1 oz. 80
   (*Price's* Pimento Spread), 1 oz. 80
   (*Snack Mate*), 4 tsp. 60
   (*Squeez-a-Snak*), 1 oz. 90
   sharp (*Kraft Old English*), 1 oz. 90
   sharp (*Squeez-a-Snak*), 1 oz. 90
   (*Velveeta*), 1 oz. 80

Cheese straws:
   1 oz. 128
   10 pieces (5″ long) 272
   (*Durkee*), 1 piece 29

Cheeseburger macaroni mix:
   dry (*Hamburger Helper*), ⅕ pkg. 180
   with meat* (*Hamburger Helper*), ⅕ pkg. 360

Cheesecake, see "Pies, frozen" and "Pies, mix"

Cherimoyers:
   raw, whole, with skin and seeds, 1 lb. 247
   raw, peeled and seeded, 4 oz. 107

Cherries:
   fresh:
      sour, red, whole, with pits and stems, 1 lb. 213
      sour, red, whole, 1 cup 60
      sour, red, pitted, 1 cup 90
      sweet, whole, with pits and stems, 1 lb. 286
      sweet, whole, 1 cup 82
      sweet, pitted, 1 cup 102
      sweet, 10 cherries 47

*Prepared according to directions on container

canned, with liquid:
  Royal Anne, in syrup (*Del Monte*), ½ cup 95
  sour, red, in syrup, pitted (*Stokely-Van Camp*),
  ½ cup 45
  sweet, in syrup, with pits (*Del Monte*), ½ cup 90
  sweet, in syrup, pitted (*Del Monte*), ½ cup 95
frozen, sour, red, unsweetened, unthawed, 8 oz. 125
frozen, sour, red, sweetened, unthawed, 8 oz. 254
Cherries, candied:
1 oz. 96
10 cherries 119
Cherries, maraschino:
bottled, with liquid, 1 oz. 33
bottled, 1 average cherry 8
Cherry, black, dessert topping:
concentrate (*Hain*), 1 tbsp. 46
Cherry brandy:
(*Bols*), 1 fl. oz. 100
(*DuBouchett*), 1 fl. oz. 88
(*Garnier*), 1 fl. oz. 86
(*Hiram Walker*), 1 fl. oz. 88
wild (*Old Mr. Boston*—70 proof), 1 fl. oz. 100
Cherry drink:
canned (*Hi-C*), 6 fl. oz. 93
mix*:
  (*Cramores*), 6 fl. oz. 68
  (*Hi-C*), 6 fl. oz. 76
  (*Kool-Aid*), 6 fl. oz. 68
  (*Wyler's*), 6 fl. oz. 68
Cherry extract:
pure (*Burton's*), 1 tsp. 9
imitation (*Ehlers*), 1 tsp. 16
Cherry fruit roll:
dried, sweetened (*Grocer's Choice*), 1 oz. 100

---

*Prepared according to directions on container

dried, sweetened (*Sahadi*), 1 oz. 90
Cherry liqueur:
  (*Bols*), 1 fl. oz. 96
  (*Cherry Heering*), 1 fl. oz. 80
  (*Dolfi*), 1 fl. oz. 87
  (*DuBouchett*), 1 fl. oz. 72
  (*Hiram Walker*), 1 fl. oz. 79
Cherry nut bread, see "Bread, sweet, mix"
Cherry pie, see "Pies"
Cherry pie filling:
  canned (*Comstock*), ⅓ cup 100
Cherry pie tart:
  frozen (*Pepperidge Farm*), 1 piece 280
Cherry turnover:
  frozen (*Pepperidge Farm*), 1 piece 340
  refrigerator (*Pillsbury*), 1 piece 180
Chervil:
  raw, 1 oz. 16
Chestnut flour:
  4 oz. 410
Chestnuts:
  in shell, 1 lb. 713
  in shell, 1 cup 189
  in shell, 10 nuts 141
  shelled, 4 oz. 220
  shelled, 1 cup 310
  dried, shelled, 4 oz. 428
Chewing gum:
  sweetened, 1 oz. 90
  (*Adams* Sour Gum), 1 piece 9
  (*Beechnut*), 1 piece 10
  (*Big Red*), 1 piece 10
  (*Bubble Yum*), 1 piece 20
  (*Bubblicious*), 1 piece 24
  (*Chicklets*), 1 piece 6
  (*Clorets*), 1 piece 6

(*Dentyne*), 1 piece 5
(*Doublemint*), 1 piece 10
(*Freedent*), 1 piece 10
(*Freshen-Up*), 1 piece 10
(*Juicy Fruit*), 1 piece 10
(*Orbit*), 1 piece 8
(*Trident*—all flavors except bubble gum), 1 piece 5
(*Trident* Bubble Gum), 1 piece 7
(*Wrigley's Spearmint*), 1 piece 10

Chianti wine:
domestic (*Italian Swiss Colony Tipo*), 4 fl. oz. 86
imported (*Brolio* Classico), 4 fl. oz. 88
imported (*Gancia* Classico), 4 fl. oz. 100

Chicken, fresh:
broilers:
  broiled, with skin, giblets, 7.1 oz.
    (yield from 1 lb. raw) 273
  broiled, meat only, 4 oz. 154
capon, raw, ready-to-cook, 1 lb. 937
fryers:
  raw, ready-to-cook, 1 lb. 382
  fried, with skin, giblets, 8 oz. (yield from 1 lb. raw) ...565
  fried, dark meat, without skin, 4 oz. 249
  fried, light meat, without skin, 4 oz. 223
  fried, 1 back (2.1 oz.) 139
  fried, ½ breast (3.3 oz.) 160
  fried, 1 drumstick (2 oz.) 88
  fried, 1 neck, (2.1 oz.) 127
  fried, ½ rib section (¾ oz.) 41
  fried, 1 thigh (2.3 oz.) 122
  fried, 1 wing (1.8 oz.) 82
  fried, skin only, 1 oz. 119
roasters:
  raw, ready-to-cook, 1 lb. 791
  roasted, with skin, giblets, 8.4 oz. (yield from
    1 lb. raw) 576

    roasted, dark meat, without skin, 4 oz. 204
    roasted, dark meat, without skin, chopped or diced,
      1 cup 258
    roasted, dark meat, without skin, ground, 1 cup 202
    roasted, light meat, without skin, 4 oz. 207
    roasted, light meat, without skin, chopped or diced,
      1 cup 255
    roasted, light meat, without skin, ground, 1 cup 200
  stewing hens or cocks:
    raw, ready-to-cook, 1 lb. 987
    stewed, with skin, giblets, 8 oz. (yield from 1 lb. raw) . .708
    stewed, dark meat, without skin, 4 oz. 235
    stewed, dark meat, without skin, chopped or diced,
      1 cup 290
    stewed, dark meat, without skin, ground, 1 cup 228
    stewed, light meat, without skin, 4 oz. 204
    stewed, light meat, without skin, chopped or diced,
      1 cup 252
    stewed, light meat, without skin, ground, 1 cup 198
Chicken, canned or refrigerated:
  boned:
    4 oz. 225
    1 cup 406
    (*Hormel Tender Chunk*), 6¾-oz. can 256
    (*Swanson*), 5 oz. 110
    chunk (*Chicken Ready*), 6½-oz. can 273
    chunk (*Swanson*), 5 oz. 110
  breast, oven-roasted (*Chef's Gourmet Norwestern*), 8 oz. ..200
  and dumplings (*Swanson*), 7½-oz. can 230
  and noodles (*Heinz*), 7½-oz. can 160
  potted:
    1 oz. 70
    1 tbsp. 32
    5½-oz. can 387
    1 cup 558
  roll, boneless, cooked (*Swift Premium*), 3½ oz. 180

101

stew, see "Chicken stew"
whole (*Ranch Table*), 8 oz. 443
Chicken, frozen:
A la king, see "Chicken a la king"
baked breast (*Stouffer's*), 16-oz. pkg. 770
cacciatore, with spaghetti (*Stouffer's*), 11¼-oz. pkg. 310
chow mein, see "Chow mein, chicken"
creamed (*Stouffer's*), 6½-oz. pkg. 300
croquettes, with fricassee sauce (*Howard Johnson's*),
    11-oz. pkg. 505
dinner, see "Chicken dinner, frozen"
divan (*Stouffer's*), 8-oz, pkg. 335
escalloped, and noodles (*Stouffer's*), 11½-oz. pkg. 500
fillets (*Buitoni*), 15-oz. pkg. 546
fried (*Banquet Buffet Suppers*), 32-oz. pkg. 2,591
fried (*Morton*), 32-oz. pkg. 1,500
fried (*Morton Country Table* Entree), 12-oz. pkg. 640
fried (*Swanson Hungry-Man* Entree), 12-oz. pkg. 620
fried, assorted pieces (*Swanson* Chicken Parts), 3.2 oz. ...260
fried, barbecue flavor (*Swanson Hungry-Man* Entree),
    12-oz. pkg. 550
fried, breast (*Morton*), 22-oz. pkg. 1,320
fried, breast (*Swanson* Chicken Parts), 3.2 oz. 250
fried, nibbles (*Swanson* Chicken Parts), 3.2 oz. 290
fried, nibbles, with french fries
    (*Swanson TV Brand* Entree), 6-oz. pkg. 370
fried, thighs and drumsticks (*Swanson* Chicken Parts),
    3.2 oz. 260
fried, with whipped potatoes
    (*Swanson TV Brand* Entree), 7-oz. pkg. 360
paprikash, with egg noodles (*Stouffer's*), 10½-oz. pkg 385
patties, breaded, and fries (*Mrs. Paul's*), 8½-oz. pkg. 390
patties, light batter-fried, and fries (*Mrs. Paul's*),
    8½-oz. pkg. 420
sliced (*Morton* Boil-in-Bag), 5-oz. pkg. 130
sticks, breaded, and fries (*Mrs. Paul's*), 8½-oz. pkg. 420

and biscuits (*Green Giant* Baked Entree), 7-oz. pkg. 200
and dumplings (*Banquet Buffet Suppers*), 32-oz. pkg. ...1,209
and noodles (*Banquet Buffet Suppers*), 32-oz. pkg. 764
and noodles (*Green Giant* Entree), 9-oz. pkg. 250

Chicken a la king:
(*Swanson*), 5¼ oz. 190
frozen (*Banquet Cookin' Bag*), 5-oz. pkg. 138
frozen (*Green Giant Toast Toppers*), 5-oz. pkg. 170
frozen (*Morton* Boil-in-Bag), 5-oz. pkg. 150
with rice, frozen (*Stouffer's*), 9½-oz. pkg. 330

Chicken chow mein, see "Chow mein, chicken"

Chicken crepe:
with mushroom sauce, frozen (*Stouffer's*), 8¼-oz. pkg. ...390
sweet and sour, with sauce (*Stouffer's*), 8½-oz. pkg. 280

Chicken dinner, frozen:
boneless (*Morton*), 10-oz. pkg. 230
boneless (*Morton* King Size), 17-oz. pkg. 530
boneless (*Swanson Hungry-Man*), 19-oz. pkg. 730
fried (*Banquet*), 11-oz. pkg. 530
fried (*Banquet Man Pleasers*), 11-oz. pkg. 1,026
fried (*Morton*), 11-oz. pkg. 460
fried (*Morton Country Table*), 15-oz. pkg. 710
fried (*Morton* King Size), 17-oz. pkg. 860
fried (*Swanson*), 15-oz. pkg. 630
fried (*Swanson Hungry-Man*), 15¾-oz. pkg. 910
fried (*Swanson TV Brand*), 11½-oz. pkg. 570
fried, barbecue flavor (*Swanson Hungry-Man*),
  16½-oz. pkg. 760
fried, barbecue flavor (*Swanson TV Brand*), 11¼-oz. pkg. ...530
fried, crispy (*Swanson TV Brand*), 10¾-oz. pkg. 650

Chicken flavor mix*:
(*Lipton Lite-Lunch*), 7 fl. oz. 140

Chicken frankfurters:
(*Longacre*), 1 frank 120

*Prepared according to directions on container

Chicken gizzards, see "Gizzards"
Chicken gravy:
    canned (*Franco-American*), 4 oz. 100
    in jars (*Heinz*), ½ cup 80
    mix*:
        (*Durkee*), ½ cup 44
        (*Ehlers*), ½ cup 42
        (*French's*), ½ cup 50
        (*McCormick/Schilling*), ½ cup 48
        (*Pillsbury*), ½ cup 50
    creamy, mix* (*Durkee*), ½ cup 78
    giblet, canned (*Franco-American*), 4 oz. 70
Chicken hearts, see "Hearts"
Chicken liver, see "Liver"
Chicken liver puff pastry:
    frozen (*Durkee*), 1 piece 48
Chicken luncheon meat:
    (*Danola* Thin Sliced), 1 oz. 45
    (*Eckrich* Slender Sliced), 1 slice 47
    breast (*Eckrich*), 6-oz. pkg. 193
Chicken pot pie, frozen:
    8-oz. pie 497
    (*Banquet*), 8-oz. pie 427
    (*Morton*) 8-oz. pie 350
    (*Stouffer's*), 10-oz. pie 500
    (*Swanson*), 8-oz. pie 450
    (*Swanson Hungry-Man*), 16-oz. pie 780
    (*Van de Kamp's*), 7½-oz. pie 520
Chicken puff pastry:
    frozen (*Durkee*), 1 piece 49
Chicken salad:
    (*Longacre*), ½ oz. 32
    (*The Spreadables*), ½ oz. 31

*Prepared according to directions on container

Chicken seasoning mix:
  cream style, dry (*Durkee Roastin' Bag*), 2-oz. packet 242
  gravy, dry (*Durkee Roastin' Bag*), 1½-oz. packet 122
  Italian style, dry (*Durkee Roastin' Bag*), 1½-oz. packet . . .144
Chicken soup, see "Soups"
Chicken spread:
  (*Chicken Ready*), ½ oz. 36
  (*Swanson*), ½ oz. 35
  (*Underwood*), ½ oz. 31
Chicken stew, canned:
  (*Swanson*), 7½ oz. 180
  with dumplings (*Heinz*), 7½ oz. .202
  with dumplings (*Libby's*), 8 oz. .199
Chickpeas (garbanzos):
  dry, raw, 8 oz. 817
  dry, raw, 1 cup 720
  canned:
    (*Hanover*), 4 oz. 110
    (*Joan of Arc* Ceci Beans), ½ cup 125
    (*Progresso*), ½ cup 98
    (*Old El Paso*), ½ cup 103
Chicory, witloof, see "Endive, French or Belgian"
Chicory greens, fresh:
  untrimmed, 1 lb. 74
  cuts, 1 cup 11
  10 inner leaves 5
Chili con carne:
  canned, with beans:
    (*Armour Star*), 7¾ oz. 347
    (*Austex*), 1 cup 353
    (*Gebhardt*), 8 oz. 493
    (*Gebhardt* Instant), 8 oz. 493
    (*Gebhardt* Longhorn), 8 oz. 452
    (*Heinz*), 1 cup 340
    (*Hormel*), 7½ oz. 321
    (*Hormel* Short Order), 7½-oz. can 300

(*Libby's*), 1 cup 276
(*Morton House*), 7½ oz. 340
(*Old El Paso*), 1 cup 420
(*Stokely-Van Camp*), 1 cup 390
(*Stokely-Van Camp Chilee Weenee*), 1 cup 330
(*Swanson*), 7¾-oz. 310
hot (*Hormel* Short Order), 7½-oz. can 300
canned, without beans:
(*Armour Star*), 7¾ oz. 424
(*Austex*), 1 cup 390
(*Gebhardt*), 8 oz. 427
(*Gebhardt* Chunky Beef), 8 oz. 492
(*Gebhardt* Longhorn), 8 oz. 452
(*Hormel*), 7½-oz. 344
(*Hormel* Short Order), 7½-oz. can 368
(*Libby's*), 1 cup 379
(*Morton House*), 7½ oz. 340
(*Old El Paso*), 8 oz. 402
(*Stokely-Van Camp*), 1 cup 430
frozen (*Stouffer's*), 8¾-oz. pkg. 270
Chili con carne spread:
(*Gebhardt* Chili Meat), 1 tbsp. 37
Chili hot dog sauce:
canned (*Gebhardt*), 4 oz. 106
Chili mac:
canned (*Hormel* Short Order), 7½-oz. can 201
Chili pepper, see ''Pepper, hot chili''
Chili pepper, ground, see ''Pepper''
Chili powder:
seasoned, 1 oz. 96
seasoned, 1 tbsp. 52
(*Mexene*), 1 tbsp. 24
Chili sauce, canned or bottled:
(*Gebhardt*), ½ cup 246
(*Heinz*), 1 tbsp. 17
(*Hunt's*), 1 tbsp. 19

Chili sauce relish:
(*Bennett's*), 1 tbsp. 15
Chili seasoning mix:
(*Durkee*), 1¾-oz. packet 148
(*Durkee* Texas), ½ cup* 386
(*French's Chili-O*), 1¾-oz. packet 150
Chili tomato dinner mix:
dry (*Hamburger Helper*), ⅕ pkg. 140
with meat* (*Hamburger Helper*), ⅕ pkg. 320
Chinese fried rice, see "Rice, flavored"
Chinese style vegetables, frozen:
(*Birds Eye*), 3.3 oz. 25
(*Birds Eye* Chinese Fried), 3.6 oz. 110
(*Birds Eye* Stir-Fry), 3.3 oz. 30
(*Green Giant*), ½ cup 65
mixed (*La Choy*), ½ cup 25
Chives, fresh:
raw, whole, 1 lb. 128
raw, chopped, 1 tbsp. 1
Chocolate almond liqueur:
(*Hiram Walker*), 1 fl. oz. 91
Chocolate, baking type:
baking (*Hershey*), 1 oz. 190
milk (*Hershey* Chips), 1 oz. 147
milk (*Nestlé* Morsels), 1 oz. 150
premelted (*Nestlé Choco-Bake*), 1 oz. 170
semisweet:
(*Baker's*), 1 oz. 130
(*Baker's* Chips), 1 oz. 130
(*Ghirardelli* Chips), 1 oz. 150
(*Hershey* Chips/Mini Chips), 1 oz. 147
(*Nestlé* Morsels), 1 oz. 150
sweet, 1 oz. 150
sweet (*Baker's* German), 1 oz. 130

Prepared according to directions on container

107

unsweetened:
   (*Baker's*), 1 oz. 140
   bitter, 1 oz. 143
   bitter, grated, ½ cup 334
Chocolate cake, see "Cakes, frozen," "Cakes, mix," and "Cakes, snack"
Chocolate candy, see "Candy"
Chocolate cherry liqueur:
   (*Hiram Walker*), 1 fl. oz. 91
Chocolate cream pie, see "Pies"
Chocolate drink mix, dry:
   high-fat or breakfast, processed, 1 oz. 84
   high-fat or breakfast, processed, 1 tbsp. 18
   medium-fat, processed, 1 oz. 74
   medium-fat, processed, 1 tbsp. 16
   low-medium-fat, processed, 1 oz. 61
   low-medium-fat, processed, 1 tbsp. 13
   low-fat, 1 oz. 53
   low-fat, 1 tbsp. 11
   with nonfat dry milk, 1 oz. 102
   with nonfat dry milk, 1 tbsp. 32
   without milk, 1 oz. 98
   without milk, 1 tbsp. 31
   for hot chocolate, 1 oz. 111
   for hot chocolate, 1 tbsp. 35
   (*Flick* Instant), 1 oz. 111
   (*Hershey* Instant), 3 tbsp. 80
   (*Nestlé Quik*), 2 tsp. 90
   (*Ovaltine*), ¾ oz. 80
Chocolate drink mix, prepared, see "Milk beverages, flavored"
Chocolate drinks, see "Milk beverages, flavored"
Chocolate extract:
   imitation (*Durkee*), 1 tsp. 7
Chocolate flavoring:
   imitation (*Ehlers*), 1 tsp. 10
Chocolate milk, see "Milk beverages, flavored"

Chocolate mint liqueur:
  (*Hiram Walker*), 1 fl. oz. 91
  (*Vandermint*), 1 fl. oz. 90
Chocolate pie filling:
  canned (*Comstock*), ⅓ cup 130
Chocolate toppings and syrups:
  (*Bosco* Milk Amplifier), 1 tbsp. 50
  (*Hershey* Syrup), 1 tbsp. 40
  (*Kraft* Topping), 1 tbsp. 50
  (*Milk Mate*), 1 tbsp. 50
  (*Smucker's*), 1 tbsp. 65
  fudge:
    (*Hershey* Topping), 1 tbsp. 50
    (*Kraft* Topping), 1 tbsp. 70
    (*Smucker's*), 1 tbsp. 65
    (*Smucker's* Swiss Milk), 1 tbsp. 70
    mint (*Smucker's*), 1 tbsp. 70
  fudge type, 1 tbsp. 62
  thin type, 1 tbsp. 46
Chop suey:
  canned, with meat, without noodles, 8 oz. 141
  canned, with meat, without noodles, 1 cup 155
  frozen (*Banquet Cookin' Bag*), 7-oz. pkg. 93
  beef, with rice, frozen (*Stouffer's*), 12-oz. pkg. 355
Chop suey seasoning mix:
  dry (*Durkee*), 1½-oz. packet 128
Chop suey vegetables:
  canned (*La Choy*), ½ cup, drained .10
Chow mein:
  canned:
    beef (*Chun King*—Divider Pak, 24 oz.), ½ pkg. 90
    beef (*Chun King*—Divider Pak, 42 oz.), ¼ of pkg. 80
    beef (*La Choy*), ¾ cup 70
    beef (*La Choy*—Bi-Pack), ¾ cup 60
    beef (*La Choy*—Dinner for 2), ½ pkg. 295
    chicken (*Chun King*—Divider Pak, 24 oz.), ½ pkg. 90

chicken (*Chun King*—Divider Pak, 42 oz.), ¼ of pkg. ...80
chicken (*La Choy*), ¾ cup 80
chicken (*La Choy*—Bi-Pack), ¾ cup 70
chicken (*La Choy*—Dinner for 2), ½ pkg. 305
pork (*Chun King*—Divider Pak), ¼ of pkg.* 110
pork (*La Choy*—Bi-Pack), ¾ cup 90
shrimp (*Chun King*—Divider Pak), ¼ of pkg. 70
shrimp (*La Choy*), ¾ cup 60
shrimp (*La Choy*—Bi-Pack), ¾ cup 70
vegetable (*La Choy*—Bi-Pack), ¾ cup 60
frozen:
   (*Banquet Cookin' Bag*), 7-oz. pkg. 89
   (*Chun King*), ⅕ of pkg. 230
   chicken (*Chun King* Pouched Entree), 6 oz. 90
   chicken (*Green Giant* Entree), 9-oz. pkg. 130
   chicken (*La Choy*), ⅔ cup 90
   chicken (*Stouffer's*), 8-oz. pkg. 145
   shrimp (*Chun King* Pouched Entree), 6 oz. 80

Chow mein dinner, frozen:
  chicken (*Chun King*), 1 dinner 320
  chicken/sweet and sour pork (*Chun King*), 1 dinner 390
  shrimp (*Chun King*), 1 dinner 300
  shrimp (*La Choy*), 1 dinner 220
  shrimp/beef pepper Oriental (*Chun King*), 1 dinner 350

Chow mein noodles, canned:
  (*Chun King*), 5-oz. can 600
  (*Chun King* Chinatown Style), 6-oz. can 800
  (*La Choy*), 1 oz., or ½ cup 153

Chow mein vegetables:
  canned (*Chun King*), 4 oz. 20

Chubs:
  smoked, flesh only (*Vita*), 2 oz. 108

Chutney, Major Grey's:
  bottled, 1 tbsp. 50

*Prepared according to directions on container

bottled (*Crosse & Blackwell*), 1 tbsp. 53
Cinnamon:
all brands, 1 tsp. 6
Cinnamon sugar:
(*French's*), 1 tsp. 16
Cisco, see "Lake herring"
Citron, candied:
1 oz. 89
Citrus flavored drink:
canned (*Hi-C* Citrus Cooler), 6 fl. oz. 93
Clam chowder, see "Soups"
Clam cocktail:
with sauce (*Sau-Sea*), 4-oz. jar. 99
Clam dip:
(*Kraft*), 2 tbsp. 50
(*Kraft* Ready to serve), 1 oz. 45
Clam juice:
(*Snow's*), 3 fl. oz. 12
Clam and lobster dip:
(*Borden*), 4-oz. container 240
Clam sandwich:
frozen, fried (*Mrs. Paul's*), 4½-oz. pkg. 420
Clam sauce:
red, canned (*Buitoni*), 4 oz. 108
white, canned (*Buitoni*), 4 oz. 144
Clam-tomato cocktail:
(*Mott's Clamato*), 6 fl. oz. 80
Clams:
fresh, raw:
hard, or round, meat only 1 pt. 363
hard, or round, meat only, 8 oz. 182
hard, or round, meat only, 4 cherrystones
or 5 littlenecks 56
soft, meat only, 1 pt. 372
soft, meat only, 8 oz. 186

canned or in jars:
  whole, meat only (*Doxsee*), 1 cup 194
  whole, half meat/half liquid (*Doxsee*), 1 cup 116
  chopped or minced, drained (*Doxsee*), 1 cup 196
  chopped or minced, half meat/half liquid (*Doxsee*),
    1 cup 118
  minced, with liquid (*Snow's*), 6½ oz. 120
frozen:
  fried (*Howard Johnson's*), 5-oz. pkg. 395
  fried (*Mrs. Paul's*), 5-oz. pkg. 540
  fried (*Mrs. Paul's*) 8-oz. pkg. 880
  fritters, batter-fried (*Mrs. Paul's*), 7¾-oz. pkg. 520

Clam, dinner, frozen:
  fried (*Taste O' Sea Platter*), 6½-oz. pkg. 540

Claret wine:
  (*Gold Seal*), 4 fl. oz. 109
  (*Italian Swiss Colony*), 4 fl. oz. 86
  (*Taylor*), 4 fl. oz. 96
  (*Taylor* Lake Country Red), 4 fl. oz. 108

Cloves:
  all brands, 1 tsp. 7

Club soda, see "Soft drinks and mixers"
Coating mixes, see "Seasoned coating mix"
Cocktail host:
  bottled (*Holland House*), 1 fl. oz. 47

Cocktail loaf:
  (*Oscar Mayer*), 1-oz. slice 65

Cocktail mix, see individual listings
Cocktail seafood sauce:
  (*Crosse & Blackwell*), 1 tbsp. 22
  (*Del Monte*), 1 tbsp. 18
  (*Pfeiffer*), ½ oz. 25
  (*Sau-Sea*), 1 tbsp. 16

Cocoa mix, dry:
  (*Hershey*), 1 oz. 120
  (*Hershey* Hot Cocoa Mix), 1 oz. 120

(*Nestlé* Hot Cocoa Mix), 1 oz. 110
(*Ovaltine* Hot Cocoa Mix), 1 oz. .120
chocolate, with marshmallows (*Nestlé*), 1 oz. 110
chocolate, with mini marshmallows
    (*Carnation* Instant Hot Cocoa Mix), 1 oz. 109
milk chocolate (*Carnation* Instant Hot Cocoa Mix),
    1 oz. 112
rich chocolate (*Carnation* Instant Hot Cocoa Mix),
    1 oz. 112

Coconut:
fresh:
    in shell, 1 coconut (4⅝″ in diam.) 1,373
    shelled, meat only, 4 oz. 392
    shelled, meat only, 1 piece (2″ × 2″ × ½″) 156
    shredded or grated, 1 cup loosely packed 277
    shredded or grated, 1 cup packed 450
dried:
    flaked (*Baker's* Angel Flake), 1 oz. 150
    grated (*Baker's Fine Grated*), 1 oz. 150
    shredded, unsweetened, 4 oz. 751
    shredded, unsweetened, 1 cup 622
    shredded, sweetened, 4 oz. 621
    shredded, sweetened, 1 cup 515
    shredded (*Durkee*), 1 cup 277
Coconut, chocolate covered, see "Candy"
Coconut cream (liquid from grated coconut meat):
 1 cup 802
 1 tbsp. 50
Coconut, cream of:
 canned (*Holland House Coco Casa*), 1 tbsp. 59
Coconut cream pie filling:
 canned (*Comstock*), ⅓ cup 120
Coconut custard pie, see "Pies"
Coconut flavoring:
 imitation (*Durkee*), 1 tsp. 8
 imitation (*Ehlers*), 1 tsp. 17

Coconut milk
(liquid from grated coconut meat and coconut water): 1 cup . . . 605
Coconut water
(liquid from coconuts): 1 cup 53
Cod:
fresh:
raw, fillets, 8 oz. 176
broiled, with butter, 1 steak (5½″ × 4″ × 1¼″) 352
broiled, with butter, fillets, 4 oz. 192
broiled with butter, 1 fillet (5″ × 2½″ × ⅞″) 111
canned:
drained, 8.5 oz. (yield from 11-oz. can) 204
drained, 4 oz. 97
drained, flaked, 1 cup 119
dehydrated and dried:
dehydrated, lightly salted, 4 oz. 424
dehydrated, lightly salted, shredded, 1 cup 158
dried, salted, 4 oz. 148
dried, salted, 1 piece (5½″ × 1½″ × ½″) 104
frozen:
breaded (*Taste O' Sea*), 1 portion 80
fillets (*Gorton*), 4 oz. 90
fillets (*Taste O' Sea*), 16-oz. pkg. 320
sticks, fried (*Taste O' Sea*), 4 sticks 230
with butter sauce (*Gorton*), 6-oz. pkg. 170
with cheese sauce (*Gorton*), 6-oz. pkg. 180
Cod dinner:
frozen, batter-fried (*Taste O' Sea Batter Dipt*), 8¾-oz. pkg. . . . 500
Coffee:
ground roasted, prepared*:
(*Chase & Sanborn*), 6 fl. oz. 2
(*Maxwell House*), 6 fl. oz. 2
(*Sanka*), 6 fl. oz. 2

*Prepared according to directions on container

(*Yuban*), 6 fl. oz. 2

instant, dry:

    regular, 1 tbsp. 3

    regular, 1 tsp. 1

    freeze-dried, 1 tbsp. 5

    freeze-dried, 1 tsp. 1

instant, prepared*:

    (*Decaf*), 6 fl. oz. 4

    (*Kava*), 6 fl. oz. 3

    (*Maxwell House*), 6 fl. oz. 3

    (*Nescafé*), 6 fl. oz. 4

    (*Nescafé* Decaffeinated), 6 fl. oz. 4

    freeze-dried (*Maxim*), 6 fl. oz. 3

    freeze-dried (*Taster's Choice*), 6 fl. oz. 4

    freeze-dried (*Taster's Choice* Decaffeinated), 6 fl. oz. 4

flavored, prepared*:

    café Francais (*General Foods* International Coffees),

        6 fl. oz. 60

    café Vienna

        (*General Foods* International Coffees), 6 fl. oz. 60

    Irish mocha mint (*General Foods* International Coffees),

        6 fl. oz. 50

    orange cappucino (*General Foods* International Coffees),

        6 fl. oz. 60

    Suisse mocha (*General Foods* International Coffees),

        6 fl. oz. 60

    imitation (*Celestial Seasonings Roastaroma*), 6 fl. oz. ...10

Coffee brandy:

    (*DuBouchett*), 1 fl. oz. 88

    (*Hiram Walker*), 1 fl. oz. 96

    (*Old Mr. Boston*—70 proof), 1 fl. oz. 74

Coffee flavoring:

    pure (*Burton's*), 1 tsp. 9

Coffee liqueur:

    (*Coffee Southern*), 1 fl. oz. 85

Prepared according to directions on container

(*Kahlua*), 1 fl. oz. 106

(*Pasha* Turkish), 1 fl. oz. 100

(*Tia Maria*), 1 fl. oz. 92

Cola, see "Soft drinks and mixers"

Cold cuts, see individual listings

Coleslaw:

  commercial, with French dressing, 4 oz. 108

  commercial, with French dressing, 1 cup 114

  commercial, with mayonnaise, 4 oz. 164

  commercial, with mayonnaise, 1 cup 173

  commercial, with mayonnaise-type salad dressing, 4 oz. . . .113

  commercial, with mayonnaise-type salad dressing, 1 cup . . .119

Collards:

  fresh:

    raw, with stems, 1 lb. 181

    raw, leaves only, 1 lb. 204

    leaves only, boiled in small amount water, drained, 1 cup 63

    leaves only, boiled in large amount water, drained, 1 cup 59

    with stems, boiled in small amount water, drained, 1 cup 42

  frozen:

    chopped (*Birds Eye*), 3.3 oz. 25

    chopped (*Seabrook Farms*), 3.3 oz. 25

    chopped (*Southland*), 3.3 oz. 30

Collins mixer, see "Soft drinks and mixers"

Concord wine:

  (*Gold Seal*), 4 fl. oz. 167

Consommé, see "Soups"

Cookie crumbs:

  gingersnap, 1 cup 483

  graham (*Keebler*), 1 oz. 122

  graham (*Nabisco*), 1 oz. 140

  graham (*Sunshine*), 1 oz. 119

  vanilla wafer, 1 cup 370

Cookies:

  almond flavor:

    (*Stella D'Oro* Almond Toast—Mandel), 1 piece 55

(*Stella D'Oro* Breakfast Treats), 1 piece 105
(*Stella D'Oro* Chinese Dessert), 1 piece 165
animal crackers:
  (*Barnum's*), 1 piece 12
  (*Dixie Bell*), 1 oz., or 15 crackers 120
  (*Keebler*), 1 piece 12
  (*Ralston*), 1 oz., or 15 crackers .120
  (*Sunshine*), 1 piece 11
  honey (*El Molino*), 1 piece 14
  iced (*Keebler 100's*), 1 piece 24
anise flavor:
  (*Stella D'Oro* Anisette Sponge), 1 piece 49
  (*Stella D'Oro* Anisette Toast), 1 piece 43
  (*Stella D'Oro* Anisette Toast—large), 1 piece 129
  (*Stella D'Oro* Roman Egg Biscuits), 1 piece 128
apple (*Stella D'Oro* Apple Pastry), 1 piece 92
arrowroot (*Nabisco*), 1 piece 60
assorted:
  (*Stella D'Oro* Hostess), 1 piece 43
  (*Stella D'Oro* Lady Stella), 1 piece 40
bran (*El Molino* Breakfast Biscuit), 1 piece 20
brown edge (*FFV*), 1 piece 40
brown edge (*Nabisco*), 1 piece 28
brown sugar, see ''sugar,'' below
butter flavor:
  (*Jacob's Petit Beurre*), 1 piece 110
  (*Nabisco*), 1 piece 23
  (*Pepperidge Farm Bordeaux*), 1 piece 37
  (*Pepperidge Farm Chessman*), 1 piece 43
  (*Sunshine*), 1 piece 28
carob chip (*El Molino*), 1 piece 80
carob, wheat-free (*El Molino*), 1 piece 80
chocolate:
  1 oz. 126
  (*Nabisco Famous Wafers*), 1 piece 28
  (*Stella D'Oro Margherite*), 1 piece 72

117

chocolate chip:
  1 oz. 134
  (*C.C. Biggs*), 1 piece 56
  (*Chip-A-Roos*), 1 piece 52
  (*Chips Ahoy!*), 1 piece 53
  (*FFV*), 1 piece 57
  (*Keebler 100's*), 1 piece 24
  (*Pepperidge Farm*), 1 piece .43
  (*Pepperidge Farm Fudge Chip*), 1 piece 57
  (*Pepperidge Farm St. Moritz*), 1 piece 47
  (*Rich n' Chips*), 1 piece 81
  (*Sunshine Chocolate Nuggets*), 1 piece 20
chocolate covered (*Keebler Fudge Stripe*), 1 piece 54
chocolate-nut (*Pepperidge Farm Chocolate Brownie*),
  1 piece 57
chocolate-nut sandwich, vanilla-filled
  (*Pepperidge Farm Capri*), 1 piece 85
cinnamon (*Nabisco Cinnamon Treats*), 1 piece 28
cinnamon-sugar (*Pepperidge Farm*), 1 piece 53
coconut:
  bars, 1 oz. 140
  (*Nabisco* Coconut Bars), 1 piece 47
  (*Pepperidge Farm Zanzibar*), 1 piece 37
  (*Stella D'Oro*), 1 piece 49
coconut-chocolate drop (*Keebler*), 1 piece 83
coconut sandwich, chocolate-filled
  (*Pepperidge Farm Tahiti*), 1 piece 85
creme sandwich:
  1 oz. 140
  (*Elfwich*), 1 piece 55
  (*FFV Duplex*), 1 piece 73
  (*Keebler* Opera), 1 piece 82
  assorted (*Cookie Break*), 1 piece 50
  chocolate (*Hydrox*), 1 piece 49
  chocolate (*Oreo*), 1 piece 50
  chocolate (*Oreo Double Stuf*), 1 piece 70
  chocolate fudge (*Keebler*), 1 piece 83

chocolate fudge (*Sunshine*), 1 piece 70
coconut (*Sunshine Coconut Cremers*), 1 piece 51
fudge (*Keebler*), 1 piece 55
oatmeal-peanut (*Sunshine*), 1 piece 82
peanut butter (*Keebler* Double Nutty), 1 piece 64
peanut butter (*Pitter Patter*), 1 piece 83
vanilla (*Cameo*), 1 piece 70
vanilla (*Cookie Break*), 1 piece 50
vanilla (*Hydrox*), 1 piece 51
vanilla (*Keebler*), 1 piece 56
vanilla (*Keebler* French Vanilla), 1 piece 83
vanilla (*Sunshine Cup Custard*), 1 piece 65
vanilla (*Vienna Fingers*), 1 piece 69
date-nute granola (*Pepperidge Farm*), 1 piece 53
devil's food (*FFV*), 1 piece 45
devil's food (*Nabisco* Cakes), 1 piece 50
egg biscuits:
  (*Stella D'Oro*), 1 piece 41
  (*Stella D'Oro* Jumbo), 1 piece 44
  flavored, see specific flavors
  sugared (*Stella D'Oro*), 1 piece 64
  sugared (*Stella D'Oro Anginetti*), 1 piece 29
fig:
  bars, 1 oz. 101
  (*Fig Newtons*), 1 piece 55
  (*Keebler*), 1 piece 74
  (*Stella D'Oro* Fig Pastry), 1 piece 95
  (*Sunshine*), 1 piece 45
ginger:
  (*Nabisco* Old Fashion Ginger Snaps), 1 piece 30
  (*Pepperidge Farm* Gingerman), 1 piece 33
  (*Sunshine* Ginger Snaps), 1 piece 16
graham crackers:
  plain, 1 oz. 109
  sugar honey, 1 oz. 116
  (*Dixie Belle* Sugar Honey Grahams), 1 oz., or 8 crackers ...110

(*Honey Maid*), 1 piece 30
(*Keebler* Honey Graham), 1 piece 17
(*Nabisco*), 1 piece 30
(*Ralston* Sugar Honey Graham), 1 oz., or 8 crackers 110
(*Sunshine* Cinnamon Grahams), 1 piece 17
(*Sunshine* Sugar Honey), 1 piece 15
chocolate covered, 1 oz. 135
chocolate covered (*Fancy Dip*), 1 piece 65
chocolate covered (*Keebler* De Luxe), 1 piece 43
chocolate covered (*Nabisco* Chocolate Grahams), 1 piece ...57
graham cracker crumbs, see "Cookies crumbs"
honey:
   and bran (*El Molino*), 1 piece 70
   and carob chip (*El Molino*), 1 piece 38
   and oatmeal (*El Molino*—large), 1 piece 80
   and oatmeal (*El Molino*—small), 1 piece 38
   and peanut butter (*El Molino*—large), 1 piece 80
   and peanut butter (*El Molino*—small), 1 piece 38
ladyfingers, 1 oz. 102
lemon:
   (*FFV* Lemon Thins), 1 piece 40
   (*Sunshine* Lemon Coolers), 1 piece 29
lemon-nut crunch (*Pepperidge Farm*), 1 piece 60
macaroons, 1 oz. 135
marshmallow:
   chocolate covered (*Mallomars*), 1 piece 55
   chocolate covered (*Nabisco* Puffs), 1 piece 85
   chocolate covered (*Pinwheels*), 1 piece 140
   with chocolate sprinkles (*Sunshine* Sprinkles),
     1 piece 59
   with coconut (*Sunshine Mallo Puffs*), 1 piece 62
   with coconut and jelly (*Sunshine* Marshmallow Bar),
     1 piece 92
   iced (*Sunshine Nut Sundae*), 1 piece 57
   iced (*Sunshine Busters*), 1 piece 84
   sandwich (*Nabisco*), 1 piece 33

mint sandwich (*Pepperidge Farm Mint Milano*), 1 piece 70
mint sandwich, chocolate covered (*Mystic*), 1 piece 85
molasses (*Pepperidge Farm* Crisps), 1 piece 30
oatmeal:
    (*Keebler* Old Fashion), 1 piece 83
    (*Nabisco*), 1 piece 75
    (*Pepperidge Farm* Irish Oatmeal), 1 piece 50
    (*Sunshine*), 1 piece 61
oatmeal-almond (*Pepperidge Farm*), 1 piece 53
oatmeal-marmalade (*Pepperidge Farm*), 1 piece 53
oatmeal-raisin (*Pepperidge Farm*), 1 piece 57
peach-apricot (*Stella D'Oro* Pastry), 1 piece 87
peanut (*Nabisco* Peanut Creme Patties), 1 piece 35
peanut (*Pepperidge Farm*), 1 piece 47
peanut butter:
    (*Sunshine* Wafers), 1 piece 39
    sandwich (*Nutter Butter*), 1 piece 75
    sandwich, chocolate filled (*Pepperidge Farm Nassau*),
      1 piece 75
pecan, see "shortbread," below
(*Pepperidge Farm Adelaide*), 1 piece 53
prune (*Stella D'Oro* Prune Pastry), 1 piece 95
raisin:
    (*Nabisco* Raisin Fruit), 1 piece 55
    (*Stella D'Oro* Golden Bars), 1 piece 107
    (*Sunshine* Golden Fruit), 1 piece 60
    iced (*Keebler* Bars), 1 piece 80
raisin, biscuit type, 1 oz. 107
raisin-bran (*Pepperidge Farm*), 1 piece 53
rum and brandy flavor (*Stella D'Oro* Roman Egg Biscuits),
    1 piece 128
sesame (*Stella D'Oro* Regina), 1 piece 47
shortbread:
    1 oz. 141
    (*Lorna Doone*), 1 piece 40
    (*Pepperidge Farm*), 1 piece 65

    iced (*Sunshine* Frosted Cakes),1 piece 60
    pecan (*Nabisco*), 1 piece 80
    pecan (*Pecan Sandies*), 1 piece .86
(*Social Tea Biscuits*), 1 piece 20
spice (*Keebler Spiced Windmills*), 1 piece 60
spice (*Nabisco* Wafers), 1 piece 33
(*Stella D'Oro Angel Puffs*), 1 piece 18
(*Stella D'Oro Angelica Goodies*), 1 piece 101
(*Stella D'Oro Como Delights*), 1 piece 143
(*Stella D'Oro Love Cookies*), 1 piece 110
(*Stella D'Oro Royal Nuggets*), 1 piece 1
(*Stella D'Oro Sorrento*), 1 piece 58
(*Stella D'Oro Taste of Vienna*), 1 piece 85
sugar:
    (*Keebler* Old Fashion), 1 piece 83
    (*Nabisco* Sugar Rings), 1 piece 70
    (*Pepperidge Farm*), 1 piece 53
    brown (*Pepperidge Farm*), 1 piece 50
sugar wafers:
    (*Bisco*), 1 piece 19
    (*Bisco* Waffle Cremes), 1 piece 43
    (*Keebler* Krisp Kreem), 1 piece 29
    (*Sunshine*), 1 piece 42
    chocolate covered (*Nabisco* Creme Wafer Sticks), 1 piece . . .50
    iced (*Sunshine Yum Yums*), 1 piece 83
sunflower-raisin (*Pepperidge Farm*), 1 piece 53
toy cookies (*Sunshine*), 1 piece 13
vanilla:
    (*FFV* Wafers), 1 piece 18
    (*Keebler* Wafers), 1 piece 19
    (*Nilla* Wafers), 1 piece 19
    (*Stella D'Oro Margherite*), 1 piece 74
    (*Stella D'Oro* Roman Egg Biscuits), 1 piece 128
    (*Sunshine Dixie Vanilla*), 1 piece 58
    (*Sunshine* Wafers), 1 piece 14
    chocolate centers (*Stella D'Oro* Swiss Fudge), 1 piece . . .67

rolls (*Pepperidge Farm Pirouette*), 1 piece 40
rolls, chocolate laced (*Pepperidge Farm Pirouette*),
  1 piece 40
sandwich, chocolate filled (*Pepperidge Farm Brussels*),
  1 piece 57
sandwich, chocolate filled (*Pepperidge Farm Lido*),
  1 piece 95
sandwich, chocolate filled (*Pepperidge Farm Milano*),
  1 piece 63
wafer, chocolate covered (*Pepperidge Farm Orleans*),
  1 piece 33
wheat-free (*El Molino*), 1 piece 80

Cookies, frozen:
chocolate chip (*Mrs. Goodcookie*), 1 piece 57
chocolate fudge (*Mrs. Goodcookie*), 1 piece 57
oatmeal, with raisin (*Mrs. Goodcookie*), 1 piece 53
peanut butter (*Mrs. Goodcookie*), 1 piece 60
sugar (*Mrs. Goodcookie*), 1 piece 53

Cookies, mix*:
chocolate (*Betty Crocker Big Batch* Double Chocolate),
  1 piece 70
chocolate chip (*Betty Crocker Big Batch*), 1 piece 75
chocolate chip (*Nestlé*), 1 piece 55
chocolate chip (*Quaker*), 1 piece 75
coconut macaroon (*Betty Crocker* Dessert Mix), 1/24 of pkg. ...80
date bar (*Betty Crocker*), 1/32 of pkg. 60
gingerbread (*Betty Crocker* Dessert Mix), 1/9 of pkg. 210
gingerbread (*Pillsbury*), 3" square 190
oatmeal (*Betty Crocker Big Batch*), 1 piece 70
oatmeal (*Quaker*), 1 piece 65
peanut butter (*Betty Crocker Big Batch*), 1 piece 70
peanut butter (*Quaker*), 1 piece 75
peanut butter with chips (*Betty Crocker Big Batch*), 1 piece ...70
sugar (*Betty Crocker Big Batch*), 1 piece 65

*Prepared according to directions on container

Vienna bar (*Betty Crocker* Vienna Dream Bar),
  ¹⁄₂₄ of pkg. 90
Cookies, refrigerator:
chocolate chip:
  (*Pillsbury Oven Lovin*), 1 piece 57
  (*Pillsbury* Slice 'N Bake), 1 piece 53
  (*Pillsbury* Slice 'N Bake Cookie Lover), 1 piece 53
oatmeal:
  (*Pillsbury Oven Lovin*), 1 piece 57
  (*Pillsbury* Slice 'N Bake), 1 piece 57
  with raisins (*Pillsbury* Slice 'N Bake), 1 piece 53
peanut butter (*Pillsbury Oven Lovin*), 1 piece 60
peanut butter (*Pillsbury* Slice 'N Bake), 1 piece 57
sugar (*Pillsbury Oven Lovin*), 1 piece 57
sugar (*Pillsbury* Slice 'N Bake), 1 piece 63
Coriander seed:
ground (all brands), 1 tsp. 6
Corn:
sweet, fresh:
  raw, on cob, with husks, 1 lb. 157
  raw, on cob, without husks, 1 lb. 240
  on cob, boiled, drained, 1 ear (5″ long, 1¾″ in diam.) ...70
  kernels, cut from cob, boiled, drained, 1 cup 138
canned:
  whole kernel (*Del Monte* Family Style), ½ cup 85
  whole kernel (*Del Monte*—vacuum pack), ½ cup 100
  whole kernel (*Green Giant*), ½ cup 80
  whole kernel (*Green Giant* Nuggets), ½ cup 75
  whole kernel (*Kounty Kist/Lindy*), ½ cup 90
  whole kernel (*Kounty Kist/Lindy*—vacuum pack), ½ cup ...80
  whole kernel (*Le Sueur*), ½ cup 85
  whole kernel (*Libby's*), ½ cup 80
  whole kernel (*Stokely-Van Camp*), ½ cup 90
  whole kernel (*Stokely-Van Camp*—vacuum pack), ½ cup ...115
  cream (*Del Monte*), ½ cup 105
  cream (*Green Giant*), ½ cup 105

cream (*Kounty Kist/Lindy*), ½ cup 115
cream (*Libby's*), ½ cup 87
cream (*Stokely-Van Camp*), ½ cup 105
white, whole kernel (*Del Monte*), ½ cup 75
white, whole kernel (*Green Giant*—vacuum pack), ½ cup . . .75
white, whole kernel (*Stokely-Van Camp*), ½ cup 95
white, cream (*Del Monte*), ½ cup 95
white, cream (*Stokely-Van Camp*), ½ cup 100
and peppers (*Del Monte*), ½ cup 95
and peppers (*Green Giant Mexicorn*), ½ cup 75
frozen:
on cob (*Birds Eye*), 1 ear 120
on cob (*Green Giant*), 5½″ ear .160
on cob (*Ore-Ida*), 6″ ear 150
on cob (*Seabrook Farms*), 5″ ear 140
on cob, small (*Birds Eye Little Ears*), 2 ears 130
on cob, small (*Green Giant Nibblers*), 2 ears 180
kernels, boiled, drained, 9.75 oz.
(yield from 10-oz. pkg.) 217
kernels, boiled, drained, 1 cup 130
whole kernel (*Birds Eye*), 3.3 oz. 80
whole kernel (*Green Giant*), ½ cup 65
whole kernel (*Hanover*), 3.2 oz. 85
whole kernel (*Kounty Kist/Lindy*), ½ cup 70
whole kernel (*Ore-Ida*), ½ cup .100
whole kernel (*Seabrook Farms*), 3.3 oz. 90
whole kernel (*Stokely-Van Camp*), 3.3 oz. 90
cream (*Green Giant*), ½ cup 90
cream (*Stokely-Van Camp*), 3.3 oz. 90
white, whole kernel (*Green Giant*), ½ cup 65
white, whole kernel (*Hanover* Shoepeg Corn), 3.2 oz. . . .90
white, whole kernel (*Kounty Kist/Lindy*), ½ cup 70
with butter sauce (*Green Giant Niblets*), ½ cup 95
white, with butter sauce (*Green Giant*), ½ cup 95
combination (*Birds Eye* Corn Jubilee), 3.3 oz. 120
combination (*Stokely-Van Camp* Chuckwagon Corn),
3.3 oz. 90

with cut green beans (*Hanover* Shoepeg Corn),
   3.2 oz. 60
with Fordhook lima beans (*Hanover* Shoepeg Corn),
   3.2 oz. 90
with green beans and pasta twists
   (*Birds Eye* Blue Ribbon), 3.3 oz. 110

Corn chips:
   (*Bachman's* Indian), 1 oz. 160
   (*Dipsy Doodles*), 1 oz. 160
   (*Frito's*), 1 oz. 160
   (*Planters*), 1 oz. 170
   (*Wise*), 1 oz. 160
   (*Wonder*), 1 oz. 162
   barbecue flavor (*Frito's* Bar-B-Q), 1 oz. 150
   barbecue flavor (*Wise*), 1 oz. 160

Corn crisps and puffs:
   (*Bachman's* Cheese Twists), 1 oz. .150
   (*Chee•tos*), 1 oz. 160
   (*Cheez Bursts*), 1 oz. 160
   (*Cheez Doodles*—crunchy), 1 oz. .160
   (*Cheez Doodles*—puffed), 1 oz. 160
   (*Cheez Doodles*—super puffed), 1 oz. 160
   (*Diggers*), 1 oz. 160
   (*Doo Dads*), 1 oz. 140
   (*Flings*), 1 oz. 160
   (*Jax*), 1 oz. 150
   (*Korkers*), 1 oz. 150
   (*Planters* Cheez Balls), 1 oz. 160
   (*Planters* Cheez Curls), 1 oz. 160

Corn flakes, see "Cereals, ready-to-eat"
Corn fritters:
   frozen (*Hanover*), 2 oz. 140
   frozen (*Mrs. Paul's*), 2 oz., or 1 fritter 130
Corn grits, degermed:
   dry, 8 oz. 821
   dry, 1 cup 579

cooked, 8 oz. 116
cooked, 1 cup 125
Corn, or hominy grits, dry:
(*Quaker* Instant), 1 packet 79
white, regular or quick (*Aunt Jemima*), 3 tbsp. 101
white, regular or quick (*Quaker*), 3 tbsp. 101
white, quick (*3-Minute Brand*), ½ oz. 100
with artificial cheese flavor (*Quaker* Instant), 1 packet 104
with imitation bacon bits (*Quaker* Instant), 1 packet 101
with imitation ham bits (*Quaker* Instant), 1 packet 99
Corn meal:
white or yellow:
whole-ground, unbolted, dry, 8 oz. 806
whole-ground, unbolted, dry, 1 cup 433
bolted, dry, 8 oz. 822
bolted, dry, 1 cup 442
degermed, dry, 8 oz. 826
degermed, dry, 1 cup 502
degermed, cooked, 1 cup 120
self-rising, whole-ground, dry, 8 oz. 788
self-rising, whole-ground, dry, 1 cup 465
self-rising, degermed, dry, 8 oz. 790
self-rising, degermed, dry, 1 cup 491
white:
(*Aunt Jemima*), 3 tbsp. 102
(*Quaker*), 3 tbsp. 102
bolted, mix (*Aunt Jemima*), ⅙ cup 99
self-rising (*Aunt Jemima*), ⅙ cup 98
self-rising, bolted (*Aunt Jemima*), ⅙ cup 99
yellow:
(*Aunt Jemima*), 3 tbsp. 102
(*Elam's* Stone Ground), 1 oz. 105
(*Quaker*), 3 tbsp. 102
Corn muffin, see "Muffins"
Corn nuggets:
toasted (*Frito-Lay's*), 1 oz. 180

Corn relish:

(*Crosse & Blackwell*), 1 tbsp. 15

Corn salad:

raw, whole, 1 lb. 91

raw, trimmed, 1 lb. 96

Corn soufflé:

frozen (*Stouffer's*), 12-oz. pkg. 465

Corn syrup:

dark (*Karo*), 1 tbsp. 60

light (*Karo*), 1 tbsp. 60

Cornbread mix*:

(*Aunt Jemima* Easy Mix), ⅙ of cornbread 220

(*Ballard*), ⅛ of cornbread 160

(*Dromedary*), 2″ × 2″ square piece 130

Cornbread stuffing, see "Bread stuffing"

Cornstarch:

(*Argo/Kingsford's/Duryea's*), 1 tbsp. 35

Corned beef, see "Beef, corned"

Cough drops, see "Candy"

Cowpeas (black-eyed peas):

immature seeds, in pods, raw, 1 lb. 317

immature seeds, shelled, raw, 8 oz. 288

immature seeds, shelled, raw, 1 cup 184

immature seeds, boiled, drained, 1 cup 178

young pods, with seeds, raw, 1 lb. 182

young pods, with seeds, boiled, drained, 1 cup 154

mature seeds, dry, uncooked, 8 oz. 779

mature seeds, dry, uncooked, 1 cup 583

mature seeds, dry, cooked, 1 cup 190

canned:

(*Hanover*), 4 oz. 105

(*Progresso*), ½ cup 83

frozen:

(*Birds Eye*), 3.3 oz. 130

**Prepared according to directions on container*

  (*Green Giant*), ½ cup 140
  (*Seabrook Farms*), 3.3 oz. 130
  (*Southland*), 3.3 oz. 120

Crab:
  fresh:
    steamed, in shell, 1 lb. 202
    steamed, meat only, 8 oz. 211
    steamed, meat only, flaked, 1 cup loosely packed 116
    steamed, meat only, pieces, 1 cup loosely packed 144
    steamed, meat only, pieces or flaked, 1 cup packed 195
  canned:
    drained, 8 oz. 229
    claw, drained, 1 cup loosely packed 116
    white or king, drained, 1 cup loosely packed 136
    claw, white or king, drained, 1 cup 162
  frozen:
    cakes, deviled (*Mrs. Paul's*), 3-oz. cake 170
    miniatures, deviled, (*Mrs. Paul's*), 1 oz. 63
    miniatures, deviled, (*Mrs. Paul's*), 7-oz. pkg. 440
    fritters (*Mrs. Paul's*), 7¾-oz. pkg. 500

Crab apples:
  raw, whole, 1 lb. 284
  raw, trimmed, flesh only, 8 oz. 154

Crab cocktail:
  with sauce (*Sau-Sea*), 4-oz. jar 107

Crab crepes:
  frozen (*Mrs. Paul's*), 5½-oz. pkg. 240

Cracker crumbs:
  butter, 1 cup 366
  cheese, 1 cup 407
  graham, see "Cookie crumbs"
  matzo meal (*Manischewitz*), 1 oz. 110
  saltines (*Premium*), 1 oz. 120
  soda, 1 cup 307

Crackers:
  (*American Harvest*), 1 piece 16

129

animal crackers, see "Cookies"
arrowroot, see "Cookies"
bacon flavor (*Keebler* Bacon Toast), 1 piece 16
bacon flavor (*Nabisco* Bacon Thins), 1 piece 11
barbecue flavor, 1 oz. 142
butter flavor:
    (*Hi-Ho*), 1 piece 19
    (*Keebler Club*), 1 piece 15
    (*Keebler* Town House), 1 piece 16
    (*Nabisco* Butter Thins), 1 piece 14
    (*Ritz*), 1 piece 17
    (*Tam-Tams*), 1 piece 14
    (*Sunshine* Banquet Wafers), 1 piece 14
butter flavor-sesame (*Nabisco* Sesame Snack), 1 piece 17
cheese filled (*Frito-Lay's*), 1½-oz. pkg. 200
cheese filled sandwich (*Cheez-Waffies*), 1 oz. 140
cheese flavor:
    (*Cheese Nips*), 1 piece 6
    (*Cheez-It*), 1 piece 6
    (*Dixie Belle* Cheese Crackers), 1 oz., or 25 crackers 140
    (*Keebler* Nacho Cheese Snack), 1 piece 11
    (*Ralston* Cheese Snack), 1 oz., or 25 crackers 140
    (*Shindigs*), 1 piece 6
    cheddar (*Pepperidge Farm* Goldfish), ¼ oz. 35
    cheddar (*Pepperidge Farm* Goldfish Thins), 1 piece 18
    Parmesan (*Nabisco* Cheese Swirls), 1 piece 11
    Parmesan (*Pepperidge Farm* Goldfish), ¼ oz. 35
    Swiss (*Nabisco* Cheese Snack), 1 piece 10
    cheese sandwich, peanut-butter filled (*Cheda-Nut*),
      1 piece 38
(*Chicken In A Biskit*), 1 piece 10
Cinnamon (*Keebler Cinnamon Crisp*), 1 piece 17
(*Dixie Belle* Snackers), 1 oz., or 8 crackers 140
(*FFV* Ocean Crisp), 1 piece 58
(*FFV* Snack Crackers), 1 piece 17
flatbread:
    (*Ideal* Ultra-Thin), 1 piece 12

bran (*Ideal*), 1 piece 19
whole grain (*Ideal*), 1 piece 19
garlic (*Manischewitz* Garlic *Tams*), 1 piece 13
garlic (*Old London* Melba Rounds), 1 piece 10
graham crackers, see "Cookies"
matzo:
  (*Manischewitz* American), 1 sheet or piece 115
  (*Manischewitz* Egg 'n Onion), 1 sheet or piece 112
  (*Manischewitz* Matzo Cracker), 1 sheet or piece 8
  (*Manischewitz* Matzo Thins), 1 sheet or piece 91
  (*Manischewitz* Passover Egg Matzo), 1 sheet or piece ...132
  (*Manischewitz* Passover Matzo), 1 sheet or piece 129
  (*Manischewitz* Passover Thin Tea Matzo),
    1 sheet or piece 103
  (*Manischewitz* Passover Whole Wheat Matzo),
    1 sheet or piece 118
  (*Manischewitz* Thin Salted), 1 sheet or piece 95
  (*Manischewitz* Thin Tea Matzo), 1 sheet or piece 103
  (*Manischewitz* Unsalted), 1 sheet or piece 112
  (*Manischewitz* Whole Wheat with Bran),
    1 sheet or piece 110
melba toast:
  bacon flavor (*Old London* Bacon Rounds), 1 piece 12
  cheese flavor (*Old London* Cheese Rounds), 1 piece 12
  garlic flavor (*Old London* Garlic Rounds), 1 piece 10
  onion flavor (*Old London* Onion Rounds), 1 piece 10
  pumpernickel (*Old London*), 1 piece 17
  rye (*Old London*), 1 piece 17
  salty rye (*Old London* Salty-Rye Rounds), 1 piece 10
  sesame (*Old London*), 1 piece 20
  sesame flavor (*Old London* Sesame Rounds), 1 piece 12
  wheat (*Old London*), 1 piece 17
  white (*Old London*), 1 piece 17
  white (*Old London* White Melba Rounds), 1 piece 10
onion flavor:
  (*Keebler* Onion Toast), 1 piece 15
  (*Nabisco* French Onion), 1 piece 12

131

(*Manischewitz* Onion *Tams*), 1 piece 13
green (*Pepperidge Farm* Goldfish Mixed Suite), ¼ oz. ... 35
oyster:
    (*Dandy*), 1 piece 3
    (*Dixie Belle*), 1 oz., or 33 crackers 120
    (*Oysterettes*), 1 piece 3
    (*Ralston*), 1 oz., or 33 crackers 120
    (*Sunshine*), 1 piece 4
    (*Zesta*), 1 piece 2
peanut butter (*Frito-Lay's*), 1½-oz. pkg. 210
peanut-butter-and-cheese sandwiches, 1 oz. 139
pizza (*FFV*), 1 piece 15
pizza (*Pepperidge Farm* Goldfish), ¼ oz. 35
potato (*Keebler* Potato Crisp), 1 piece 16
potato (*Tater Puffs*), 1 piece 7
pumpernickel (*Keebler* Pumpernickel Toast), 1 piece 15
(*Ralston* Snackers), 1 oz. or 8 crackers 140
rusks, 1 oz. 119
rye:
    (*Finn Crisp* Bread Wafers), 1 piece 20
    (*Keebler* Rye Toast), 1 piece 16
    (*Nabisco* Rye Wafers), 1 piece 20
    (*Pepperidge Farm* Goldfish Thins), 1 piece 17
    (*Ry-Krisp*), 1 piece 25
    (*Wasa* Golden Rye Crisp Bread), 1 piece 37
    (*Wasa* Hearty Rye Crisp Bread), 1 piece 54
    (*Wasa* Lite Rye Crisp Bread), 1 piece 30
    dark, with caraway (*Finn Crisp* Bread Wafers), 1 piece ..20
    seasoned (*Nabisco* Rye Wafers), 1 piece 23
    seasoned (*Ry-Krisp*), 1 piece 30
    seasoned (*Wasa* Rye Crisp Bread), 1 piece 34
    sesame (*Ry-Krisp*), 1 piece 30
saltines:
    (*Dixie Belle*), 1 oz., or 10 crackers 120
    (*FFV*), 1 piece 13
    (*Krispy*), 1 piece 12
    (*Krispy* Unsalted), 1 piece 13

(*Pepperidge Farm* Goldfish), ¼ oz. 35
(*Pepperidge Farm* Goldfish Thins), 1 piece 17
(*Premium*), 1 piece 12
(*Premium* Unsalted), 1 piece 12
(*Ralston*), 1 oz., or 10 crackers .120
(*Zesta*), 1 piece 13
sesame:
(*FFV* Sesame Crisp), 1 piece 14
(*Keebler* Savory Sesame and Poppy Seed), 1 piece 12
(*Keebler* Sesame Stick Snack), 1 piece 6
(*Keebler* Sesame Toast), 1 piece .15
(*Old London* Melba Toast), 1 piece 20
(*Teeko* Glazed Sesame Crisp), 1 piece 22
(*Wasa* Crisp Bread), 1 piece 60
sesame-cheese (*Pepperidge Farm* Goldfish Mixed Suite),
¼ oz. 35
sesame-garlic (*Pepperidge Farm* Goldfish), ¼ oz. 35
(*Skittle Chips*), 1 piece 14
(*Sociables*), 1 piece 10
soda and water biscuits:
1 oz. 124
(*Crown Pilot*), 1 piece 70
(*Jacob's* Biscuits for Cheese), 1 piece 35
(*Jacob's* English Cream), 1 piece 110
(*Jacob's* Large Water Biscuits), 1 piece 35
(*Milk Lunch*), 1 piece 27
(*Royal Lunch*), 1 piece 55
(*Sea Toast*), 1 piece 60
(*Waldorf*), 1 piece 14
soup and oyster, see "oyster," above
sour cream-onion (*Keebler*), 1 piece 7
sourdough (*Wasa* Toast), 1 piece 45
taco (*Pepperidge Farm* Goldfish), ¼ oz. 35
toasted peanut butter (*Frito-Lay's*), 1½-oz. pkg. 210
(*TUC*), 1 piece 25
(*Uneeda*), 1 piece 22

(*Wasa* Mora Crisp Bread), 1 piece 33
(*Wasa* Sport Crisp Bread), 1 piece 43
(*Waverly*), 1 piece 18
wheat:
    (*Dixie Belle* Wheat Snacks), 1 oz., or 15 crackers 140
    (*FFV* Stoned Wheat Wafers), 1 piece 15
    (*Keebler Harvest Wheats*), 1 piece 24
    (*Keebler* Wheat Crisps), 1 piece 13
    (*Keebler* Wheat Toast), 1 piece 15
    (*Manischewitz* Wheat Crackers), 1 piece 8
    (*Manischewitz* Wheat *Tams*), 1 piece 13
    (*Nabisco* Wheat Thins), 1 piece 9
    (*Pepperidge Farm* Goldfish Thins), 1 piece 17
    (*Ralston* Wheat Snacks), 1 oz., or 15 crackers 140
    (*Sunshine* Wheat Wafers), 1 piece 9
    (*Triscuit*), 1 piece 20
zwieback (*Nabisco*), 1 piece 30
Cranberries:
fresh:
    whole, with stems, 1 lb. 200
    whole, without stems, 1 cup 52
    chopped, 1 cup 51
canned, fresh-pack (*Ocean Spray*), ½ cup 25
dehydrated, 1 oz. 104
Cranberry-apple juice:
bottled (*Ocean Spray Cranapple*), 6 fl. oz. 130
Cranberry-apricot juice:
bottled (*Ocean Spray Cranicot*), 6 fl. oz. 110
Cranberry bread, see "Bread, sweet, mix"
Cranberry dessert topping:
concentrate (*Hain*), 1 tbsp. 19
Cranberry juice cocktail:
6 fl. oz. 124
1 cup 164
(*Ocean Spray*), 6 fl. oz. 110
(*Welch's*), 6 fl. oz. 110

Cranberry-orange relish:
uncooked, 4 oz. 202
uncooked, 1 cup 498
(*Ocean Spray*), 2 oz. 100
Cranberry-prune juice:
bottled (*Ocean Spray Cranprune*), 6 fl. oz. 120
Cranberry sauce, canned:
jellied (*Ocean Spray*), 2 oz. 90
whole (*Ocean Spray*), 2 oz. 90
Crayfish:
raw, in shell, 1 lb. 39
raw, meat only, 4 oz. 82
Cream:
half and half:
  10.5% fat (*Foremost*), 1 tbsp. 19
  10.5% fat (*Sealtest*), 1 tbsp. 19
  12% fat (*Foremost*), 1 tbsp. 21
  12% fat (*Meadow Gold*), 1 tbsp. 30
heavy, whipping, unwhipped:
  (*Foremost*), 1 tbsp. 54
  36% fat (*Meadow Gold*), 1 tbsp. 50
  36% fat (*Sealtest*) 1 tbsp. 52
heavy, whipping, whipped:
  1 cup 419
  1 tbsp. 27
light, table or coffee:
  18% fat (*Foremost*), 1 tbsp. 28
  18% fat (*Sealtest*), 1 tbsp. 28
  20% fat (*Foremost*), 1 tbsp. 31
light, whipping, unwhipped:
  1 cup 717
  1 tbsp. 45
light, whipping, whipped:
  1 cup 357
  1 tbsp. 23
medium, whipping, unwhipped (*Sealtest*), 1 tbsp. 44
whipped, aerosol (*Redi-Wip*), 1 tbsp. 8

Cream, imitation:
powdered, 1 tbsp. 30
Cream, nondairy:
dry:
    (*Coffee-mate*), 1 tbsp. 30
    (*Coffee-mate*), 1 packet 16
    (*Cremora*), 1 tbsp. 36
    (*IGA*), 1 tbsp. 33
    (*Pet*), 1 tbsp. 30
liquid form:
    (*Coffee-mate*), reconstituted*, 1 tbsp. 13
    (*Coffee Rich*), 1 tbsp. 20
    (*Coffee Twin*), 1 tbsp. 18
    (*Jerzee*), 1 fl. oz. 43
    (*Poly Rich*), 1 fl. oz. 43
    (*Sanna*), 1 tbsp. 24
    frozen, 1 tbsp. 20
    half and half (*Foremost*), 1 tbsp. 20
    half and half (*Meadow Gold*), 1 tbsp. 27
whipped:
    (*Birds Eye Cool Whip*), 1 tbsp. 14
    (*Kraft*), ¼ cup 35
    (*Kraft* Real Cream), ¼ cup 25
    (*Pet*), 1 tbsp. 14
    (*Richwhip*), 1 tbsp. 10
    (*Rich's Spoon 'N Serve*), ¼ oz. 24
    aerosol (*Lucky Whip*), 1 tbsp. 12
    aerosol (*Rich's*), ¼ oz. 20
    mix* (*Dream Whip*), 1 tbsp. 8
    mix* (*D-Zerta*), 1 tbsp. 8
Cream, sour:
(*Breakstone*), 1 tbsp. 29
(*Foremost*), 1 tbsp. 30
(*Hood*), 1 tbsp. 25

Prepared according to directions on container

(*Meadow Gold*), 1 tbsp. 29
(*Sealtest*), 1 tbsp. 30
half and half:
    (*Foremost*), 1 tbsp. 22
    (*Hood Nuform*), 1 tbsp. 20
imitation (*Pet*), 1 tbsp. 25
imitation, dressing, 1 tbsp. 20
with chives (*Foremost*), 1 tbsp. 30
Cream, whipped, see "Cream"
Creamers, see "Cream, nondairy"
Crème de almond liqueur:
    (*Bols* Crème de Noyaux), 1 fl. oz. 115
    (*DuBouchett*), 1 fl. oz. 101
    (*Garnier* Crème d'Amande), 1 fl. oz. 111
    (*Hiram Walker* Crème de Noyaux), 1 fl. oz. 99
Crème de apricot liqueur:
    (*Old Mr. Boston*), 1 fl. oz. 66
Crème de banana liqueur:
    (*Dolfi* Crème de Banane), 1 fl. oz. 100
    (*Garnier* Crème de Banane), 1 fl. oz. 96
    (*Hiram Walker*), 1 fl. oz. 96
    (*Old Mr. Boston*), 1 fl. oz. 66
Crème de black cherry liqueur:
    (*Old Mr. Boston*), 1 fl. oz. 66
Crème de blackberry liqueur:
    (*Old Mr. Boston*), 1 fl. oz. 66
Crème de cacao liqueur:
brown or white:
    (*Bols*), 1 fl. oz. 101
    (*Dolfi*), 1 fl. oz. 100
    (*DuBouchett*), 1 fl. oz. 101
    (*Garnier*), 1 fl. oz. 97
    (*Old Mr. Boston*—54 proof), 1 fl. oz. 95
    (*Old Mr. Boston* Connoisseur—42 proof), 1 fl. oz. 84
brown (*Hiram Walker*), 1 fl. oz. 102
brown (*Leroux*), 1 fl. oz. 100

white (*Hiram Walker*), 1 fl. oz. 96
white (*Leroux*), 1 fl. oz. 94
Crème de cassis liqueur:
(*Dolfi*), 1 fl. oz. 97
(*DuBouchett*), 1 fl. oz. 79
(*Garnier*), 1 fl. oz. 83
(*Hiram Walker*), 1 fl. oz. 95
Crème de coffee liqueur:
(*Old Mr. Boston* Connoisseur), 1 fl. oz. 66
Crème de menthe liqueur:
green or white:
(*Bols*), 1 fl. oz. 112
(*DuBouchett*—46 proof), 1 fl. oz. 95
(*DuBouchett*—60 proof), 1 fl. oz. 101
(*Garnier*), 1 fl. oz. 110
(*Hiram Walker*), 1 fl. oz. 96
(*Old Mr. Boston*—60 proof), 1 fl. oz. 94
(*Old Mr. Boston* Connoisseur—42 proof), 1 fl. oz. 66
green (*Dolfi*), 1 fl. oz. 103
green (*Leroux*), 1 fl. oz. 110
white (*Dolfi*), 1 fl. oz. 104
white (*Leroux*), 1 fl. oz. 104
Crème de noisette liqueur:
(*Dolfi*), 1 fl. oz. 91
Crème de noyaux liqueur, see "Crème de almond liqueur"
Crème de peach liqueur:
(*Old Mr. Boston*), 1 fl. oz. 66
Crepes, see individual listings
Cress, garden:
raw, untrimmed, 1 lb. 103
raw, trimmed, 4 oz. 36
boiled in small amount water, drained, 1 cup 31
boiled in large amount water, drained, 1 cup 30
Cress, water, see "Watercress"
Croaker, Atlantic:
raw, whole, 1 lb. 148

raw, meat only, 4 oz. 109
baked, 4 oz. 152
Croaker, white:
raw, meat only, 4 oz. 95
Croaker, yellow:
raw, meat only, 4 oz. 101
Croutons:
plain:
  (*Bel-Air*), ¼ cup 30
  (*Brownberry* "Buttery" Toasted), ¼ cup 45
  (*Pepperidge Farm*), ⅓ oz. 47
bacon (*Bel-Air*), ¼ cup 40
Caesar salad (*Brownberry*), ¼ cup 45
cheese:
  (*Brownberry*), ¼ cup 45
  cheddar (*Pepperidge Farm*), ⅓ oz. 43
  Italian (*Bel-Air*), ¼ cup 50
cheese-garlic (*Bel-Air*), ¼ cup 50
cheese-garlic (*Pepperidge Farm*), ⅓ oz. 47
garlic (*Bel-Air*), ¼ cup 40
herb seasoned (*Croutettes*), .7 oz. 70
onion-garlic (*Brownberry*), ¼ cup 45
onion-garlic (*Pepperidge Farm*), ⅓ oz. 47
seasoned:
  (*Bel-Air*), ¼ cup 45
  (*Brownberry*), ¼ cup 45
  (*Pepperidge Farm*), ⅓ oz. 47
Crowder peas, see "Peas, crowder"
Cucumber, fresh:
with skin, 1 lb. 65
with skin, 1 large (8¼" long) 45
with skin, 1 small (6⅜" long) 25
with skin, sliced, 6 large or 8 small slices (1 oz.) 4
with skin, sliced, 1 cup 16
pared, 1 lb. 64
pared, 1 large (8¼" long) 39

pared, 1 small (6⅜″ long) 22
pared, sliced, 6½ large or 8 small slices (1 oz.) 4
pared, sliced or diced, 1 cup 20
Cucumber-onion dip:
(*Kraft*), 1 oz. 50
Cucumber, pickled, see "Pickles"
Cumin seed:
ground (all brands), 1 tsp. 7
Cupcakes:
chocolate (*Drake's*), 1½-oz. piece 170
chocolate (*Drake's Yankee Doodles*), 1-oz. piece 105
chocolate (*Hostess*), 1¾-oz. piece 160
chocolate (*Tastykake*), 2-oz. pkg. 200
orange (*Hostess*), 1½-oz. piece 150
Cupcakes, frozen:
chocolate (*Sara Lee*), 1¾-oz. piece 190
double chocolate (*Sara Lee*), 1¾-oz. piece 191
yellow (*Sara Lee*), 1¾-oz. piece 174
Cupcake mix*:
with egg, milk, without icing, 1 cupcake (2¾″ in diam.) ...116
with egg, milk, without icing, 1 cupcake (2½″ in diam.) ...88
with egg, milk, chocolate icing, 1 cupcake (2¾″ in diam.) ...172
with egg, milk, chocolate icing, 1 cupcake (2½″ in diam.) ...129
yellow, with eggs, chocolate icing,
1 cupcake (2¾″ in diam.) 155
yellow, with eggs, chocolate icing,
1 cupcake (2½″ in diam.) 118
(*Flako*), 1 cake 150
Curaçao liqueur:
blue (*Bols*), 1 fl. oz. 105
orange (*Bols*), 1 fl. oz. 100
orange (*Dolfi*), 1 fl. oz. 107
orange (*DuBouchett*), 1 fl. oz. 86
orange (*Garnier*), 1 fl. oz. 100

*Prepared according to directions on container

orange (*Hiram Walker*), 1 fl. oz. 95
orange (*Leroux*), 1 fl. oz. 87
Currants:
  fresh:
    black, with stems, 1 lb. 240
    black, trimmed, 1 cup 60
    red or white, with stems, 1 lb. 220
    red or white, trimmed, 1 cup 55
  dried:
    zante (*Del Monte*), ½ cup 190
    zante (*Sun•Maid*), 1 oz. 83
    zante (*Sun•Maid*), ½ cup 206
Curry powder:
  (*Crosse & Blackwell*), 1 tbsp. 26
Cusk:
  raw, meat only, 4 oz. 85
  steamed, meat only, 4 oz. 120
Custard, see "Pies, frozen," "Pudding," and "Pudding mix"
Custard, frozen, see "Ice cream"

D

Dates, domestic:
with pits, 1 lb. 1,081
pitted, 1 lb. 1,243
chopped, 1 cup 488
10 average dates 219
dried:
    pitted (*Bordo*), 1 oz. 83
    pitted (*Dromedary*), 1 oz. 94
    chopped (*Dromedary*), 1 oz. 99
    diced (*Bordo*), 1 oz. 82
Dates, Chinese, see "Jujubes"
Delaware wine:
(*Gold Seal*), 4 fl. oz. 116
Deviled ham, see "Ham, deviled"
Dewberries, see "Blackberries"
Dill pickle, see "Pickles"
Dill pickle dip:
(*Kraft* Ready Dip), 8-oz. container 536
Dill seed:
ground (all brands), 1 tsp. 9
Dim sum, frozen:
shrimp-bamboo shoot (*Royal Dragon—Hargow*), ½-oz. piece ...27
turkey-shrimp-vegetable (*Royal Dragon—Shaomai*), .6 oz. ...27
turkey-vegetable (*Royal Dragon—Potsticker*), 1-oz. piece ...45
Dinner rolls, see "Rolls and buns"
Distilled liquor, see "Liquor, pure distilled"
Dock, or sorrel:
raw, with stems, 1 lb. 89
boiled, drained, 1 cup 38
Doughnuts:
plain (*Hostess*), 1-oz. piece 110
cinnamon (*Hostess*), 1-oz. piece 110
enrobed (*Hostess*), 1-oz. piece 130
krunch (*Hostess*), 1-oz. piece 100
old-fashioned (*Hostess*), 1½-oz. piece 170
powdered sugar (*Hostess*), 1-oz. piece 110

143

Doughnuts, frozen:
  Bavarian creme (*Morton*), 2-oz. piece 180
  Boston creme (*Morton*), 2⅓-oz. piece 210
  chocolate, iced (*Morton*), 1½-oz. piece 150
  chocolate, iced (*Morton Morning Light*), 2-oz. piece 200
  devil's food (*Morton Donut Holes*), 1.55-oz. piece 160
  glazed (*Morton*), 1½-oz. piece 150
  glazed (*Morton Morning Light*), 2-oz. piece 200
  honey wheat (*Morton Donut Holes*), 1.55-oz. piece 160
  jelly (*Morton*), 1.8-oz. piece 180
  jelly (*Morton Morning Light*), 2.6-oz. piece 250
  mini (*Morton*), 1.1-oz. piece 120
  vanilla (*Morton Donut Holes*), 1.55-oz. piece 160
(*Drambuie*) liqueur:
  1 fl. oz. 110
Drum:
  freshwater, raw, whole, 1 lb. 143
  freshwater, raw, meat only, 4 oz. 138
  red, raw, whole, 1 lb. 149
  red, raw, meat only, 4 oz. 91
Duck:
  domesticated, raw, meat only. 4 oz. 188
  domesticated, roasted, meat only, 4 oz. 352
  wild, raw, meat only, 4 oz. 157
(*Durkee Famous Sauce*):
  1 tbsp. 69

E

Eggnog, nonalcoholic:
  canned:
    4.7% fat (*Borden*), 4 fl. oz. 132
    6% fat (*Borden*), 4 fl. oz. 154
    8% fat (*Borden*), 4 fl. oz. 171
  dairy pack:
    6% fat (*Foremost*), 4 fl. oz. 206
    6% fat (*Meadow Gold*), 4 fl. oz. 164
    6% fat (*Sealtest*), 4 fl. oz. 174
Eggnog flavored drink mix:
  dry (*Ovaltine*), 1 oz. 113
Eggplant:
  fresh:
    raw, whole, 1 lb. 92
    raw, diced, 1 cup 50
    boiled, drained, 4 oz. 22
    boiled, drained, diced, 1 cup 38
  frozen, fried sticks (*Mrs. Paul's*), 3.5 oz. 260
Eggplant Parmesan:
  frozen (*Buitoni*), 12-oz. pkg. 624
  frozen (*Mrs. Paul's*), 9-oz. pkg. 690
Eggs:
  fresh:
    raw, whole, 1 extra-large egg 94
    raw, whole, 1 large egg 82
    raw, whole, 1 medium egg 72
    raw, white of 1 extra-large egg 19
    raw, white of 1 large egg 17
    raw, white of 1 medium egg 15
    raw, yolk of 1 extra-large egg 66
    raw, yolk of 1 large egg 59
    raw, yolk of 1 medium egg 52
    boiled or poached, 1 extra-large egg 94
    boiled or poached, 1 large egg 82
    boiled or poached, 1 medium egg 72
  dried:
    whole, ½ cup 320

whole, 1 oz. 168
whole, 1 tbsp. 41
white, flakes, 1 oz. 99
white, powdered, 1 oz. 105
white, powdered, 1 tbsp. 26
yolk, 1 oz. 188
yolk, 1 tbsp. 47
frozen:
scrambled, and sausages, with coffee cake (*Swanson*),
  6¼-oz. pkg. 460
mix:
imitation, fat free (*Egg Beaters*), ¼ cup 40
omelet, cheese (*McCormick/Schilling* Seasoning Mix),
  1 serving* 168
omelet, with bacon (*Durkee*), 1 pkg. dry 128
omelet, with bacon (*Durkee*), yield from ½ pkg. * 310
omelet, puffy (*Durkee*), 1 pkg. dry 112
omelet, puffy (*Durkee*), yield from ½ pkg.* 302
omelet, western (*Durkee*), 1¼-oz. pkg.* 170
omelet, western (*McCormick/Schilling* Seasoning Mix),
  1 serving* 164
scrambled (*Durkee*), ⅞-oz. pkg.* 124
scrambled, with bacon bits (*Durkee*), 1¼-oz. pkg.* 181
Eggs, duck:
raw, whole, 1 egg 134
Eggs, goose:
raw, whole, 1 egg 266
Eggs, turkey:
raw, whole, 1 egg...................................135
Elderberries:
fresh, with stems, 1 lb. 307
fresh, without stems, 4 oz. 82
Enchilada, beef:
canned (*Old El Paso*), 2.4-oz. enchilada 119

Prepared according to directions on container

frozen, with chili gravy (*Banquet Buffet Suppers*),
  32-oz. pkg. 1,118
frozen, with sauce (*Banquet Cookin' Bag*), 6-oz. pkg. 207
Enchilada dip:
(*Frito's*), 3⅛-oz. serving 120
Enchilada dinner, frozen:
beef:
  (*Banquet*), 12-oz. pkg. 479
  (*Morton*), 11-oz. pkg. 280
  (*Swanson TV Brand*), 15-oz. pkg. 570
  (*Van de Kamp's*), 12-oz. pkg. 420
cheese (*Banquet*), 12-oz. pkg. 459
cheese (*Van de Kamp's*), 12-oz. pkg. 430
Enchilada sauce:
canned (*Gebhardt*), 4 oz. 214
canned, hot, (*Old El Paso*), ½ cup .49
canned, mild, (*Old El Paso*), ½ cup 49
mix* (*Durkee*), ½ cup 29
Enchilada seasoning mix:
dry (*French's*), 1⅜-oz. packet 120
dry (*McCormick/Schilling*), 1½-oz. packet 113
Endive, curly, see "Escarole"
Endive, French or Belgian, bleached, fresh:
trimmed, 1 lb. 68
1 head (5″–7″ long) 8
10 small leaves 5
chopped, 1 cup 14
English muffins, see "Muffins"
Escarole, fresh:
untrimmed, 1 lb. 80
4 large outer leaves 20
7 small leaves 4
cuts or small pieces, 1 cup 10
Eulachon (smelt):
raw, meat only, 4 oz. 135

*Prepared according to directions on container

F

Food and Measure   *Calories*

Farina, see "Cereals, cooked" and "Cereals, cooking type, dry"
Fats, cooking, see "Lard," "Oil," "Shortening," etc.
Fennel leaves:
  raw, untrimmed, 1 lb. 118
  raw, trimmed, 4 oz. 32
Fennel seed:
  ground (all brands), 1 tsp. 8
Fettuccine Alfredo:
  frozen (*Ronzoni*), 16-oz. pkg. 760
  frozen (*Ronzoni* Single Serving), 8-oz. pkg. 430
  frozen (*Stouffer's*), 10-oz. pkg. 270
(Fiddle Faddle):
  1 oz. 125
Figs:
  raw:
    whole, 1 lb. 363
    1 large (2½″ in diam.) 52
    1 medium (2¼″ in diam.) 40
    1 small (1½″ in diam.) 32
  candied, 1 oz. 85
  canned:
    in water, with liquid, 8 oz. 109
    in water, with liquid, 1 cup 119
    in water, 3 figs and 1¾ tbsp. liquid 38
    in syrup, whole (*Del Monte*), ½ cup 105
    in heavy syrup, with liquid, 8 oz. 191

in heavy syrup, with liquid, 1 cup 218
in heavy syrup, 3 figs and 1¾ tbsp. liquid 71
dried, 4 oz. 311
dried, 1 fig (2″ × 1″) 57
Filberts (hazelnuts):
in shell, 4 oz. 331
in shell, 10 nuts 87
shelled, 4 oz. 719
shelled, whole, 1 cup 856
shelled, whole, 1 oz. 180
shelled, chopped, 1 cup 729
shelled, chopped, 1 tbsp. 44
shelled, ground, 1 cup 476
Finnan haddie:
meat only, 4 oz. 117
Fish, see individual listings
Fish, frozen (see also individual listings):
miniatures, light batter-fried (*Mrs. Paul's*), 1 oz. 51
miniatures, light batter-fried (*Mrs. Paul's*), 9-oz. pkg. 450
ocean snacks, batter-fried (*Gorton*), 3 oz. 270
portions, batter-fried (*Gorton*), 3 oz. 240
portions, beer batter-fried (*Booth*), 3 oz. 250
portions, buttermilk french-fried (*Booth*), 3 oz. 218
portions, fried (*Booth*), 3 oz. 171
portions, with shrimp stuffing (*Gorton*), 3 oz. or 1 portion . . .250
Fish au gratin:
frozen (*Mrs. Paul's*), 10-oz. pkg. 500
Fish balls:
canned (*King Oscar*), 14-oz. can .137
Fish cakes, frozen:
(*Gorton*), 4 oz., or 2 cakes 250
(*Mrs. Paul's*), 4 oz., or 2 cakes 210
(*Mrs. Paul's Beach Haven*), 4 oz., or 2 cakes 210
thins (*Mrs. Paul's*), 5 oz., or 2 cakes 320
Fish and chips, frozen:
(*Swanson TV Brand*), 5-oz. pkg. 290

batter-fried (*Van de Kamp's*), 8 oz. 500
light batter-fried (*Mrs. Paul's*), 8½-oz. pkg. 450
light batter-fried (*Mrs. Paul's*), 14-oz. pkg. 740

Fish dinner, frozen:
(*Banquet*), 8¾-oz. pkg. 382
(*Morton*), 9-oz. pkg. 260
batter-fried (*Van de Kamp's*), 11-oz. pkg. 540
cakes, fried (*Taste O'Sea*), 8-oz. pkg. 380
and chips (*Swanson Hungry-Man*), 15¾-oz. pkg. 760
and chips (*Swanson TV Brand*), 10¼-oz. pkg. 450
fillets (*Van de Kamp's*), 12-oz. pkg. 300
fried (*Taste O'Sea Moby Dick*), 9-oz. pkg. 430

Fish fillets, frozen:
batter-fried (*Mrs. Paul's*), 4½ oz., or 2 fillets 280
batter-fried (*Mrs. Paul's* Supreme), 3⅝-oz. fillet 220
batter-fried (*Van de Kamp's*), 3-oz. fillet 220
batter-fried miniatures (*Mrs. Paul's*), 9-oz. pkg. 450
buttered (*Mrs. Paul's*), 5 oz., or 2 fillets 310
country seasoned (*Van de Kamp's*), 4¾ oz., or 2 fillets ...360
fried (*Gorton*), 3.6 oz., or 2 fillets 220
fried (*Mrs. Paul's*), 4 oz., or 2 fillets 220
light batter-fried, crunchy (*Mrs. Paul's*), 4½ oz.,
    or 2 fillets 350
sandwich (*Mrs. Paul's*), 4⅛-oz. pkg. 200

Fish flakes:
canned, 7-oz. can 220
canned, 1 cup 183

Fish flour:
from whole fish, 1 oz. 95
from fish fillets, 1 oz. 113
from fish-fillet waste, 1 oz. 86

Fish kabobs, frozen:
batter-fried (*Van de Kamp's*), 4 oz., or 10 pieces 260
country seasoned (*Van de Kamp's*), 4 oz., or 10 pieces ...290
light batter-fried (*Mrs. Paul's*), 3⅝-oz. fillet 220
light batter-fried (*Mrs. Paul's* Supreme), ⅓ of 10-oz. pkg. ..200

Fish Parmesan:
　frozen (*Mrs. Paul's*), 10-oz. pkg. 440
Fish sticks, frozen:
　(*Booth*), 4 oz., or 4 sticks 216
　(*Gorton*), 3.2 oz., or 4 sticks 180
　(*Mrs. Paul's*), 3 oz., or 4 sticks 150
　(*Van de Kamp's*), 5 oz., or 5 sticks 310
　batter-fried (*Booth*), 3.6 oz., or 2 sticks 305
　batter-fried (*Gorton*), 2 oz. 160
　batter-fried (*Gorton*), 3 oz. 230
　batter-fried (*Mrs. Paul's*), 3 oz., or 4 sticks 150
　fried (*Taste O' Sea*), 4 sticks 254
　light batter-fried, crunchy (*Mrs. Paul's*), 3½ oz.,
　　or 4 sticks 280
　sandwich (*Mrs. Paul's*), 6½-oz. pkg. 400
　with shrimp stuffing (*Gorton*), 3 oz. 240
Fishburger:
　frozen (*Booth*), 3 oz. 137
Flatfish, see "Flounder," "Sand dab," and "Sole"
Flounder:
　fresh:
　　fillets, raw, 4 oz. 89
　　fillets, baked with butter, 4 oz. 229
　　fillets, baked with butter, 1 fillet (6″ × 2½″ × ¼″) 115
　　fillets, baked with butter, 1 fillet (8¼″ × 2¾″ × ¼″) 202
　frozen:
　　breaded (*Taste O' Sea*), 1 portion 90
　　fillets (*Taste O' Sea*), 16-oz. pkg. 360
　　fillets, fried (*Mrs. Paul's*), 4 oz., or 2 fillets 220
　　with lemon butter (*Mrs. Paul's*), 9-oz. pkg. 300
Flounder almandine:
　frozen (*Gorton*), ½ pkg. 210
Flounder dinner:
　frozen, fried (*Taste O' Sea*), 9-oz. pkg. 350
Flour (see also individual listings):
　all purpose and bread, see "white," below

buckwheat:
   whole-grain, 4 oz. 382
   whole-grain, sifted, 1 cup 335
   dark, 4 oz. 380
   dark, sifted, spooned into cup, 1 cup 326
   light, 4 oz. 395
   light, sifted, spooned into cup, 1 cup 340
   (*Elam's* Pure), 4 oz. 401
cake or pastry, see "white," below
carob (Saint-John's-bread):
   4 oz. 205
   1 cup 252
   1 tbsp. 14
corn, 4 oz. 419
corn, 1 cup 431
gluten, see "white," below
(*King Midas*), 1 cup 400
(*Occident*), 1 cup 400
(*Peavey* High Altitude Hungarian), 1 cup 400
plain (*Ballard*), 1 cup 400
rye:
   dark, 4 oz. 373
   dark, spooned into cup, 1 cup 419
   light, 4 oz. 407
   light, sifted, spooned into cup, 1 cup 314
   light, unsifted, spooned into cup, 1 cup 364
   medium, 4 oz. 399
   medium, sifted, spooned into cup, 1 cup 308
   medium (*Pillsbury Best*), 1 cup 420
   wheat (*Pillsbury Best* Bohemian), 1 cup 400
   whole (*Elam's* Stone Ground 100%), 4 oz. 405
sauce and gravy (*Pillsbury Best*), 2 tbsp. 50
self-rising:
   4 oz. 401
   unsifted, spooned into cup, 1 cup 440
   sifted, spooned into cup, 1 cup 405
   (*Aunt Jemima*), 1 cup 436

(*Ballard*), 1 cup 380
(*Pillsbury Best*), 1 cup 380
unbleached (*Pillsbury Best*), 1 cup 380
soybean:
    full-fat, 4 oz. 478
    full-fat, not stirred, 1 cup 358
    full-fat, stirred, 1 cup 295
    low-fat, 4 oz. 401
    low-fat, stirred, 1 cup 313
    defatted, 4 oz. 370
    defatted, stirred, 1 cup 326
sunflower seed, partially defatted, 4 oz. 386
tortilla (*Pinata*), 4 oz. 320
unbleached, all purpose (*Pillsbury Best*), 1 cup 400
unbleached, white, with wheat germ (*Elam's*), 4 oz. 414
white:
    all-purpose, 4 oz. 415
    all-purpose, unsifted, dipped with cup, 1 cup 499
    all-purpose, unsifted, spooned into cup, 1 cup 455
    all-purpose, sifted, spooned into cup, 1 cup 419
    all-purpose, instant-blending, unsifted, 1 cup 470
    all-purpose (*Ballard*), 1 cup 400
    all-purpose (*Pillsbury Best*), 1 cup 400
    bread, 4 oz. 416
    bread, unsifted, dipped with cup, 1 cup 500
    bread, sifted, spooned into cup, 1 cup 420
    bread (*Pillsbury Best*), 1 cup 410
    cake or pastry, 4 oz. 415
    cake or pastry, unsifted, dipped with cup, 1 cup 430
    cake or pastry, unsifted, spooned into cup, 1 cup 397
    cake or pastry, sifted, spooned into cup, 1 cup 349
    cake (*Swans Down*), 1 cup 400
    cake, self-rising (*Presto*), 1 cup 400
    cake, self-rising (*Swans Down*), 1 cup 360
    gluten (45%), 4 oz. 431
    gluten (45%), unsifted, dipped with cup, 1 cup 529
    gluten (45%), unsifted, spooned into cup, 1 cup 510

whole wheat:
  hard wheat, 4 oz. 380
  hard wheat, stirred, spooned into cup, 1 cup 400
  (*Elam's* Stone Ground), 4 oz. 416
  (*Pillsbury Best*), 1 cup 400
(*Fournier Nature*) wine:
  4 fl. oz. 109
Frankfurters:
  without binders (all meat):
    not smoked, 1-lb. pkg. (8 or 10 frankfurters) 1,343
    not smoked, 5½-oz. pkg. (about 16 frankfurters) 462
    not smoked, 1 frankfurter (5″ long, ⅞″ in diam.) 169
    not smoked, 1 frankfurter (5″ long, ¾″ in diam.) 133
    not smoked, 1 frankfurter (1¾″ long, ½″ in diam.) 30
    half-smoked, 11-oz. pkg. (about 5 frankfurters) 924
    half-smoked, 1 frankfurter (5″ long, 1″ in diam.) 184
    smoked, 12-oz. pkg. (8 or 10 frankfurters) 1,006
    smoked, 5-oz. pkg. (about 16 frankfurters) 420
    smoked, 1 frankfurter (4¾″ long, ¾″ in diam.) 124
    smoked, 1 frankfurter (4½″ long, ¾″ in diam.) 101
    smoked, 1 frankfurter (1¾″ long, ⅝″ in diam.) 27
  with nonfat dry milk:
    1-lb. pkg. (8 or 10 frankfurters) 1,361
    1 frankfurter (5″ long, ⅞″ in diam.) 171
    1 frankfurter (5″ long, ¾″ in diam.) 135
  with cereal:
    1-lb. pkg. (8 or 10 frankfurters) 1,125
    1 frankfurter (5″ long, ⅞″ in diam.) 141
    1 frankfurter (5″ long, ¾″ in diam.) 112
  (*Armour Star* Hog Dogs), 1 link 142
  (*Eckrich*), 1 link 120
  (*Eckrich* Jumbo), 1 link 190
  (*Eckrich* Skinless), 1 link 150
  (*Kahn's* Wieners), 1 link 150
  (*Kahn's* Jumbo Wieners), 1 link 187
  (*Kahn's Lauderdale* Jumbo Wieners), 1 link 184

(*Oscar Mayer* Wieners), 1 link .145
(*Oscar Mayer* Wieners—Imperial Size), 1 link 177
(*Wilson Certified* Skinless), 1-lb. pkg. 1,398
(*Wilson* Western Style), 1-lb. pkg. 1,400
with cheese (*Oscar Mayer* Wieners), 1 link 145
beef:
    (*Eckrich*), 1 link 150
    (*Eckrich* Jumbo), 1 link 190
    (*Hormel*—12-oz. pkg.), 1 link 104
    (*Hormel*—1-lb. pkg.), 1 link 139
    (*Kahn's*), 1 link 148
    (*Kahn's* Jumbo), 1 link 185
    (*Oscar Mayer*—1-lb. pkg.), 1 link 140
    (*Oscar Mayer* Machiaeh), 1 link 180
    (*Vienna*), 3½ oz. 311
    (*Wilson Certified*), 1-lb. pkg. .1,358
    (*Wilson Certified* Skinless), 1-lb. pkg. 1,400
    (*Wilson Corn King*), 1-lb. pkg. 1,358
chicken, see "Chicken Frankfurters"
cocktail, see "Frankfurters, canned"
fried, on stick (*Oscar Mayer* Corn Dogs), 1 piece 330
meat:
    (*Hormel*—12-oz. pkg.), 1 link 106
    (*Hormel*—1-lb. pkg.), 1 link 142
    (*Wilson Certified*), 1-lb. pkg. .1,398
    (*Wilson Corn King*), 1-lb. pkg. 1,398
smoked, see "Sausages"
turkey, see "Turkey frankfurters"
Frankfurters, canned:
12-oz. can (7 frankfurters) 751
1 frankfurter (4⅞" long, ⅞" in diam.) 106
cocktail (*Vienna*), 1 oz. 88
Frankfurters, frozen:
batter-wrapped (*Hormel Corn Dogs*), 1 link 231
batter-wrapped (*Hormel Tater Dogs*), 1 link 187
in pastry (*Durkee* Franks-N-Blankets), 1 piece 45

Frankfurter rolls, see "Rolls and buns"
Franks and beans, see "Beans, baked, canned"
French toast:
  frozen:
    (*Aunt Jemima*), 1 slice 85
    (*Downyflake*), 1 slice 135
    cinnamon swirl (*Aunt Jemima*), 1 slice 97
    with sausages (*Swanson*), 4½-oz. pkg. 300
    mix* (*McCormick/Schilling* Batter Mix), 1 slice 119
Frogs' legs:
  raw, whole, with bone, 1 lb. 215
  raw, meat only, 4 oz. 83
Frosting, see "Icings, cake"
Fruit, see individual listings
Fruit cocktail, canned:
  in syrup, with liquid (*Del Monte*), ½ cup 85
  in syrup, with liquid (*Libby's*), ½ cup 94
  in syrup, with liquid (*Stokely-Van Camp*), ½ cup 95
  in water, with liquid (*Libby's*), ½ cup 40
Fruit dessert topping:
  (*Smucker's*), 1 tbsp. 50
Fruit flavor drinks:
  all flavors, mix* (*Funny Face*), 6 fl. oz. 60
  all flavors, mix* (*Kool-Aid*), 6 fl. oz. 75
  punch, bottled (*Bama*), 6 fl. oz. 90
  punch, bottled (*Wyler's*), 6 fl. oz. 85
Fruit mix:
  freeze-dried (*Mountain House*), ⅔ oz. 70
Fruit, mixed:
  canned (*Del Monte Fruit Cup*), 5-oz. can 100
  frozen, sweetened, 8-oz. pkg. 250
  frozen (*Birds Eye* Quick Thaw), 5 oz. 130
Fruit for salad, canned or in jars:
  in syrup, with liquid (*Del Monte*), ½ cup 85

*Prepared according to directions on container

in syrup, with liquid (*Libby's*), ½ cup 90
in syrup, with liquid (*Stokely-Van Camp*), ½ cup 95
Fruit salad, canned or in jars:
in juice (*Kraft*), ½ cup 50
in water, with liquid, 8 oz. 80
in water, with liquid, 1 cup 86
in heavy syrup, with liquid, 8 oz. 170
in heavy syrup, with liquid, 1 cup 191
tropical, in syrup (*Del Monte*), ½ cup 100
Fudge, see "Candy"
Fudge syrup, see "Chocolate toppings and syrups"

G

Food and Measure   *Calories*

Garbanzos, see ''Chickpeas''
Garden spice dip:
  (*Borden*), 4-oz. container 264
Garlic:
  raw, whole, 2 oz. (weighed with skin) 68
  raw, peeled, 1 oz. 39
  raw, peeled, 5 cloves 14
Garlic dip:
  (*Kraft*), 2 tbsp. 60
Garlic flavoring:
  liquid (*Burton's*), ½ tsp. 21
Garlic and onion dip:
  mix (*McCormick/Schilling*), 1¼-oz. pkg. 158
Garlic powder:
  all brands, 1 tsp. 5
Garlic salt:
  (*French's*), 1 tsp. 4
  parslied (*French's*), 1 tsp. 6
Garlic spread:
  (*Lawry's*), 1 tbsp. 88
Gefilte fish, canned or in jars:
  (*Manischewitz*—4 piece/12-oz. jar), 1 piece 53
  (*Manischewitz*—8 piece/24-oz. jar), 1 piece 53
  (*Manischewitz*—24 piece/4-lb. jar), 1 piece 48
  (*Manischewitz* Homestyle—4 piece/12-oz. jar), 1 piece 55
  (*Manischewitz* Homestyle—8 piece/24-oz. jar), 1 piece 55
  (*Manischewitz* Homestyle—24 piece/4-lb. jar), 1 piece 50

(*Mother's*—4 piece/12-oz. jar), 1 piece 41
(*Mother's*—6 piece/15-oz. jar), 1 piece 34
(*Mother's*—4 piece/1-lb. jar), 1 piece 55
(*Mother's*—6 piece/1-lb. jar), 1 piece 37
(*Mother's*—6 piece/24-oz. jar), 1 piece 55
(*Mother's*—8 piece/24-oz. jar), 1 piece 41
(*Mother's*—5 piece/27-oz. jar), 1 piece 74
(*Mother's*—8 piece/2-lb. jar), 1 piece 55
(*Mother's*—12 piece/2-lb. jar), 1 piece 37
sweet (*Manischewitz*—4 piece/12-oz. jar), 1 piece 65
sweet (*Manischewitz*—8 piece/24-oz. jar), 1 piece 65
sweet (*Manischewitz*—24 piece/2-lb. jar), 1 piece 59
sweet, whitefish and pike
    (*Manischewitz*—4 piece/12-oz. jar), 1 piece 64
sweet, whitefish and pike
    (*Manischewitz*—8 piece/24-oz. jar), 1 piece 64
sweet, whitefish and pike
    (*Manischewitz*—24 piece/2-lb. jar), 1 piece 58
whitefish and pike (*Manischewitz*—4 piece/12-oz. jar),
    1 piece 49
whitefish and pike (*Manischewitz*—8 piece/24-oz. jar),
    1 piece 49
whitefish and pike (*Manischewitz*—24 piece/2-lb. jar),
    1 piece 44
Gefilte fish balls:
cocktail (*Manischewitz Fishlets*), 1 oz. 30
Gelatin:
unflavored (*Carmel* Kosher), 1 envelope 30
unflavored (*Knox*), 1 envelope 25
Gelatin desserts, flavored:
all flavors, mix*:
    (*Carmel* Kosher Gelatin Dessert), 4 oz. 80
    (*Jell-O*), ½ cup 80
    (*Jells Best*), ½ cup 77
    (*Royal*), ½ cup 80

*Prepared according to directions on container

vegetable gelatin, all flavors, mix* (*Carmel* Kosher), 4 oz. 90
Gelatin drink:
  orange (*Knox*), 1 envelope 70
German style dinner:
  frozen (*Swanson TV Brand*), 11¾-oz. pkg. 430
Gimlet cocktail mix:
  bottled (*Holland House*), 1 fl. oz. 40
  instant (*Holland House*), 1 packet 69
Gin, see "Liquor, pure distilled"
Gin, flavored, see individual listings
Gin sour cocktail:
  (*Calvert*—60 proof), 1 fl. oz. 65
Ginger:
  crystallized, candied, 1 oz. 96
  ground (all brands), 1 tsp. 6
Ginger brandy:
  (*DuBouchett*), 1 fl. oz. 75
  (*Garnier*), 1 fl. oz. 74
  (*Hiram Walker*), 1 fl. oz. 71
  (*Old Mr. Boston*—70 proof), 1 fl. oz. 74
  (*Old Mr. Boston* Connoisseur—42 proof), 1 fl. oz. 75
Ginger root:
  fresh, unpeeled, 1 lb. 207
  fresh, peeled, 1 oz. 14
Ginger ale, see "Soft drinks and mixers"
Gingerbread, see "Cookies, mix"
Gizzards:
  chicken:
    simmered, 11⅞ oz. (yield from 1 lb. raw) 497
    simmered, 4 oz. 168
    simmered, chopped or diced, 1 cup 215
  goose, raw, 1 lb. 631
  turkey:
    simmered, 11⅞ oz. (yield from 1 lb. raw) 659

*Prepared according to directions on container

161

simmered, 4 oz. 222

simmered, chopped or diced, 1 cup 284

Gluten flour, see "Flour"

Goat's milk, see "Milk, goat's"

Goldwasser liqueur:

(*Dolfi*), 1 fl. oz. 104

Goose, domesticated:

raw, whole, ready-to-cook, 1 lb. 1,172

roasted, whole, 8½ oz. (yield from 1 lb. raw) 1,022

roasted, meat only, 4 oz. 266

roasted, meat and skin, 4 oz. 503

Gooseberries:

fresh, 1 lb. 177

fresh, 1 cup 59

canned, in water, with liquid, 8 oz. 59

canned, in heavy syrup, with liquid, 8 oz. 204

Gourd, see "Towel gourd"

Gourmet loaf:

(*Eckrich*—8-oz. pkg.), 1-oz. slice 40

(*Eckrich Smorgas Pac*), 1 slice 30

Graham crackers, see "Cookies"

Grain chips:

(*Hain* 7-Grain Chips), 1 oz. 131

Granadillas, purple (passion fruit):

raw, whole, in shell, 1 lb. 212

raw, whole, 1 average fruit 16

raw, shelled, 4 oz. 102

Granola, see "Cereals, ready-to-eat"

Granola bars, see "Breakfast bars"

Grape-cranberry drink:

bottled (*Ocean Spray Crangrape*), 6 fl. oz. 110

Grape drink:

bottled (*Bama*), 6 fl. oz. 80

bottled (*Welch's*), 6 fl. oz. 110

bottled (*Welchade*), 6 fl. oz. 90

canned (*Hi-C*), 6 fl. oz. 89

dairy pack (*Tropicana*), 6 fl. oz. 70
mix*:
  (*Hi-C*), 6 fl. oz. 76
  (*Kool-Aid*), 6 fl. oz. 68
  (*Tang*), 6 fl. oz. 90
  (*Wyler's*), 6 fl. oz. 68
red, bottled (*Welchade*), 6 fl. oz. .90
Grape fruit roll:
dried, sweetened (*Grocer's Choice*), 1 oz. 90
dried, sweetened (*Sahadi*), 1 oz. 90
Grape juice:
canned or bottled:
  (*Heinz*), 6 fl. oz. 122
  (*Seneca*), 6 fl. oz. 120
  (*Welch's*), 6 fl. oz. 120
frozen:
  (*Minute Maid*), 6 fl. oz.* 99
  (*Seneca*), 6 fl. oz.* 100
reconstituted 1 + 1 (*Welch's*), 6 fl. oz. 200
reconstituted 1 + 3 (*Welch's*), 6 fl. oz. 100
Grapes, fresh:
all varieties, seeds removed, halves, 1 cup 117
American type (slipskin), Concord, Delaware, Niagara, etc:
  seeded, whole, 1 lb. 197
  seeded, 1 cup 70
  seeded, 10 grapes (¾″ in diam.) .18
European type (adherent skin), Malaga, muscat,
  Thompson seedless:
  whole, 1 lb. 270
  seeded, 1 cup 102
  seedless, 1 cup 107
  seedless, 10 grapes (⅝″ in diam.) 34
Grapes, canned (Thompson seedless):
in water, with liquid, 8 oz. 116

Prepared according to directions on container

in water, with liquid, 1 cup 125
in heavy syrup, with liquid, 8 oz. 175
in heavy syrup, with liquid, 1 cup 197

Grapefruit, fresh:
pink or red, seeded:
   whole, with skin, 1 lb. 87
   ½ medium (4³⁄₁₆″ in diam.) 58
   sections, 1 cup 80
   sections, with 2 tbsp. juice, 1 cup 92
pink or red, seedless:
   whole, with skin, 1 lb. 93
   ½ medium (3¾″ in diam.) 49
   sections, 1 cup 80
   sections, with 2 tbsp. juice, 1 cup 92
white, seeded:
   whole, with skin, 1 lb. 84
   ½ medium (4³⁄₁₆″ in diam.) 56
   sections, 1 cup 82
   sections, with 2 tbsp. juice, 1 cup 94
white, seedless:
   whole, with skin, 1 lb. 87
   ½ medium (3¾″ in diam.) 46
   sections, 1 cup 78
   sections, with 2 tbsp. juice, 1 cup 90

Grapefruit, canned or bottled:
sections, in juice, with liquid (*Del Monte*), ½ cup 45
sections, in juice, with liquid (*Kraft*), ½ cup 50
sections, in syrup, with liquid (*Del Monte*), ½ cup 70

Grapefruit drink:
dairy pack (*Tropicana*), 6 fl. oz. 70
mix* (*Tang*), 6 fl. oz. 90

Grapefruit juice, fresh:
pink or red, seeded:
   1 cup 93

*Prepared according to directions on container

juice from 1 medium grapefruit 110
pink or red, seedless:
  1 cup 96
  juice from 1 medium grapefruit 96
white, seeded:
  1 cup 98
  juice from 1 medium grapefruit 108
white, seedless:
  1 cup 93
  juice from 1 medium grapefruit 90
Grapefruit juice, canned or bottled:
(*Del Monte*), 6 fl. oz. 70
(*Ocean Spray*), 6 fl. oz. 70
dairy pack (*Hood*), 6 fl. oz. 70
dairy pack (*Kraft*), 6 fl. oz. 70
dairy pack (*Tropicana*), 6 fl. oz. 75
pink (*Texsun*), 6 fl. oz. 77
sweetened (*Del Monte*), 6 fl. oz. 80
Grapefruit juice, dehydrated:
dry form, 1 oz. 107
dry form, 1 tbsp. 30
diluted with water, 1 cup 99
Grapefruit juice, frozen:
sweetened, diluted with 3 parts water, 1 cup 117
unsweetened, diluted with 3 parts water, 1 cup 101
(*Minute Maid*), 6 fl. oz.* 75
Grapefruit-orange drink:
canned (*Musselman's* Breakfast Cocktail), 6 fl. oz. 68
Grapefruit-orange juice, see "Orange-grapefruit juice"
Grapefruit peel:
candied, 1 oz. 90
Grapefruit-pineapple drink, see "Pineapple-grapefruit drink"
Grasshopper cocktail mix:
instant (*Holland House*), 1 packet 69

*Prepared according to directions on container

Gravy, see individual listings
(*Gravymaster*):
  1 tbsp. 12
Green goddess dip:
  (*Kraft Teez* Dip), 8-oz. container 368
Green pepper see "Peppers, sweet, green"
Grenadine syrup:
  (*Garnier*), 1 tsp. 17
  (*Hollnd House*), 1 tsp. 15
Griddle cakes, see "Pancakes" and "Pancake and waffle mix"
Grits, see **"Corn grits"**
Ground cherries, raw:
  with husks, 1 lb. 221
  without husks, 1 lb. 240
  without husks, 1 cup 74
Grouper, raw:
  whole, 1 lb. 170
  meat only, 4 oz. 99
Guacamole, see "Avocado dip"
Guavas, common, fresh:
  whole, with stems, 1 lb. 273
  trimmed, 4 oz. 70
  1 small (about 2¾ oz.) 48
Guavas, strawberry, fresh:
  whole, with stems, 1 lb. 289
  trimmed, 4 oz. 74
Guinea hen, raw:
  whole, ready to cook, 1 lb. 594
  meat and skin, 4 oz. 179
Gum, see "Chewing gum"

H

                                    Calories

Haddock:
  fresh:
    whole, raw, 1 lb. ...172
    fillets, raw, 1 lb. ...360
    fried, fillets, breaded, 12⅘ oz. (yield from 1 lb. raw) ...597
    fried, fillets, breaded, 4 oz. ...187
  frozen:
    batter-fried (*Van de Kamp's*), 4¾ oz., or 2 pieces ...330
    breaded (*Taste O' Sea*), 1 portion ...80
    fillets (*Taste O' Sea*), 16-oz. pkg. ...400
    fillets, fried (*Mrs. Paul's*), 4 oz., or 2 fillets ...230
    sticks, fried (*Taste O' Sea*), 4 sticks ...230
    in lemon butter (*Gorton*), ½ pkg. ...180

Haddock au gratin:
  frozen (*Howard Johnson's*), 10-oz. pkg. ...318

Haddock dinner:
  frozen, fried (*Taste O' Sea*), 9-oz. pkg. ...380

Haddock, smoked, see "Finnan haddie"
Half and half, see "Cream"
Half and half mixer, see "Soft drinks and mixers"

Halibut:
  Atlantic or Pacific, fresh:
    whole, raw, 1 lb. ...268
    fillets, raw, 1 lb. ...452
    fillets, broiled with butter, 12⅞ oz.
      (yield from 1 lb. raw). ...624
    fillets, broiled with butter, 4 oz. ...194

frozen:
    batter-fried (*Van de Kamp's*), 4 oz., or 3 pieces 270
Halibut, smoked:
    4 oz. 254
Halvah:
    original and marble (*Sahadi*), 1 oz. 150
Ham, retail cuts (see also "Pork"):
    fresh, lean with fat:
      baked, with bone and skin, 9.2 oz.
        (yield from 1 lb. raw). 980
      baked, without bone and skin, 10.9 oz.
        (yield from 1 lb. raw) 1,152
      baked, without bone and skin, 4 oz. 424
      baked, chopped or diced, 1 cup 524
      baked, ground, 1 cup 411
    fresh, lean only (trimmed of fat):
      baked, with bone and skin, 6.8 oz.
        (yield from 1 lb. raw with fat) 421
      baked, without bone and skin, 8.1 oz.
        (yield from 1 lb. raw with fat) 495
      baked, without bone and skin, 4 oz. 246
      baked, chopped or diced, 1 cup 304
      baked, ground, 1 cup 239
    light-cured, lean with fat:
      baked, with bone and skin, 11.3 oz.
        (yield from 1 lb. raw) 925
      baked, without bone and skin, 13.1 oz.
        (yield from 1 lb. raw) 1,075
      baked, without bone and skin, 4 oz. 328
      baked, chopped or diced, 1 cup 405
      baked, ground, 1 cup 318
    light-cured, lean only (trimmed of fat):
      baked, with bone and skin, 8.7 oz.
        (yield from 1 lb. raw with fat) 460
      baked, without bone and skin, 10.2 oz.
        (yield from 1 lb. raw with fat) 539

baked, without bone and skin, 4 oz. 212
baked, chopped or diced, 1 cup 262
baked, ground, 1 cup 206
long-cured, dry, unbaked:
   medium-fat, lean with fat, with bone and skin, 4 oz. ...394
   relatively lean, lean with fat, with bone and skin, 4 oz. ...302
picnic, see "Pork"
Ham and asparagus crepe:
frozen (*Stouffer's*), 6¼-oz. pkg. 325
Ham, boiled, see "Ham luncheon meat"
Ham, canned:
(*Armour Star*), 8 oz. 416
(*Armour Star Golden*), 8 oz. 304
(*Armour Star Parti Style*), 8 oz. 336
(*Hormel—3-lb. can*), 8 oz. 255
(*Hormel* Bone-In), 8 oz. 418
(*Hormel Cure-81*), 8 oz. 388
(*Hormel Curemaster*), 8 oz. 274
(*Hormel Holiday Glaze*), 8 oz. 279
(*Hormel Tender Chunk*), 6¾-oz. can 314
(*Oscar Mayer Jubilee*), 8 oz. 280
(*Swift Premium*), 8 oz. 499
(*Swift Premium Hostess*), 8 oz. 318
(*Swift Premium Hostess—boneless*), 8 oz. 340
(*Wilson Certified—3- or 5-lb. can*), 8 oz. 386
(*Wilson Certified Boneless*), 8 oz. 382
(*Wilson Corn King—3- or 5-lb. can*), 8 oz. 386
(*Wilson Corn King Boneless*), 8 oz. 382
(*Wilson Masterpiece—3-lb. can*), 8 oz. 250
(*Wilson Masterpiece Boneless*), 8 oz. 250
(*Wilson Tender Made*), 8 oz. 344
Ham and cheese loaf:
(*Hormel*), 1-oz. slice 77
(*Oscar Mayer*), 1-oz. slice 75
Ham and cheese spread:
(*Oscar Mayer*), ½ oz. 36

Ham, deviled, canned:
  (*Armour Star*), 1 tbsp. 48
  (*Hormel*), 1 tbsp. 33
  (*Libby's*), ½ oz. 42
  (*Underwood*), 1 tbsp. 47
Ham dinner, frozen:
  (*Banquet*), 10-oz. pkg. 369
  (*Morton*), 10-oz. pkg. 440
  (*Swanson TV Brand*), 10¼-oz. pkg. 380
Ham luncheon meat:
  (*Oscar Mayer* Thin Sliced), 3-oz. bag 113
  chopped (*Oscar Mayer*), 1-oz. slice 65
  chopped, canned (*Armour Star*), 12-oz. can 1,004
  chopped, canned (*Hormel*), 12-oz. can 917
  cooked (*Danola*), 1 oz. 56
  cooked (*Eckrich*), 1 slice 40
  cooked (*Hormel*), .8-oz. slice 28
  cooked (*Oscar Mayer*), ¾-oz. slice 25
  minced (*Oscar Mayer*), .8-oz. slice 56
  sausage roll (*Oscar Mayer*), .8-oz. slice 35
  sectioned, formed (*Oscar Mayer Jubilee*), 1 oz. 30
  smoked (*Eckrich*), 1 slice 40
  smoked (*Oscar Mayer Jubilee*), 1 oz. 50
Ham, minced:
  4 oz. 259
Ham patties:
  canned (*Wilson Certified*), 2 oz. 146
Ham salad:
  (*Oscar Mayer*), ½ oz. 30
  (*The Spreadables*), ½ oz. 26
Ham, spiced:
  canned, 7-oz. can 582
  canned, 1 slice (⅓ of 7-oz. can) 176
Ham steak:
  canned (*Oscar Mayer Jubilee*), 2-oz. slice 70

Ham and swiss cheese crepe:
  frozen (*Stouffer's*), 7½-oz. pkg. 410
Ham, turkey, see "Turkey ham"
Hamburger, fresh, see "Beef"
Hamburger hash mix:
  dry (*Hamburger Helper*), ⅕ pkg. 130
  with meat* (*Hamburger Helper*), ⅕ pkg. 300
Hamburger and meatloaf seasoning mix:
  dry (*McCormick/Schilling*), 1½-oz. packet 119
Hamburger patties, frozen:
  (*Pierre* Beef Patties), 3½ oz. 247
  breaded (*Pierre*), 3½ oz. 319
  breaded (*Pierre Chuckwagon*), 3½ oz. 297
  hoagie (*Pierre* Hoagie Beef Patties), 3½ oz. 246
  with red and green peppers
    (*Pierre* Zesty Hoagie Beef Patties), 3½ oz. 226
Hamburger pizza mix:
  dry (*Hamburger Helper*), ⅕ pkg. 160
  with meat* (*Hamburger Helper*), ⅕ pkg. 340
Hamburger relish:
  (*Crosse & Blackwell*), 1 tbsp. 20
  (*Heinz*), 1 tbsp. 17
Hamburger rolls, see "Rolls and buns"
Hamburger seasoning mix, dry:
  (*Durkee*), 1-oz. packet 110
  (*French's*), 1-oz. packet 100
  regular and with onion (*Grocer's Choice*), ⅓ oz. 30
Hamburger steaks:
  (*Pierre* 100% Beef), 3½ oz. 248
Hamburger stew mix:
  dry (*Hamburger Helper*), ⅕ pkg. 110
  with meat* (*Hamburger Helper*), ⅕ pkg. 290
Hard candy, see "Candy"

*Prepared according to directions on container

171

Hard sauce dessert topping:
(*Crosse & Blackwell*), 1 tbsp. 64
Hawaiian style vegetables:
frozen (*Birds Eye*), 3.3 oz. 50
frozen (*Green Giant*), ½ cup 100
Hazelnuts, see "Filberts"
Head cheese:
(*Oscar Mayer*), 1-oz. slice 55
Hearts, fresh:
beef, lean only, braised, 4 oz. 213
beef, lean only, braised, chopped or diced, 1 cup 273
calf, braised, 4 oz. 236
calf, braised, chopped or diced, 1 cup 302
chicken, simmered, 4 oz. 196
chicken, simmered, chopped or diced, 1 cup 251
hog, braised, 4 oz. 221
hog, braised, chopped or diced, 1 cup 283
lamb, braised, 4 oz. 295
lamb, braised, chopped or diced, 1 cup 377
turkey, simmered, 4 oz. 245
turkey, simmered, chopped or diced, 1 cup 313
Herb gravy mix*:
(*McCormick/Schilling*), ½ cup 41
Herring:
fresh:
Atlantic, raw, whole, 1 lb. 407
Atlantic, raw, meat only, 4 oz. 200
Pacific, raw, meat only, 4 oz. 111
canned:
plain, with liquid, 15-oz. can 884
plain, with liquid, 4 oz. 236
in tomato sauce, 4 oz. 200
in tomato sauce, 1 tbsp. sauce and 1 herring
(4¾″ × 1⅛″ × ⅝″) 97

*Prepared according to directions on container

172

kippered, see "smoked," below
pickled:
   Bismarck or marinated, 4 oz. 253
   Bismarck, 1 herring (7″ × 1½″ × ½″) 112
   Bismarck (*Vita*), 5-oz. jar 210
   cocktail (*Vita*), 8-oz. jar 350
   lunch (*Vita*), 8-oz. jar 326
   marinated pieces, 1 piece (1¾″ × ⅞″ × ½″) 33
   party snacks (*Vita*), 8-oz. jar 361
   roll mops (*Vita*), 8-oz. jar 242
   schmaltz, old-fashioned (*Vita*), 16-oz. jar 630
   in sour cream (*Danola*), 2 oz. 140
   in sour cream (*Vita*), 8-oz. jar 415
   tastee bits (*Vita*), 8-oz. jar 340
   in wine sauce (*Danola*), 2 oz. 90
salted or brined, 4 oz. 247
smoked:
   bloaters, 4 oz. 222
   hard, 4 oz. 340
   kippered, 4 oz. 239
   kippered, canned (*King Oscar*), 8-oz. can 480
   kippered, snacks, canned (*King Oscar* Kippered Snacks),
     3¾-oz. can 205
Herring, lake, see "Lake herring"
Herring salad:
   pickled (*Vita*), 7½-oz. jar 493
Hickory nuts:
   in shell, 4 oz. 267
   shelled, 4 oz. 763
Hickory smoke salt:
   (*French's*), 1 tsp. 2
Hollandaise sauce mix*:
   (*Durkee*), ½ cup 115
   (*French's*), ½ cup 120
   (*McCormick/Schilling*), ½ cup 170

---

*Prepared according to directions on container

Homestyle gravy mix*:
  (*Durkee*), ½ cup 35
  (*French's*), ½ cup 50
  (*Pillsbury*), ½ cup 30
Homestyle sauce mix:
  dry (*Durkee* Simmer Sauce), 2-oz. pkg. 133
Hominy grits, see "Corn grits"
Honey, strained or extracted:
  4 oz. 345
  1 cup 1,031
  1 tbsp. 64
  1 packet (½ oz.) 43
Honey loaf:
  (*Eckrich*), 1 slice 45
  (*Oscar Mayer*), 1-oz. slice 35
Honey roll sausage:
  (*Oscar Mayer*), .8-oz. slice 40
Honeydew melon, fresh:
  whole, with rind and seeds, 1 lb. 94
  1 wedge (2″ × 7″) 49
  cubed or diced, 1 cup 56
Horseradish:
  raw, whole, 1 lb. 288
  raw, pared, 1 oz. 25
  prepared, 1 oz. 11
  prepared, 1 tbsp. 6
  prepared, 1 tsp. 2
  prepared (*Kraft*), 1 tbsp. 4
  prepared, cream style (*Kraft*), 1 tbsp. 8
Horseradish with bacon dip:
  mix (*McCormick/Schilling*), 1¼-oz. pkg. 153
Horseradish mustard:
  (*Kraft*), 1 tbsp. 4

*Prepared according to directions on container

Horseradish sauce:
  (*Kraft*), 1 tbsp. 50
Hot dogs, see ''Frankfurters''
Hot dog relish:
  (*Crosse & Blackwell*), 1 tbsp. 22
  (*Heinz*), 1 tbsp. 22
Hot pepper relish:
  (*Crosse & Blackwell*), 1 tbsp. 22
Hot sauce:
  (*Frank's*), 1 tsp. 1
  (*Gebhardt*), 1 tsp. 1
  (*Tabasco*), 1 tsp. 1
Hot sauce relish:
  (*Bennett's*), 1 tbsp. 16
Hyacinth beans, raw:
  mature seeds, dry, 4 oz. 383
  young pods, untrimmed, 1 lb. 140
  young pods, cuts, 1 cup 32

I

Ice cream:
   all flavors, hardened, 10% fat, ½ cup 128
   all flavors, hardened, 12% fat, ½ cup 138
   all flavors, hardened, rich, 16% fat, ½ cup 165
   all flavors, soft-serve (frozen custard), ½ cup 167
   almond (*Foremost Almond Roca*), ½ cup 160
   banana (*Foremost Banana Susannah*), ½ cup 140
   banana nut (*Foremost*), ½ cup 130
   blackberry (*Foremost* Wild Mountain Blackberry),
     ½ cup 140
   black cherry (*Good Humor*), ½ cup 130
   black walnut (*Foremost*), ½ cup 140
   butter almond (*Breyer's*), ½ cup 170
   butter almond and chocolate (*Breyer's*), ½ cup 160
   butter pecan (*Good Humor*), ½ cup 150
   cherry (*Foremost Cherry Cherie*), ½ cup 130
   cherry vanilla (*Breyer's*), ½ cup 140
   chocolate (*Breyer's*), ½ cup 160
   chocolate (*Foremost*), ½ cup 130
   chocolate (*Foremost Chocolate Brazil*), ½ cup 150
   chocolate (*Good Humor*), ½ cup 130
   chocolate (*Meadow Gold*), ½ cup 129
   chocolate (*Sealtest*), ½ cup 140
   chocolate (*Swift's* Sweet Cream), ½ cup 130
   chocolate almond (*Foremost Parfait*), ½ cup 150
   chocolate chip (*Foremost*), ½ cup 145
   chocolate chip (*Good Humor*), ½ cup 150

chocolate chip (*Sealtest*), ½ cup 150
chocolate chip mint (*Breyer's*), ½ cup 170
chocolate eclair (*Sealtest*), ½ cup 160
chocolate peanut sundae (*Sealtest*), ½ cup 170
coffee (*Breyer's*), ½ cup 140
coffee (*Foremost Kona Coffee*), ½ cup 130
coffee (*Sealtest*), ½ cup 140
cotton candy (*Foremost*), ½ cup 160
heavenly hash (*Sealtest*), ½ cup 150
macadamia nut (*Foremost*), ½ cup 140
maple nut (*Foremost*), ½ cup 140
mint (*Foremost San Francisco Mint*), ½ cup 140
Neapolitan (*Foremost*), ½ cup 120
peach (*Breyer's*), ½ cup 140
peach (*Foremost Peach Crate*), ½ cup 120
peach (*Sealtest*), ½ cup 130
pecan (*Foremost Pecan Dandy*), ½ cup 130
pineapple (*Foremost*), ½ cup 120
rocky road (*Foremost*), ½ cup 145
strawberry (*Breyer's*), ½ cup 130
strawberry (*Foremost*), ½ cup 110
strawberry (*Foremost Strawberry Blonde*), ½ cup 140
strawberry (*Good Humor*), ½ cup 120
strawberry (*Meadow Gold*), ½ cup 126
strawberry (*Swift's* Sweet Cream), ½ cup 120
toffee (*Foremost English Toffee*), ½ cup 140
toffee fudge (*Good Humor Swirl*), ½ cup 130
vanilla (*Breyer's*), ½ cup 150
vanilla (*Foremost*), ½ cup 130
vanilla (*Good Humor*), ½ cup 140
vanilla (*Hood*), ½ cup 130
vanilla (*Hood Coronet*), ½ cup 150
vanilla (*Meadow Gold*), ½ cup 126
vanilla (*Swift's* Sweet Cream), ½ cup 130
vanilla fudge (*Breyer's* Fudge Royale), ½ cup 150
vanilla fudge (*Breyer's* Vanilla Fudge Twirl), ½ cup 160

vanilla fudge (*Good Humor* Royal Fudge), ½ cup 120
vanilla fudge (*Good Humor* Swirl), ½ cup 140
Ice cream, imitation:
  all flavors (*Meadow Gold*), ½ cup 126
  chocolate (*Foremost Dutch Pride*), ½ cup 130
  rocky road (*Foremost Dutch Pride*), ½ cup 130
  strawberry (*Foremost Dutch Pride*), ½ cup 120
  vanilla (*Foremost Dutch Pride*), ½ cup 130
Ice cream bars:
  (*Foremost Sidewalk Sundae*), 4 oz. 330
  (*Good Humor* Milky Pop), 1.5 fl. oz. 60
  assorted (*Good Humor Whammy*), 1.6 fl. oz. 100
  chocolate chip, crunch-coated
    (*Good Humor Whammy* Chip Crunch), 1.6 fl. oz. 110
  strawberry ripple, cake-coated
    (*Good Humor* Strawberry Shortcake), 3 fl. oz. 200
  vanilla, chocolate-coated (*Eskimo Pie*), 3 fl. oz. 180
  vanilla, chocolate-coated (*Good Humor*), 3 fl. oz. 170
  vanilla, toasted almond-coated
    (*Good Humor* Toasted Almond), 3 fl. oz. 220
  vanilla fudge, cake-coated (*Good Humor* Chocolate Eclair),
    3 fl. oz. 220
Ice cream cone:
  (*Foremost Nutty Buddy*), 3 fl. oz. 290
Ice cream cone (biscuit only):
  1 average 19
  all flavors (*Comet*), 1 cone 18
  rolled sugar, 1 average 37
  rolled sugar (*Comet*), 1 cone 45
Ice cream cups:
  chocolate (*Foremost*), 3-oz. cup 100
  orange (*Foremost*), 3-oz. cup 80
  raspberry (*Foremost*), 3-oz. cup 80
  strawberry (*Foremost*), 3-oz. cup 90
  vanilla (*Foremost*), 3-oz. cup 100

Ice cream cups (biscuit only):
  all flavors (*Comet*), 1 cup 18
Ice cream sandwich:
  (*Good Humor*), 2.5 fl. oz. 200
  chocolate chip cookie (*Good Humor*), 1 sandwich 480
  mint (*Foremost San Francisco Mint*), 1 sandwich 140
  vanilla (*Foremost*), 3 fl. oz. 140
  vanilla (*Foremost* Dandy), 3 fl. oz. 190
Ice milk:
  all flavors, hardened, 5.1% fat, ½ cup 100
  all flavors, soft-serve, 5.1% fat, ½ cup 133
  banana nut (*Foremost Big Dip*), ½ cup 120
  butter brickle (*Foremost Big Dip*), ½ cup 120
  chocolate (*Foremost Big Dip*), ½ cup 100
  chocolate (*Light 'N Easy*), ½ cup 110
  marble fudge (*Foremost Big Dip*), ½ cup 130
  rocky road (*Foremost Big Dip*), ½ cup 120
  strawberry (*Foremost Big Dip*), ½ cup 110
  strawberry (*Light 'N Easy*), ½ cup 100
  vanilla (*Foremost Big Dip*), ½ cup 110
  vanilla (*Hood Nuform*), ½ cup 110
  vanilla (*Light 'N Easy*), ½ cup 110
  vanilla (*Meadow Gold*), ½ cup 95
Ice milk, imitation:
  all flavors (*Meadow Gold*), ½ cup 106
  chocolate (*Foremost Dutch Maid*), ½ cup 100
  marble fudge (*Foremost Dutch Maid*), ½ cup 130
  Neapolitan (*Foremost Dutch Maid*), ½ cup 110
  strawberry (*Foremost Dutch Maid*), ½ cup 100
  toffee (*Foremost Dutch Maid*), ½ cup 110
  vanilla (*Foremost Dutch Maid*), ½ cup 110
Ice milk bars:
  vanilla (*Foremost Carousel*), 3 fl. oz. 65
  vanilla (*Foremost Dixie Doodle*), 2.5 fl. oz. 120
Ice sherbet, see "Sherbet"

Ice bars:
   all flavors (*Good Humor* Lite Fruit Stix), 1.5 oz. 35
   lemon, orange, or grape (*Foremost*), 2.5 fl. oz. 70
Ices:
   lime, ½ cup 124
Icing, cake, mix*:
   banana (*Betty Crocker Chiquita* Fluffy), ¹⁄₁₂ of pkg. 170
   butter (*Betty Crocker Butter Brickle* Fluffy), ¹⁄₁₂ of pkg. ...170
   butter pecan (*Betty Crocker* Fluffy), ¹⁄₁₂ of pkg. 170
   caramel (*Pillsbury Rich 'n Easy*), ¹⁄₁₂ of pkg. 140
   cherry, creamy (*Betty Crocker* Fluffy), ¹⁄₁₂ of pkg. 170
   chocolate and fudge:
      dark fudge (*Betty Crocker*), ¹⁄₁₂ of pkg. 170
      double Dutch (*Pillsbury Rich 'n Easy*), ¹⁄₁₂ of pkg. 150
      double Dutch (*Pillsbury* Smooth and Creamy),
         ¹⁄₁₂ of pkg. 180
      fudge (*Betty Crocker*), ¹⁄₁₂ of pkg. 180
      fudge (*Pillsbury Rich 'n Easy*), ¹⁄₁₂ of pkg. 150
      fudge (*Pillsbury* Smooth and Creamy), ¹⁄₁₂ of pkg. 180
      milk chocolate (*Betty Crocker*), ¹⁄₁₂ of pkg. 170
      milk chocolate (*Pillsbury Rich 'n Easy*), ¹⁄₁₂ of pkg. 150
      milk chocolate (*Pillsbury* Smooth and Creamy),
         ¹⁄₁₂ of pkg. 190
   coconut almond (*Pillsbury*), ¹⁄₁₂ of pkg. 170
   coconut pecan (*Betty Crocker* Fluffy), ¹⁄₁₂ of pkg. 140
   coconut pecan (*Pillsbury*), ¹⁄₁₂ of pkg. 150
   lemon:
      (*Betty Crocker Sunkist*), ¹⁄₁₂ of pkg. 170
      (*Pillsbury Rich 'n Easy*), ¹⁄₁₂ of pkg. 140
      (*Pillsbury* Smooth and Creamy), ¹⁄₁₂ of pkg. 180
   sour cream, chocolate (*Betty Crocker*), ¹⁄₁₂ of pkg. 170
   sour cream, white (*Betty Crocker*), ¹⁄₁₂ of pkg. 180
   strawberry (*Pillsbury Rich 'n Easy*), ¹⁄₁₂ of pkg. 140
   strawberry (*Pillsbury* Smooth and Creamy), ¹⁄₁₂ of pkg. ...180

*Prepared according to directions on container

vanilla (*Pillsbury Rich 'n Easy*), ¹⁄₁₂ of pkg. 150
vanilla (*Pillsbury* Smooth and Creamy), ¹⁄₁₂ of pkg. 180
white:
  (*Betty Crocker* Fluffy), ¹⁄₁₂ of pkg. 60
  (*Pillsbury* Fluffy), ¹⁄₁₂ of pkg. 70
  creamy (*Betty Crocker* Fluffy), ¹⁄₁₂ of pkg. 190

Icing, cake, ready-to-spread:
butter pecan (*Betty Crocker Creamy Deluxe*),
  ¹⁄₁₂ of container 170
cherry (*Betty Crocker Creamy Deluxe*), ¹⁄₁₂ of container . . .170
chocolate and fudge:
  (*Betty Crocker Creamy Deluxe*), ¹⁄₁₂ of container 170
  dark Dutch fudge (*Betty Crocker Creamy Deluxe*),
    ¹⁄₁₂ of container 170
  double Dutch (*Pillsbury Frosting Supreme*),
    ¹⁄₁₂ of container 160
  fudge (*Pillsbury Frosting Supreme*), ¹⁄₁₂ of container 160
  milk chocolate (*Betty Crocker Creamy Deluxe*),
    ¹⁄₁₂ of container 170
  milk chocolate (*Pillsbury Frosting Supreme*),
    ¹⁄₁₂ of container 160
  nut (*Betty Crocker Creamy Deluxe*), ¹⁄₁₂ of container 170
cream cheese (*Pillsbury Frosting Supreme*),
  ¹⁄₁₂ of container 160
decorator, all colors (*Pillsbury*), 1 tbsp. 70
lemon (*Betty Crocker Sunkist Creamy Deluxe*),
  ¹⁄₁₂ of container 170
lemon (*Pillsbury Frosting Supreme*), ¹⁄₁₂ of container 160
orange (*Betty Crocker Creamy Deluxe*), ¹⁄₁₂ of container . . .170
sour cream:
  chocolate (*Betty Crocker Creamy Deluxe*),
    ¹⁄₁₂ of container 170
  chocolate (*Pillsbury Frosting Supreme*),
    ¹⁄₁₂ of container 160
  vanilla (*Pillsbury Frosting Supreme*), ¹⁄₁₂ of container . . .160

white (*Betty Crocker Creamy Deluxe*),
   1/12 of container 160
strawberry (*Pillsbury Frosting Supreme*), 1/12 of container ..160
vanilla (*Betty Crocker Creamy Deluxe*), 1/12 of container ...170
vanilla (*Pillsbury Frosting Supreme*), 1/12 of container 160
Inconnu (sheefish):
raw, whole, 1 lb. 417
raw, meat only, 4 oz. 166
India relish:
(*Crosse & Blackwell*), 1 tbsp. 26
(*Heinz*), 1 tbsp. 28
Italian sauce, see "Spaghetti sauce"
Italian style dinner:
frozen (*Banquet*), 11-oz. pkg. 446
frozen (*Swanson TV Brand*), 13-oz. pkg. 420
Italian style mixed vegetables, frozen:
(*Birds Eye*), 3.3 oz. 60
(*Stokely-Van Camp* Vegetables Milano), 3.2 oz. 45
(*Stokely-Van Camp* Vegetables Romano), 3.2 oz. 40
northern (*Birds Eye*), 3.6 oz. 110

J

Jack fruit:
  fresh, whole, 1 lb. 124
  fresh, peeled and seeded, 4 oz. 111
Jack mackerel:
  raw, meat only, 4 oz. 162
Jalapeño dip:
  (*Frito's*), 3⅛-oz. serving 110
  (*Gebhardt*), 8-oz. container 240
  (*Kraft*), 2 tbsp. 50
  (*Kraft* Ready to Serve), 1 oz. 60
  (*Old El Paso*), 7½-oz. container 263
Jam:
  all flavors (*Kraft*), 1 tsp. 16
  all flavors (*Smuckers*), 1 tbsp. 53
  all flavors, except apricot, peach, pear, and plum (*Bama*),
    1 tbsp. 54
  apricot, peach, pear, and plum (*Bama*), 1 tbsp. 51
  grape (*Welch's*), 1 tbsp. 53
  strawberry (*Musselman's*), 1 tbsp. 54
  strawberry (*Welch's*), 1 tbsp. 53
Japanese style vegetables, frozen:
  (*Birds Eye*), 3.3 oz. 40
  (*Birds Eye* Stir-Fry), 3.3 oz. 30
  (*Green Giant*), ½ cup 65
  (*Stokely-Van Camp*), 3.2 oz. 25
Jellies:
  all flavors (*Bama*), 1 tbsp. 45

all flavors (*Crosse & Blackwell*), 1 tbsp. 51
all flavors (*Kraft*), 1 tsp. 16
all flavors (*Ma Brown*), 1 tbsp. 49
all flavors (*Musselman's*), 1 tbsp. 53
all flavors (*Smucker's*), 1 tbsp. 53
grape (*Welch's*), 1 tbsp. 53
and peanut butter (*Bama*), 1 tbsp. 75
Jerusalem artichokes:
fresh, whole, with skin, 1 lb. 207
fresh, pared, 4 oz. 75
Juices, see individual listings
Jujubes (Chinese dates):
fresh, whole, 1 lb. 443
fresh, without seeds, 4 oz. 119
dried, whole, with seeds, 1 lb. 1,159
dried, seeded, 4 oz. 325

K

Kale:
  fresh:
    raw, whole, with stems, 1 lb. 128
    raw, whole, without stems, 1 lb. 154
    raw, trimmed, leaves only, 4 oz. 80
    boiled, drained, with stems, 1 cup 31
    boiled, drained, leaves only, 1 cup 43
  frozen:
    chopped (*Birds Eye*), 3.3 oz. 25
    chopped (*Seabrook Farms*), 3.3 oz. 30
    chopped or leaf (*Southland*), 3.3 oz. 30
Ketchup, see "Catsup"
Kidneys, fresh:
  beef, raw, 8 oz. 294
  beef, braised, 4 oz. 286
  beef, braised, pieces, 1 cup 353
  calf, raw, 8 oz. 256
  hog, raw, 8 oz. 240
  lamb, raw, 8 oz. 238
Kielbasa:
  (*Eckrich* Polska), 1 oz. 100
  (*Eckrich* Polska Skinless), 2-oz. link 190
  (*Hormel* Kolbase), 1 oz. 81
  (*Kahn's* Polska), 1 oz. 92
  (*Vienna*), 3½ oz. 290
Kingfish (whiting):
  fresh, raw, whole, 1 lb. 210

fresh, raw, meat only, 4 oz. 119
frozen, breaded (*Taste O' Sea*), 1 portion 90
frozen, fillets (*Taste O' Sea*), 16-oz. pkg. 320
smoked, flesh only (*Vita*), 2 oz. 96

Kippers, see "Herring"

Kirsch liqueur:
(*Dolfi*), 1 fl. oz. 78
(*Dolfi* Cordon d'Or), 1 fl. oz. 83
(*Garnier*), 1 fl. oz. 83
(*Hiram Walker* Kirschwasser), 1 fl. oz. 74

Knockwurst:
packaged, 12-oz. pkg. (about 5 links) 945
packaged, 1 link (4″ long 1⅛″ in diam.) 189
(*Oscar Mayer Chubbies*), 2.4-oz. link 214

Kohlrabi, fresh:
raw, whole, without leaves, 1 lb. 96
raw, pared, 4 oz. 33
raw, pared, diced, 1 cup 41
boiled, drained, 4 oz. 27
boiled, drained, diced, 1 cup 40

Kosher wine:
all dry varieties (*Manischewitz*), 4 fl. oz. 91
all medium varieties (*Manischewitz*), 4 fl. oz. 112
all sweet varieties (*Manischewitz*), 4 fl. oz. 170
Concord (*Mogen David*), 4 fl. oz. 200

Kummel liqueur:
(*DuBouchett*—48 proof), 1 fl. oz. 65
(*DuBouchett*—70 proof), 1 fl. oz. 83
(*Garnier*), 1 fl. oz. 75
(*Hiram Walker*), 1 fl. oz. 71
(*Old Mr. Boston*), 1 fl. oz. 78

Kumquats, fresh:
whole, with seeds, 1 lb. 274
trimmed, with seeds, 4 oz. 74
1 medium 12

L

Lake herring (Cisco):
   raw, whole, 1 lb. 226
   raw, meat only, 4 oz. 109
   smoked (*Vita*), 2 oz. 88
Lake trout:
   raw, drawn, 1 lb. 282
   raw, meat only, 4 oz. 191
   smoked, flesh only (*Vita*), 2 oz. 178
Lake trout (siscowet):
   raw, under 6.5 lb., whole, 1 lb. 404
   raw, under 6.5 lb. meat only, 4 oz. 273
   raw, over 6.5 lb., whole, 1 lb. 856
   raw, over 6.5 lb. meat only, 4 oz. 594
Lamb:
   leg, lean with fat:
     roasted, with bone, 9.4 oz. (yield from 1 lb. raw) 745
     roasted, boneless, 11.2 oz. (yield from 1 lb. raw) 887
     roasted, boneless, 4 oz. 317
     roasted, chopped or diced, 1 cup 391
   leg, lean only (trimmed of fat):
     roasted, with bone, 7.8 oz.
       (yield from 1 lb. raw with fat) 411
     roasted, boneless, 9.3 oz.
       (yield from 1 lb. raw with fat) 491
     roasted, boneless, 4 oz. 211
     roasted, chopped or diced, 1 cup 260
   loin chops, with bone, lean with fat:
     broiled, 10.1 oz. (yield from 1 lb. raw) 1,023

broiled, 4 oz. 407
broiled, 1 chop, 3.4 oz. (3 chops per lb.) 341
broiled, 1 chop, 2.5 oz. (4 chops per lb.) 255
loin chops, with bone, lean only (trimmed of fat):
broiled, 6.9 oz. (yield from 1 lb. raw with fat) 368
broiled, 4 oz. 213
broiled, 1 chop, 2.3 oz. (3 chops per lb.) 122
broiled, 1 chop, 1.7 oz. (4 chops per lb.) 92
rib chops, with bones, lean with fat:
broiled, 9.5 oz. (yield from 1 lb. raw) 1,091
broiled, 4 oz. 462
broiled, 1 chop, 3.1 oz. (3 chops per lb.) 362
broiled, 1 chop, 2.4 oz. (4 chops per lb.) 273
rib chops, with bone, lean only (trimmed of fat):
broiled, 6 oz. (yield from 1 lb. raw with fat) 361
broiled, 4 oz. 239
broiled, 1 chop, 2 oz. (3 chops per lb.) 120
broiled, 1 chop, 1.5 oz. (4 chops per lb.) 91
shoulder, lean with fat:
roasted, with bone, 9.5 oz. (yield from 1 lb. raw) 913
roasted, boneless, 11.2 oz. (yield from 1 lb. raw) 1,075
roasted, boneless, 4 oz. 383
roasted, chopped or diced, 1 cup 473
shoulder, lean only (trimmed of fat):
roasted, with bone, 7 oz.
   (yield from 1 lb. raw with fat) 410
roasted, boneless, 8.3 oz.
   (yield from 1 lb. raw with fat) 482
roasted, boneless, 4 oz. 233
roasted, chopped or diced, 1 cup 287
Lamb's-quarters:
raw, trimmed, 1 lb. 195
boiled, drained, 4 oz. 36
boiled, drained, 1 cup 64
Lard:
8 oz. 2,045

1 cup 1,849
1 tbsp. 117
Lasagna:
  canned (*Hormel* Short Order), 7½-oz. can 262
  frozen:
    (*Stouffer's*), 10½-oz. pkg. 385
    (*Stouffer's*), 21-oz. pkg. 770
    (*Swanson Hungry-Man* Entree), 12¾-oz. pkg. 540
    beef (*Hormel*), 10-oz. pkg. 370
    with meat sauce (*Buitoni*), 14-oz. pkg. 596
    with meat and sauce (*Green Giant* Baked Entree),
      9-oz. pkg. 310
    with ricotta cheese (*Ronzoni*), 23-oz. pkg. 800
Lasagna dinner:
  with meat, frozen (*Swanson Hungry-Man*), 17¾-oz. pkg. . . . 740
Lasagna dinner and side dish mix:
  dry (*Hamburger Helper*), ⅕ pkg. 150
  with meat* (*Hamburger Helper*), ⅕ pkg. 330
Leeks:
  raw, untrimmed, 1 lb. 123
  raw, bulb and lower leaf, 4 oz. 59
  raw, 3 average 52
Lemon extract:
  (*Virginia Dare*), 1 tsp. 14
  pure (*Ehlers*), 1 tsp. 30
  imitation (*Durkee*), 1 tsp. 17
Lemon flavored gin:
  (*DuBouchett*), 1 fl. oz. 59
  (*Old Mr. Boston*), 1 fl. oz. 76
Lemon flavored vodka:
  (*Old Mr Boston*), 1 fl. oz. 100
Lemon juice:
  fresh:
    1 cup 61

Prepared according to directions on container

1 tbsp. 4
(*Sunkist*), 2 tbsp. 8
canned or bottled:
(*ReaLemon*), 2 tbsp. 6
(*Seneca*), 2 tbsp. 8
frozen:
full-strength (*Minute Maid*), 2 tbsp. 7
Lemon-lime drink mix*:
(*Country Time*), 6 fl. oz. 68
Lemon-limeade:
frozen* (*Minute Maid*), 6 fl. oz. .75
Lemon peel:
candied, 1 oz. 90
Lemon-pepper seasoning:
(*French's*), 1 tsp. 6
Lemon pie, see "Pies, frozen," "Pies, mix," and "Pies, snack"
Lemon pie tart:
frozen (*Pepperidge Farm*), 1 piece 320
Lemons, fresh:
whole, 1 lb. 90
pulp only, 1 large (2⅜″ in diam.) .29
pulp only, 1 medium (2⅛″ in diam.) 20
1 slice (³⁄₁₆″ thick) 2
1 wedge, ¼ of large lemon 7
1 wedge, ⅙ of large lemon 5
1 wedge, ½ of medium lemon 5
1 wedge, ⅙ of medium lemon 3
Lemonade:
canned or dairy pack:
(*Country Time*), 6 fl. oz. 68
(*Hood*), 6 fl. oz. 75
(*Lipton Lemon Tree*), 6 fl. oz. 68
(*Sealtest*), 6 fl. oz. 83
(*Wyler's*), 6 fl. oz. 65

*Prepared according to directions on container

frozen*:
   (*Country Time*), 6 fl. oz. 68
   (*Minute Maid*), 6 fl. oz. 74
mix*:
   (*Borden Prize*), 6 fl. oz. 68
   (*Country Time*), 6 fl. oz. 68
   (*Cramores*), 6 fl. oz. 68
   (*Hi-C*), 6 fl. oz. 76
   (*Kool-Aid*), 6 fl. oz. 68
   (*Lipton Lemon Tree*), 6 fl. oz. 68
   (*Minute Maid* Crystals), 6 fl. oz. 80
   (*Wyler's*), 6 fl. oz. 75

Lemonade, pink:
frozen* (*Country Time*), 6 fl. oz. 68
mix*:
   (*Cramores*), 6 fl. oz. 68
   (*Kool-Aid*), 6 fl. oz. 68
   (*Minute Maid* Crystals), 6 fl. oz. 80
   (*Wyler's*), 6 fl. oz. 68

Lentils:
whole, dry, 8 oz. 771
whole, dry, 1 cup 646
whole, cooked, 1 cup 212
split, without seed coat, dry, 8 oz. 783
split, without seed coat, dry, 1 cup 656

Lettuce:
Boston or bibb:
   untrimmed, 1 lb. 47
   1 head (5″ in diam.) 23
   1 large, 2 medium, or 3 small leaves 2
   chopped or shredded, 1 cup 8
iceberg:
   untrimmed, 1 lb. 56
   1 head trimmed (6″ in diam.) 70

Prepared according to directions on container

1 leaf (5″ × 4½″) 3
chopped or shredded, 1 cup 7
small chunks, 1 cup 10
1 wedge (¼ of 6″ head) 18
1 wedge (⅙ of 6″ head) 12
loose leaf:
untrimmed, 1 lb. 52
2 large leaves 9
chopped or shredded, 1 cup 10
romaine or cos:
untrimmed, 1 lb. 52
3 leaves (8″ long) 5
chopped or shredded, 1 cup 10
Lichee nuts:
raw, in shell, 1 lb. 174
raw, shelled, 4 oz. 73
raw, 6 average nuts 41
dry, in shell, 1 lb. 578
dry, shelled, 4 oz. 316
Licorice, see ''Candy''
Liebfraumilch wine:
(*Anheuser & Fehrs*), 4 fl. oz. 84
(*Dienhard & Co.*), 4 fl. oz. 96
Lima beans, see ''Beans, lima''
Limeade:
frozen* (*Minute Maid*), 6 fl. oz. 75
Lime flavored vodka:
(*Old Mr. Boston*), 1 fl. oz. 100
Lime juice:
fresh, 1 cup 64
fresh, 1 tbsp. 4
bottled (*ReaLime*), 2 tbsp. 4
bottled, sweetened (*Rose's*), 2 tbsp. 49
Limes:
fresh, whole, 1 lb. 107

*Prepared according to directions on container

fresh, pulp only, 1 lime (2″ in diam.) 19
Ling cod:
raw, whole, 1 lb. 130
raw, meat only, 4 oz. 95
Linguine, plain, see "Pasta, plain"
Linguine with clam sauce:
frozen (*Ronzoni*), 16-oz. pkg. 480
frozen (*Stouffer's*), 10½-oz. pkg. 285
Liqueurs, see individual listings
Liquor, pure distilled (brandy, gin, rum, whiskey, vodka, etc.):
80 proof, 1 fl. oz. 67
80 proof, 1½-fl. oz. jigger 97
84 proof, 1 fl. oz. 70
86 proof, 1 fl. oz. 72
86 proof, 1½-fl. oz. jigger 105
86.8 proof, 1 fl. oz. 72
90 proof, 1 fl. oz. 75
90 proof, 1½-fl. oz. jigger 110
90.4 proof, 1 fl. oz. 75
94 proof, 1 fl oz. 78
94 proof, 1½-fl. oz. jigger 116
94.6 proof, 1 fl. oz. 79
97 proof, 1 fl. oz. 81
100 proof, 1 fl. oz. 83
100 proof, 1½-fl. oz. jigger 124
104 proof, 1 fl. oz. 87
Liver, fresh:
beef, raw, 1 lb. 635
beef, fried, 4 oz. 260
beef, fried, 1 slice (6½″ × 2⅜″ × ⅜″) 195
calves, raw, 1 lb. 635
calves, fried, 4 oz. 296
calves, fried, 1 slice (6½″ × 2⅜″ × ⅜″) 222
chicken, raw, 1 lb. 585
chicken, simmered, 4 oz. 187
chicken, simmered, 1 liver (2″ × 2″ × ⅝″) 41
chicken, simmered, chopped, 1 cup 231

goose, raw, 1 lb. 826
hog, raw, 1 lb. 594
hog, fried, 4 oz. 273
hog, fried, 1 slice (6½″ × 2⅜″ × ⅜″) 205
lamb, raw, 1 lb. 617
lamb, broiled, 4 oz. 296
lamb, broiled, 1 slice (3½″ × 2″ × ⅜″) 117
turkey, raw, 1 lb. 626
turkey, simmered, 4 oz. 197
turkey, simmered, 1 liver from 20–25-lb. turkey 212
turkey, simmered, 1 liver from 17-lb. turkey 191
turkey, simmered, 1 liver from 12–13-lb. turkey 131
turkey, simmered, chopped, 1 cup 244

Liver cheese:
(*Oscar Mayer*), 1.3-oz. slice 115
Liver, chopped:
chicken (*Reese*), 1 oz. 47
Liver loaf:
(*Hormel*), 1-oz. slice 80
Liver pâté, see "Pâté, canned or in jars"
Liver, sliced:
canned (*Swift's Tru Tender*), 2.6 oz. 140
Liverwurst:
fresh, 4 oz. 348
smoked, see "Braunschweiger"
Liverwurst spread:
(*Underwood*), 1 tbsp. 45
Lobster:
northern, raw, in shell, 1 lb. 107
northern, cooked, in shell, 1 lb. 112
northern, cooked or canned, meat only, 4 oz. 108
northern, cooked or canned, meat only, cubed, 1 cup 138
Lobster Newburg:
frozen (*Stouffer's*), 6½-oz. pkg. 350
Lobster paste:
canned, 1 oz. 51

canned, 1 tsp. 13
Loganberries:
fresh:
    untrimmed, 1 lb. 267
    trimmed, 4 oz. 71
    trimmed, 1 cup 89
canned, in water, with liquid, 8 oz. 90
canned, in heavy syrup, with liquid, 8 oz. 202
Longans:
fresh, in shell, 1 lb. 147
fresh, shelled, without seeds, 4 oz. 69
dried, in shell, 1 lb. 467
dried, shelled, without seeds, 4 oz. 326
Loquats, fresh:
whole, 1 lb. 168
without seeds, 4 oz. 54
without seeds, 10 fruits 59
Lox, see "Salmon, smoked"
Luncheon loaf, turkey, see "Turkey luncheon loaf"
Luncheon meat (see also individual listings):
    (*Oscar Mayer*), 1-oz. slice 95
    (*Spam*), 12-oz. can 1,055
    (*Treet*), 12-oz. can 1,014
    (*Wilson Certified*), 12-oz. can 1,060
    (*Wilson Corn King*), 12-oz. can 1,060
    with cheese chunks (*Spam*), 12-oz. can 1,044
    smoked (*Spam*), 12-oz. can 1,051
    spiced (*Hormel*), 1-oz. slice 76
Luncheon meat, deviled:
    (*Spam*), 1 tbsp. 36
    (*Treet*), 1 tbsp. 44
Luncheon sausage:
    pressed (*Oscar Mayer*), .8-oz. slice 35
    roll (*Oscar Mayer*), .8-oz. slice 35
Luxury loaf:
    (*Oscar Mayer*), 1-oz. slice 40
Lychees, see "Lichee nuts"

M

Macadamia nuts:
  in shell, 1 lb. 972
  shelled, 4 oz. 784
  6 average nuts 104
Macaroni:
  dry, 8-oz. pkg. 838
  dry (*American Beauty*), 2 oz. 210
  dry (*La Rosa*), 2 oz. 210
  cooked, firm stage (8–10 minutes), hot, 1 cup 192
  cooked, tender stage (14–20 minutes), cold, 1 cup 117
  cooked, tender stage (14–20 minutes), hot, 1 cup 155
Macaroni and beef:
  canned, with tomato sauce (*Franco-American* Beefy Mac),
    7½ oz. 220
  frozen, with tomato sauce (*Green Giant* Entree),
    9-oz. pkg. 240
  frozen, with tomato sauce (*Stouffer's*), 11½-oz. pkg. 380
Macaroni and beef dinner:
  frozen (*Morton*), 10-oz. pkg. 260
  frozen (*Swanson TV Brand*), 12-oz. pkg. 400
Macaroni and cheese:
  canned:
    (*Franco-American*), 7¼ oz. 180
    (*Hormel* Short Order), 7½-oz. can 169
    with cheese sauce (*Heinz*), 1 cup 180
  frozen:
    (*Banquet Buffet Supper*), 32-oz. pkg. 1,027
    (*Banquet Cookin' Bag*), 8-oz. pkg. 261

(*Banquet* Entree), 8-oz. pkg. 279
(*Green Giant* Baked Entree), 8-oz. pkg. 290
(*Green Giant* Entree), 9-oz. pkg. 380
(*Howard Johnson's*), 10-oz. pkg. 542
(*Howard Johnson's*), 19-oz. pkg. 1,029
(*Stouffer's*), 12-oz. pkg. 520
casserole (*Banquet*), 8-oz. pkg. .279
casserole (*Morton*), 8-oz. pkg. .270
mix*:
    (*Betty Crocker*), ¼ pkg. 310
    (*Golden Grain* Stir & Serve), ½ cup 183
    (*Kraft* Dinner), ¾ cup 300
    (*Kraft* Deluxe Dinner), ¾ cup .250
    (*Lipton*), ½ cup 210
    (*Mug•O•Lunch*), 1 pouch 230
    (*Pennsylvania Dutch*), ½ cup .160
    cheddar (*Mac-A-Roni*), ¾ cup 141
Macaroni and cheese dinner:
    frozen (*Morton*), 8 oz. 260
Macaroni and cheese pot pie:
    frozen (*Swanson*), 7-oz. pie 230
Macaroni and eggplant casserole:
    frozen (*Ronzoni* Single Serving), 8-oz. pkg. 260
Macaroni and meatballs:
    canned, with tomato sauce (*Franco-American* Beefy Mac),
    7½ oz. 220
Mace:
    ground (all brands), 1 tsp. 10
Mackerel, Atlantic:
    fresh:
        raw, whole, 1 lb. 468
        raw, fillets, 1 lb. 866
        fillets, broiled with butter, 12⅞ oz.
           (yield from 1 lb. raw) 861
        fillets, broiled with butter, 4 oz. 268

Prepared according to directions on container

fillets, broiled with butter, 1 fillet (8½″ × 2½″ × ½″) ...248
canned, with liquid, 8 oz. 416
Mackerel, jack, see ''Jack mackerel''
Mackerel, Pacific:
fresh, raw, dressed, 1 lb. 519
fresh, raw, meat only, 4 oz. 181
canned, drained, 15-oz. can 765
canned, drained, 4 oz. 204
Mackerel, salted:
fillets, 4 oz. 345
fillets, 1 piece (7¾″ × 2½″ × ½″) 342
Mackerel, smoked:
meat only, 4 oz. 248
Madeira wine:
(*Hiram Walker*), 2 fl. oz. 84
(*Leacock*), 2 fl. oz. 80
(*Sandeman & Co.*), 2 fl. oz. 84
Mai-tai cocktail:
bottled (*Lemon Hart*—48 proof), 1 fl. oz. 60
Mai-tai cocktail mix:
bottled (*Holland House*), 1 fl. oz. 33
instant (*Holland House*), 1 packet 69
Malt:
dry, 1 oz. 104
Malt extract:
dry, 1 oz. 104
Malt liquor:
(*Champale*), 12 fl. oz. 156
(*Colt .45*), 12 fl. oz. 160
(*Country Club*), 12 fl. oz. 163
(*Malt Duck Apple*), 12 fl. oz. 250
(*Malt Duck Grape*), 12 fl. oz. 210
(*Mickeys*), 12 fl. oz. 160
Malted flavor mix:
dry (*Ovaltine*), ¾ oz. 80
dry, chocolate (*Carnation* Instant), ¾ oz. 85
dry, natural (*Carnation* Instant), ¾ oz. 90

Mandarin oranges, see "Tangerines, fresh"
Mangoes, fresh:
  whole, 1 lb. 201
  whole, 1 average (10.6 oz.) 152
  diced or sliced, 1 cup 109
Manhattan cocktail:
  bottled (*Calvert*—60 proof), 1 fl. oz. 54
Manhattan cocktail mix:
  bottled (*Holland House*), 1 fl. oz. 29
Manicotti, frozen:
  jumbo (*Buitoni*), 18-oz. pkg. 887
  with ricotta cheese (*Ronzoni*), 15-oz. pkg. 720
  in sauce (*Buitoni*), 13-oz. pkg. .570
Maple extract:
  imitation (*Durkee*), 1 tsp. 6
Maple flavor syrup, see "Pancake syrup"
Maple flavoring:
  imitation (*Ehlers*), 1 tsp. 9
Maple syrup:
  1 cup 794
  1 tbsp. 50
  pure (*Cary's*), 1 tbsp. 50
  blended (*Log Cabin*), 1 tbsp. 52
  imitation (*Karo*), 1 tbsp. 55
Maraschino cherries, see "Cherries, maraschino"
Maraschino liqueur:
  (*DuBouchett*), 1 fl. oz. 85
  (*Garnier*), 1 fl. oz. 94
Margarine:
  regular:
    1 cup, or 8 oz. 1,634
    1 stick, or 4 oz. 816
    1 tbsp. 102
    1 tsp. 34
    1 pat (1″ × 1″ × ⅓″) 36
  whipped:
    8-oz. container 1,634

1 cup	1,087
1 stick or ½ cup	544
1 tbsp.	68
1 tsp.	23
1 pat (1¼″ × 1¼″ × ⅓″)	27

Margarita cocktail:
bottled (*Calvert*—55 proof), 1 fl. oz. 59

Margarita cocktail mix:
bottled (*Holland House*), 1 fl. oz. 39
instant (*Holland House*), 1 packet 69

Marinade, meat, mix*:
(*Durkee*), ½ cup 47
dry (*Durkee*), 1-oz. packet 47
dry (*French's*), 1 packet 80

Marinara sauce, see "Spaghetti sauce"
Marjoram:
ground (all brands), 1 tsp. 4

Marmalade:
all flavors (*Crosse & Blackwell*), 1 tbsp. 60
orange (*Bama*), 1 tbsp. 54
orange (*Kraft*), 1 tbsp. 52
orange (*Ma Brown*), 1 tbsp. 49
orange (*Smucker's*), 1 tbsp. 53

Marmalade plums, see "Sapotes"
Marshmallow dessert topping:
(*Kraft*), 1 tbsp. 35
creme (*Kraft*), 1 oz. 90

Marshmallows, see "Candy"
Martini cocktail:
gin, bottled (*Calvert* Martini—70 proof), 1 fl. oz. 59
vodka, bottled (*Calvert* Vodka Martini—75 proof),
1 fl. oz. 63

Martini cocktail mix:
bottled (*Holland House*), 1 fl. oz. 10

Matai, see "Water chestnuts, Chinese"

*Prepared according to directions on container

Matzo, see "Crackers"
Mayonnaise:
  (*Bama*), 1 tbsp. 100
  (*Bennett's*), 1 tbsp. 110
  (*Best Foods*), 1 tbsp. 100
  (*Cains*), 1 tbsp. 100
  (*Hain*—safflower or unsalted), 1 tbsp. 100
  (*Hellmann's*), 1 tbsp. 100
  (*Kraft*), 1 tbsp. 100
  (*Mrs. Filberts*), 1 tbsp. 100
  (*Saffola*), 1 tbsp. 101
  imitation, see "Salad dressing"
Meat, see individual listings
Meat-fish-poultry sauce:
  (*A.1.*), 1 tbsp. 12
  (*Crosse & Blackwell*), 1 tbsp. 21
  (*Escoffier Sauce Diable*), 1 tbsp. 20
  (*Escoffier Sauce Robert*), 1 tbsp. 19
  (*Heinz 57*), 1 tbsp. 14
  (*Heinz* Savory Sauce), 1 tbsp. 21
  (*HP*), 1 tbsp. 21
Meat, potted (see also individual listings):
  (*Armour Star*), 1 tbsp. 35
  (*Hormel*), 1 tbsp. 29
  (*Libby's*), ½ oz. 29
Meat loaf, frozen:
  with tomato sauce (*Banquet Buffet Suppers*),
    32-oz. pkg. 1,445
  with tomato sauce (*Banquet Cookin' Bag*), 5-oz. pkg. 224
  with tomato sauce (*Morton*), 8 oz. 200
  with tomato sauce and potatoes
    (*Swanson TV Brand* Entree), 9-oz. pkg. 330
Meat loaf dinner, frozen:
  (*Banquet*), 11-oz. pkg. 412
  (*Banquet Man Pleaser*), 19-oz. pkg. 916
  (*Morton*), 11-oz. pkg. 340
  (*Swanson TV Brand*), 10¾-oz. pkg. 530

201

Meat loaf luncheon meat:
  4 oz. 227
Meat loaf seasoning mix, dry
(see also "Hamburger and meatloaf seasoning mix"):
  (*Contadina*), 3¾-oz. packet 363
Meatball dinner:
  frozen (*Swanson TV Brand*), 11¾-oz. pkg. 400
  (*Durkee Roastin' Bag*), 1½-oz. packet 129
  (*French's*), 1½-oz. packet 160
Meat marinade, see "Marinade, meat"
Meat tenderizer, see "Tenderizer, meat"
Meatball sandwich:
  frozen (*Stouffer's*), 7¾-oz. pkg. 410
Meatball seasoning mix:
  dry (*French's*), 1 packet 140
  Italian, dry (*Durkee*), 1-oz. packet 22
Meatball stew, canned:
  (*Dinty Moore*), 7½ oz. 245
  (*Libby's*), 8 oz. 275
  (*Morton House*), 8 oz. 290
Meatballs:
  frozen, with gravy and potatoes
    (*Swanson TV Brand* Entree), 9¼-oz. pkg. 330
Meatballs and spaghetti, see "Spaghetti and meatballs"
Meatballs, Swedish:
  frozen, with parsley noodles (*Stouffer's*), 11-oz. pkg. 475
Melba toast, see "Crackers"
Melon, see individual listings
Melon balls (cantaloupe and honeydew):
  frozen, in syrup, unthawed, 1 cup 143
Mexican style dinner, frozen:
  (*Banquet*), 12-oz. pkg. 608
  (*Morton*), 11-oz. pkg. 300
  (*Van de Kamp's*), 12-oz. pkg. 480
  combination (*Banquet*), 12-oz. pkg. 571
  combination (*Swanson TV Brand*), 16-oz. pkg. 600
  combination (*Van de Kamp's*), 11-oz. pkg. 420

Milk:
  buttermilk:
    Bulgarian (*Foremost*), 1 cup 160
    cultured (*Foremost*), 1 cup 140
    dry, cultured, 1 cup 464
    dry, cultured, 1 tbsp. 25
    .5% fat (*Meadow Gold*), 8 fl. oz. 105
    1.5% fat (*Foremost*), 8 fl. oz. 110
  condensed, canned:
    (*Borden*), ½ cup 480
    (*Borden Dime Brand*), ½ cup 504
    (*Borden Eagle Brand*), ½ cup 480
    (*Borden Magnolia Brand*), ½ cup 504
  evaporated, canned:
    (*Borden*), ½ cup 173
    (*Carnation*), ½ cup 173
    (*Pet*), ½ cup 170
    (*Wilson's*), ½ cup 170
    filled (*Dairymate*), ½ cup 150
    low-fat (*Carnation*), ½ cup 110
    skimmed (*Carnation*), ½ cup 100
    skimmed (*Pet*), ½ cup 100
  half and half, see "Cream"
  nonfat, dry:
    regular, dry, 1 cup 436
    instant, 1 envelope (3.2 oz.) 327
    instant, high-density (3.2 oz. yields ⅞ cup), 1 cup 373
    instant, low-density (3.2 oz. yields 1⅓ cup), 1 cup 244
    reconstituted (*Carnation*), 8 fl. oz. 80
    reconstituted (*Foremost Milkman*), 8 fl. oz. 97
    reconstituted (*Pet* Instant), 8 fl. oz. 80
    reconstituted (*Sanalac*), 8 fl. oz. 80
  skim and low-fat:
    (*Borden Lite Line*), 8 fl. oz. 120
    (*Borden Pro-Line*), 8 fl. oz. 140
    (*Foremost* Acidophilus Lowfat 2%), 1 cup 140
    (*Foremost* 1%), 1 cup 100

(*Foremost* 2%), 1 cup 120
(*Foremost* Nonfat), 1 cup 90
(*Foremost Profile*), 8 fl. oz. 99
(*Foremost Profile* Lowfat, 1%), 1 cup 100
(*Foremost Profile* Nonfat), 1 cup 90
(*Foremost Profile* Tape Watchers Nonfat), 1 cup 90
(*Foremost So-Lo*—2% fortified), 1 cup 140
(*Foremost So-Lo*—2% unfortified), 1 cup 130
(*Foremost* Tape Watchers Nonfat), 1 cup 90
(*Hood Nuform* Lowfat), 8 fl. oz. 110
(*Hood Silouet* Skim), 8 fl. oz. 110
(*Light N' Lively*), 8 fl. oz. 110
(*Meadow Gold*), 8 fl. oz. 87
(*Viva*), 8 fl. oz. 137
whole:
(*Cream O' Gold* Extrarich), 1 cup 170
(*Dellwood*), 8 fl. oz. 150
(*Foremost*), 1 cup 150
(*Hood*), 8 fl. oz. 150
3.3% fat (*Foremost*), 8 fl. oz. 148
3.3% fat (*Meadow Gold*), 8 fl. oz. 150
3.5% fat (*Borden*), 8 fl. oz. 150
3.5% fat (*Foremost*), 8 fl. oz. 153
3.7% fat (*Sealtest*), 8 fl. oz. 157
dry, regular, 1 cup 643
dry, regular, 1 tbsp. 35
dry, instant, high-density (¼ cup to 1 cup water), 1 cup 527
dry, instant, low-density (4¼ oz. to 3⅔ cups water),
    1 cup 351
Milk beverages, flavored:
banana, canned (*Sego*), 10-fl.-oz. can 225
butterscotch, canned (*Sego*), 10-fl.-oz. can 225
cherry-vanilla, mix* (*Foremost* Instant Breakfast), 8 fl. oz. 290
chocolate:
    drink, .7% fat, dairy pack (*Foremost*), 8 fl. oz. 161

Prepared according to directions on container

drink, 2% fat, dairy pack (*Meadow Gold*), 8 fl. oz. 185
milk (*Foremost*), 1 cup 220
milk, dairy pack (*Sealtest*), 8 fl. oz. 200
milk, 3.3% fat, dairy pack (*Foremost*), 8 fl. oz. 218
milk, 3.3% fat, dairy pack (*Meadow Gold*), 8 fl. oz. ...200
milk, low-fat (*Foremost So-Lo* 1%), 1 cup 170
milk, low-fat (*Foremost So-Lo* 2%), 1 cup 190
milk, low-fat (*Foremost So-Lo* 1½%), 1 cup 160
milk, low-fat, dairy pack (*Hood*), 8 fl. oz. 160
milk, nonfat (*Foremost*), 1 cup ....,...140
canned (*Borden* Dutch Chocolate Drink), 7¾-fl.-oz. can ...200
canned (*Borden Frosted Shake*), 7½-fl. oz. can 270
canned (*Sego*), 10-fl. oz. can 225
canned (*Sego* Dutch and Very Chocolate), 10-fl.-oz. can ...225
mix* (*Carnation* Instant Breakfast), 8 fl. oz. 280
mix* (*Foremost* Instant Breakfast), 8 fl. oz. 290
mix* (*Pillsbury* Instant Breakfast), 8 fl. oz. 290
chocolate fudge:
  canned (*Borden Frosted Shake*), 7½-fl.-oz. can 270
  mix* (*Foremost* Instant Breakfast), 8 fl. oz. 290
chocolate malt:
  canned (*Sego*), 10 fl. oz. 225
  mix* (*Carnation* Instant Breakfast), 8 fl. oz. 280
  Mix* (*Pillsbury* Instant Breakfast), 8 fl. oz. 290
chocolate marshmallow, canned (*Sego*), 10-fl.-oz. can 225
cocoa, see "Chocolate drink mix, dry"
coffee:
  milk, low-fat dairy pack (*Hood*), 8 fl. oz. 160
  canned (*Borden Frosted Shake*), 7½-fl.-oz. can 270
  mix* (*Carnation* Instant Breakfast), 8 fl. oz. 280
  mix* (*Foremost* Instant Breakfast), 8 fl. oz. 290
strawberry:
  canned (*Borden Frosted Shake*), 7½-fl.-oz. can 270
  canned (*Sego*), 10-fl.-oz. can 225
  mix* (*Carnation* Instant Breakfast), 8 fl. oz. 280

Prepared according to directions on container

mix* (*Foremost* Instant Breakfast), 8 fl. oz. 290
mix* (*Pillsbury* Instant Breakfast), 8 fl. oz. 290
vanilla:
   canned (*Borden Frosted Shake*), 7½-fl.-oz. can 270
   canned (*Sego*), 10-fl.-oz. can 225
   canned (*Sego* Very Vanilla), 10-fl.-oz. can 225
   mix* (*Carnation* Instant Breakfast), 8 fl. oz. 280
   mix* (*Foremost* Instant Breakfast), 8 fl. oz. 290
   mix* (*Pillsbury* Instant Breakfast), 8 fl. oz. 290

Milk, goat's:
   whole, 1 cup 163

Milk, malted:
   beverage, 1 cup 244
   dry powder, 3 heaping tsp. (1 oz.) 116

Milk, reindeer:
   1 cup 580

Millet:
   whole-grain, 4 oz. 371

Minced roll sausage:
   (*Oscar Mayer*), 1-oz. slice 68

Mincemeat pie, see "Pies, frozen"

Mincemeat pie filling, canned:
   (*Borden None Such*), ⅓ cup 220
   (*Comstock*), ⅓ cup 150
   with brandy and rum (*Borden None Such*), ⅓ cup 220
   condensed (*Borden None Such*), ¼ pkg. 220

Mint flavored gin:
   (*DuBouchett*), 1 fl. oz. 70
   (*Old Mr. Boston*), 1 fl. oz. 100

Mint julep cocktail mix:
   instant (*Holland House*), 1 packet 67

Mints, see "Candy"

Mint sauce:
   (*Crosse & Blackwell*), 1 tbsp. 16

Miso, see "Soybeans, fermented"

Prepared according to directions on container

Mixed flavors fruit drink:
  canned (*Mott's "A.M."*), 6 fl. oz. 90
Mixed nuts, see "Nuts, mixed"
Mixed vegetables, see "Vegetables, mixed"
Molasses:
  first extraction (light):
    1 fl. oz. 103
  - 1 tbsp. 50
    (*Brer Rabbit*), 1 tbsp. 60
  second extraction (medium):
    1 tbsp. 46
    1 fl. oz. 95
  third extraction (blackstrap):
    1 tbsp. 43
    1 fl. oz. 87
  dark (*Brer Rabbit*), 1 tbsp. 53
  Barbados:
    1 tbsp. 54
    1 fl. oz. 111
Mortadella:
  4 oz. 357
  1 slice (4⅞" in diam., ³⁄₃₂" thick) 79
Moselle Bernkasteler wine:
  (*Dienhard & Co.*), 4 fl. oz. 92
Mostaccioli and meat sauce:
  frozen entree (*Banquet Buffet Suppers*), 32-oz. pkg. 814
Muffins:
  packaged:
    blueberry (*Howard Johnson's Toastees*), 1 piece 121
    blueberry (*Thomas' Toast-r-Cakes*), 1 piece 110
    bran (*Arnold Bran'nola*), 1 piece 160
    bran (*Thomas' Toast-r-Cakes*), 1 piece 120
    corn (*Howard Johnson's Toastees*), 1 piece 112
    corn (*Thomas'*), 1 piece 190
    corn (*Thomas' Toast-r-Cakes*), 1 piece 120
    English (*Arnold*), 1 piece 130
    English (*Home Pride*), 1 piece 140

English (*Monk's*), 1 piece 130
English (*Pepperidge Farm*), 1 piece 130
English (*Thomas'*), 1 piece 130
English (*Wonder*), 1 piece 130
English, apple granola (*Oroweat*), 1 piece 181
English, cinnamon-raisin (*Pepperidge Farm*), 1 piece . . .140
English, extra-sour (*Oroweat*), 1 piece 150
English, high-fiber (*Monk's*), 1 piece 120
English, honey-butter (*Oroweat*), 1 piece 151
English, honey-wheat (*Oroweat* Honey Wheat Berry),
    1 piece 152
English, onion (*Thomas'*), 1 piece 130
English, raisin (*Oroweat*), 1 piece 163
English, sourdough (*Oroweat*), 1 piece 143
English, wheat (*Home Pride*), 1 piece 140
orange (*Howard Johnson's Toastees*), 1 piece 127
raisin (*Arnold*), 1 piece 160
raisin (*Wonder* Raisin Rounds), 1 piece 150
sourdough (*Wonder*), 1 piece 130
frozen:
    blueberry (*Howard Johnson's Toastees*), 1 piece 121
    blueberry (*Morton*) 1½-oz. piece 110
    blueberry, rounds (*Morton*), 1.58-oz. piece 120
    corn (*Howard Johnson's Toastees*), 1 piece 112
    corn (*Morton*), 1½-oz. piece 130
    corn, rounds (*Morton*), 1⅔-oz. piece 130
    orange (*Howard Johnson's Toastees*), 1 piece 127
mix*:
    blueberry, wild (*Betty Crocker*), ¹⁄₁₂ of pkg. 120
    blueberry, wild (*Duncan Hines*), 1 piece 110
    corn (*Betty Crocker*), ¹⁄₁₂ of pkg. 160
    corn (*Dromedary*), 1 piece 130
    corn (*Flako*), 1 piece 140
Mullet (see also ''Sucker mullet''):
raw, whole, 1 lb. 351

*Prepared according to directions on container

raw, meat only, 4 oz. 166
Mulligan stew:
canned (*Dinty Moore's* Short Order), 7½-oz. can 227
Mung beans, see "Beans, mung" and "Bean sprouts"
Muscatel wine:
(*Gold Seal*), 2 fl. oz. 105
Mushroom crepe:
frozen (*Stouffer's*), 6¼-oz. pkg. 255
Mushroom gravy:
canned (*Franco-American*), 4 oz. 70
in jars (*Heinz*), ½ cup 50
mix*:
(*Durkee*), ½ cup 30
(*French's*), ½ cup 40
(*McCormick/Schilling*), ½ cup 40
Mushroom sauce mix:
dry (*Durkee* Simmer Sauce), 2-oz. pkg. 223
Mushroom steak sauce:
canned (*Dawn Fresh*), 4 oz. 36
Mushrooms:
fresh, raw, untrimmed, 1 lb. 123
fresh, raw, sliced, chopped or diced, 1 cup 20
canned:
with liquid, 8 oz. 38
with liquid, 1 cup 41
whole, sliced or pieces and stems (*Green Giant*), 2 oz. ...14
freeze-dried (*Mountain House*), ⅓ oz. dry 25
frozen, with butter sauce (*Green Giant*), 2 oz. 30
Mushrooms, cocktail:
(*Reese* Buttons), 4-oz. jar, drained 25
Muskellunge:
raw, whole, 1 lb. 242
raw, meat only, 4 oz. 124
Muskmelon, see "Canteloupe," "Casaba melon" and "Honeydew melon"

Prepared according to directions on container

Muskrat:
  roasted, 4 oz. 174
Mussels:
  Atlantic and Pacific:
    fresh, raw, in shell, 1 lb. 153
    fresh, raw, meat only, 4 oz. 108
    canned, meat only, 4 oz. drained 130
Mustard, prepared:
  (*French's* Medford), 1 tbsp. 16
  (*Grey Poupon*), 1 tbsp. 15
  brown:
    (*French's* Bold 'n Spicy), 1 tbsp. 16
    (*Heinz*), 1 tbsp. 11
  with horseradish (*French's*), 1 tbsp. 16
  hot (*Mister Mustard*), 1 tbsp. 11
  with onion (*French's*), 1 tbsp. 25
  yellow:
    (*French's*), 1 tbsp. 10
    (*Heinz*), 1 tbsp. 10
Mustard greens:
  fresh:
    raw, untrimmed, 1 lb. 98
    raw, trimmed, 4 oz. 35
    leaves, boiled, drained, 8 oz. 52
    leaves, boiled, drained, 1 cup 32
  frozen:
    chopped (*Birds Eye*), 3.3 oz. 20
    chopped (*Seabrook Farms*), 3.3 oz. 25
    chopped (*Southland*), 3.3 oz. 20
Mustard powder:
  ground (all brands), 1 tsp. 9
Mustard relish:
  (*Crosse & Blackwell* Chow Chow), 1 tbsp. 6
Mustard spinach (tendergreens):
  fresh, raw, 1 lb. 100
  fresh, boiled, drained, 8 oz. 37
  fresh, boiled, drained, 1 cup 29

N

Natal plums, see "Carissas"
Natto, see "Soybeans, fermented"
Near beer, see "Bear, near"
Nectarines, fresh:
   whole, 1 lb. 267
   whole, 1 nectarine (2½″ in diam.) 88
   pitted, 4 oz. 73
New England loaf:
   (*Hormel*), 1-oz. slice 55
New England sausage:
   (*Oscar Mayer New England*), .8-oz. slice 35
New Zealand spinach, fresh:
   raw, 1 lb. 86
   boiled, drained, 8 oz. 30
   boiled, drained, 1 cup 23
Newburg sauce:
   with sherry, canned (*Snow's*), 3½ oz. 100
Noodles:
   plain (all varieties):
      uncooked (*American Beauty*), 2 oz. 220
      uncooked (*Buitoni*), 2 oz. 220
      uncooked (*La Rosa*), 2 oz. 220
      uncooked (*Pennsylvania Dutch*), 2 oz. 210
      cooked, 1 cup 200
   mix*:
      beef flavor (*Oodles of Noodles*), 3-oz. pkg. 390

Prepared according to directions on container

and beef flavor sauce (*Lipton*), ½ cup 190
and beef flavor sauce (*Mug•O•Lunch*), 1 pouch 170
and beef flavor sauce (*Pennsylvania Dutch*), ½ cup 130
and butter and herb sauce (*Lipton*), ½ cup 180
and butter sauce (*Lipton*), ½ cup 190
and butter sauce (*Pennsylvania Dutch*), ½ cup 150
and cheese (*Kraft*), ⅔ cup 250
and cheese sauce (*Lipton*), ½ cup 200
and cheese sauce (*Pennsylvania Dutch*), ½ cup 150
and cheese sauce, with tuna (*Tuna Helper*), ⅕ pkg. 230
and chicken, with chicken flavor sauce
  (*Pennsylvania Dutch*), ½ cup 150
chicken flavor (*Kraft* Dinner), ¾ cup 240
chicken flavor (*Oodles of Noodles*), 3-oz. pkg. 150
and chicken flavor sauce (*Lipton*), ½ cup 190
creamy, and tuna, with tuna (*Tuna Helper*), ⅕ pkg. 280
dumpling, and tuna, with tuna (*Tuna Helper*), ⅕ pkg. 230
onion flavor (*Oodles of Noodles*), 3-oz. pkg. 390
Oriental, beef flavor (*Ramen Pride*), 3-oz. pkg. 396
Oriental, chicken flavor, (*Ramen Pride*), 3-oz. pkg. 401
Oriental, and sauce (*Mug•O•Lunch*), 1 pouch 190
Oriental flavor (*Oodles of Noodles*), 3-oz. pkg. 390
Parmesano (*Noodle-Roni*), ¾ cup 195
Pork flavor (*Oodles of Noodles*), 3-oz. pkg. 390
Romanoff (*Betty Crocker*), ¼ pkg. 230
Romanoff (*Noodle-Roni*), ½ cup 181
with sour cream and chive sauce (*Lipton*), ½ cup 190
Stroganoff (*Betty Crocker*), ¼ pkg. 230
Stoganoff, with meat (*Noodle-Roni*), ½ cup 120
Noodles and beef:
canned (*Hormel* Short Order), 7½-oz. can 229
canned, with sauce (*Heinz*), 8½-oz. can 171
frozen, with gravy (*Banquet Buffet Supper*), 32-oz. pkg. 754
Noodles and chicken:
canned (*Dinty Moore* Short Order), 7½-oz. can 205
canned, in gravy (*Heinz*), 8½-oz. can 186

Noodles and chicken dinner:
  frozen (*Swanson TV Brand*), 10¼-oz. pkg. 390
Noodles, chow mein, see "Chow mein noodles"
Noodles, rice:
  canned (*La Choy*), 1 oz., or ½ cup 130
Noodles Romanoff:
  frozen (*Stouffer's*), 12-oz. pkg. 510
Nut bread, see "Bread, sweet, mix"
Nutmeg:
  ground (all brands), 1 tsp. 11
Nuts, see individual listings
Nut and snack mix:
  (*Flavor Tree*), 1 oz. 160
Nuts, mixed:
  dry roasted (*Planters*), 1 oz. 160
  with peanuts (*Planters*), 1 oz. 180
  without peanuts (*Planters*), 1 oz. .180
  unsalted (*Planters*), 1 oz. 170

O

Oats and oatmeal, see "Cereals, cooked" and "Cereals, ready-to-eat"

Ocean perch, Atlantic (redfish):
  fresh:
    raw, whole, 1 lb. 124
    raw, meat only, 4 oz. 100
    breaded, fried, 4 oz. 258
    frozen, fillets, breaded, fried, reheated, 4 oz. 382
    frozen, fillets, breaded, fried, reheated,
      1 fillet (6¾″ × 1¾″ × ⅝″) 281

Ocean perch, Pacific:
  fresh, raw, whole, 1 lb. 116
  fresh, raw, meat only, 4 oz. 108
  frozen, fillets (*Taste O' Sea*), 16-oz. pkg. 400
  frozen, fillets, fried (*Mrs. Paul's*), 4 oz., or 2 fillets 250

Octopus:
  raw, 4 oz. 83

Oils, cooking or salad:
  corn, cottonseed, safflower, sesame, or soybean, 1 cup . .1,927
  corn, cottonseed, safflower, sesame, or soybean, 1 tbsp. 120
  olive or peanut, 1 cup 1,909
  olive or peanut, 1 tbsp. 119

Okra:
  fresh:
    raw, untrimmed 1 lb. 140
    raw, fully trimmed, 4 oz. 41
    raw, crosscut slices, 1 cup 36

boiled, drained, crosscut slices, 1 cup 46
boiled, drained, 10 pods (3″ × ⅝″) 31
boiled, drained, 4 oz. 33
frozen:
    whole (*Birds Eye*), 3.3 oz. ...:.....................30
    whole (*Hanover*), 3.2 oz. 35
    whole (*Seabrook Farms*), 3.3 oz. 35
    whole (*Southland*), 3.3 oz. 35
    cut (*Birds Eye*), 3.3 oz. 25
    cut (*Hanover*), 3.2 oz. 25
    cut (*Seabrook Farms*), 3.3 oz. 30
    cut (*Southland*), 3.3 oz. 25

Okra gumbo:
frozen (*Green Giant*), ½ cup 110

Old-fashioned cocktail mix:
bottled (*Holland House*), 1 fl. oz. 36

Old-fashioned loaf:
(*Eckrich*), 1-oz. slice 75
(*Oscar Mayer*), 1-oz. slice 65

Oleomargarine, see "Margarine"

Olive loaf:
(*Hormel*), 1-oz. slice 75
(*Oscar Mayer*), 1-oz. slice 65

Olive oil, see "Oils, cooking or salad"

Olives, pickled, canned or bottled, drained:
green, 2 oz. 66
green, Manzanilla (*Grandee*), 1 medium 4
green, Manzanilla, pimento-stuffed (*Grandee*), 1 queen-size ..14
ripe:
    Ascolano, pitted, 2 oz. 73
    Ascolano, pitted, sliced, 1 cup 174
    Manzanilla, pitted, 2 oz. 73
    Manzanilla, pitted, sliced, 1 cup 174
    Mission, pitted, 2 oz. 105
    Mission, pitted, sliced, 1 cup 248
    Sevillano, pitted, 2 oz. 53

Sevillano, pitted, sliced, 1 cup 126
salt-cured, Greek style, pitted, 2 oz. 193
salt-cured, Greek style, 10 medium 65
(*Lindsay*),1 large 5
(*Lindsay*), 1 extra-large 5
(*Lindsay*), 1 giant 8
(*Lindsay*), 1 jumbo 10
(*Lindsay*), 1 colossal 13
(*Lindsay*), 1 super-colossal 16
(*Lindsay*), 1 super-supreme 18

Omelets, see "Eggs, mix"

Onion dip:
(*Kraft* Ready-to-Serve), 1 oz. 50
French (*Kraft*), 2 tbsp. 50
French (*Kraft* Ready-to-Serve), 1 oz. 45
green (*Kraft*), 2 tbsp. 50
mix, toasted (*McCormick/Schilling*), 1¼ oz. 103

Onion flavor snack rings:
(*Funyuns*), 1 oz. 140
(*Old London*), 1 oz. 130
(*Wise*), 1 oz. 130

Onion flavoring
liquid (*Burton's*), ½ tsp. 21

Onion gravy:
in jars (*Heinz*), ½ cup 60
mix*:
  (*Durkee*), ½ cup 42
  (*French's*), ½ cup 50
  (*McCormick/Schilling*), ½ cup 51

Onion powder:
all brands, 1 tsp. 8

Onion rings, frozen:
fried (*Mrs. Paul's*), 2.5 oz. 150
fried (*Mrs. Paul's* Family), 3 oz. 180

---

*Prepared according to directions on container

fried (*Mrs. Paul's* Party-Pak), 4 oz. 240
fried (*Ore-Ida* Onion Ringers), 4 rings 147
Onion salt:
  (*French's*), 1 tsp. 6
Onions:
  mature, fresh:
    raw, untrimmed, 1 lb. 157
    raw, trimmed, 4 oz. 43
    raw, 1 medium onion (2½″ in diam.) 40
    raw, chopped, 1 cup 65
    raw, chopped or minced, 1 tbsp. .4
    raw, grated or ground, 1 cup 89
    raw, sliced, 1 cup 44
    boiled, halves, large, drained, 1 cup 52
    boiled, whole, large, drained, 1 cup 61
    boiled, pearl, drained, whole, 1 cup 54
  young green, fresh:
    bulb and entire top, untrimmed, 1 lb. 157
    bulb and entire top, trimmed, 1 lb. 163
    bulb and entire top, chopped or sliced, 1 cup 36
    bulb and entire top, chopped, 1 tbsp. 2
    bulb and white portion of top, 2 medium (4⅛″ long) 14
    bulb and white portion of top, chopped or sliced, 1 cup . .45
    bulb and white portion of top, chopped, 1 tbsp. 3
    tops only (green portion), chopped, 1 cup 27
    tops only (green portion), chopped, 1 tbsp. 2
  canned:
    boiled (*O & C*), 1 oz. 8
    french fried (*O & C*), 1 oz. 178
    in cream sauce (*O & C*), 1 oz. .143
  dehydrated:
    flakes, 1 cup 224
    instant (*French's* Salad Onions), 1 tbsp. 15
  frozen:
    whole, small (*Birds Eye*), 4 oz. 40
    chopped (*Birds Eye*), 1 oz. 8

chopped (*Ore-Ida*), ¼ cup 10
chopped (*Southland*), 1 oz. 10
in cheese flavor sauce (*Green Giant*), ½ cup 70
small, with cream sauce (*Birds Eye*), 3 oz. 100
Onions, cocktail:
sour (*Crosse & Blackwell*), 1 tbsp. 9
sour (*Heinz*), 1 onion ....tr.
Onions, spiced:
(*Heinz*), 1 onion 2
Onions, Welsh:
raw, untrimmed, 1 lb. 100
raw, trimmed, 4 oz. 39
Opossum:
roasted, meat only, 4 oz. 252
Orange-apricot drink, canned:
(*BC*), 6 fl. oz. 75
(*Musselman's* Breakfast Cocktail), 6 fl. oz. 75
Orange drink:
canned (*Bama*), 6 fl. oz. 90
canned (*Hi-C*), 6 fl. oz. 92
dairy pack (*Sealtest*), 6 fl. oz. 87
dairy pack (*Tropicana*), 6 fl. oz. 70
mix*:
(*Borden* Instant Breakfast Drink), 6 fl. oz. 90
(*Cramores*), 6 fl. oz. 68
(*Hi-C*), 6 fl. oz. 76
(*Kool-Aid*), 6 fl. oz. 68
(*Tang*), 6 fl. oz. 90
(*Wilson's* Instant Breakfast Drink), 4 fl. oz. 62
frozen*:
imitation juice (*Birds Eye Awake*), 6 fl. oz. 90
imitation juice (*Birds Eye Orange Plus*), 6 fl. oz. 100
imitation juice (*Bright & Early*), 6 fl. oz. 90

Prepared according to directions on container

Orange extract:
  (*Virginia Dare*), 1 tsp. 15
  pure (*Ehlers*), 1 tsp. 30
  imitation (*Durkee*), 1 tsp. 14
Orange flavored gin:
  (*DuBouchett*), 1 fl. oz. 67
  (*Old Mr. Boston*), 1 fl. oz. 76
Orange flavored vodka:
  (*Old Mr. Boston*), 1 fl. oz. 100
Orange-grapefruit juice:
  bottled (*Kraft*), 6 fl. oz. 80
  canned (*Del Monte*), 6 fl. oz. 80
  canned, sweetened (*Del Monte*), 6 fl. oz. 80
  frozen* (*Minute Maid*), 6 fl. oz. 76
Orange juice, fresh:
  all commercial varieties, 1 cup 112
  California, navels (winter oranges):
    1 cup 120
    juice from 1 medium orange (2⅞″ in diam.) 41
  California, Valencias (summer oranges):
    1 cup 117
    juice from 1 medium orange (2⅝″ in diam.) 37
  Florida, all commercial varieties, 1 cup 106
  Florida, early and mid-season (Hamlin, Parson Brown, etc.):
    1 cup 98
    juice from 1 medium orange (2¹¹⁄₁₆″ in diam.) 39
  Florida, late season (Valencias):
    1 cup 112
    juice from 1 medium orange (2¹¹⁄₁₆″ in diam.) 48
  Florida temple:
    1 cup 134
    juice from 1 medium orange (2⅞″ in diam.) 65
Orange juice, canned or bottled:
  (*Del Monte*), 6 fl. oz. 70
  (*Hood*), 6 fl. oz. 80

Prepared according to directions on container

(*Kraft*), 6 fl. oz. 80
(*Sunkist*), 6 fl. oz. 78
(*Texsun*), 6 fl. oz. 83
(*Tropicana*), 6 fl. oz. 83
sweetened (*Del Monte*), 6 fl. oz. 80

Orange juice, dehydrated:
crystals, dry, 1 oz. 108
crystals, prepared with water, 1 cup 114

Orange juice, frozen:
(*Minute Maid*), 6 fl. oz. 90
(*Snow Crop*), 6 fl. oz. 90
from concentrate (*Minute Maid*), 6 fl. oz. 83

Orange peel:
candied, 1 oz. 90

Orange-pineapple drink:
canned (*Hi-C*), 6 fl. oz. 94
canned (*Musselman's* Breakfast Cocktail), 6 fl. oz. 75

Orange-pineapple juice:
bottled (*Kraft*), 6 fl. oz. 80
canned (*Texsun*), 6 fl. oz. 89

Oranges, fresh:
California, navels (winter oranges):
whole, 1 lb. 157
whole, 1 medium orange (2⅞″ in diam.) 71
sections, with membranes, 1 cup 77
sections, without membranes, 1 cup 84
diced, 1 cup 107
sliced, peeled, 1 slice (2½″ in diam., ¼″ thick) 11
wedge, ¼ of medium orange 18
California, Valencia (summer oranges):
whole, 1 lb. 174
whole, 1 medium orange (2⅝″ in diam.) 62
sections, without membranes, 1 cup 92
diced, 1 cup 107
sliced, peeled, 1 slice (2″ in diam., ¼″ thick) 8
wedge, ¼ of medium orange 15

Florida, all commercial varieties:
  whole, 1 lb. 158
  whole, 1 medium orange (2¹¹⁄₁₆″ in diam.) 71
  sections, without membranes, 1 cup 87
  diced, 1 cup 99
  sliced, peeled, 1 slice (2″ in diam., ¼″ thick) 7
  wedge, ¼ of medium orange 18
Oranges, canned:
  sections, in juice (*Kraft*), ½ cup 60
  mandarin, solids and liquid, in syrup (*Del Monte*), 5½ oz. . . .100
Orangeade:
  frozen* (*Minute Maid*), 6 fl. oz. .94
  mix* (*Wyler's*), 6 fl. oz. 75
Oregano:
  ground (all brands), 1 tsp. 6
Orgeat syrup:
  (*Granier*), 1 tsp. 17
Oriental style vegetables, (see also specific listings):
  frozen (*Stokely-Van Camp* Vegetables Orient), 3.2 oz. 30
Oyster plant, see "Salsify"
Oyster stew, see "Soups, canned" and "Soups, frozen"
Oysters:
  raw:
    eastern, in shell, 1 lb. 30
    eastern, meat only, 8 oz. 150
    eastern, meat only, 1 cup 158
    eastern, meat only, 1 oz. 19
    Pacific and western, meat only, 8 oz. 207
    Pacific, meat only, 1 cup 218
  canned:
    eastern, 12-fl.-oz. can, drained 224
    (*High Sea*), 4 oz. 100
    whole (*Bumble Bee*), 1 cup 160
    Pacific, drained, 12-fl.-oz. can 309

*Prepared according to directions on container

P

Pancake syrup (maple flavored):
  (*Aunt Jemima*), 1 tbsp. 53
  (*Golden Griddle*), 1 tbsp. 50
  (*Happy Jack*), 1 tbsp. 50
  (*Karo*), 1 tbsp. 60
  (*Log Cabin* Country Kitchen), 1 tbsp. 50
  (*Smucker's*), 1 tbsp. 43
  buttered (*Log Cabin*), 1 tbsp. 54
  buttered (*Mrs. Butterworth's*), 1 tbsp. 53
  with honey (*Log Cabin* Maple Honey), 1 tbsp. 50
Pancakes:
  frozen (*Downyflake*), 1 pancake 80
  frozen, and sausages (*Swanson*), 6-oz. pkg. 500
  frozen batter:
    plain (*Aunt Jemima*), 4″ pancake .70
    blueberry (*Aunt Jemima*), 4″ pancake 68
    buttermilk (*Aunt Jemima*), 4″ pancake 71
  pancake and waffle mix*:
    plain (*Aunt Jemima* Complete), ⅓ cup 198
    plain (*Aunt Jemima* Complete), 4″ pancake 67
    plain (*Aunt Jemima* Original), ¼ cup 108
    plain (*Aunt Jemima* Original), 4″ pancake 73
    plain (*Hungry Jack* Complete), 4″ pancake 60
    plain (*Hungry Jack Extra Lights*), 4″ pancake 67
    plain (*Hungry Jack Panshakes*), 4″ pancake 83

Prepared according to directions on container

plain (*Log Cabin*), 4″ pancake 63
plain (*Log Cabin* Complete), 4″ pancake 60
blueberry (*Hungry Jack*), 4″ pancake 110
buckwheat (*Aunt Jemima*), ¼ cup 107
buckwheat (*Aunt Jemima*), 4″ pancake 67
buttermilk (*Aunt Jemima*), ⅓ cup 175
buttermilk (*Aunt Jemima*), 4″ pancake 100
buttermilk (*Aunt Jemima* Complete), ⅓ cup 236
buttermilk (*Aunt Jemima* Complete), 4″ pancake 80
buttermilk (*Betty Crocker*), ⅓ cup 170
buttermilk (*Betty Crocker*), 4″ pancake 93
buttermilk (*Betty Crocker* Complete),½ cup 210
buttermilk (*Betty Crocker* Complete), 4″ pancake 70
buttermilk (*Hungry Jack*), 4″ pancake 80
buttermilk (*Hungry Jack* Complete), 4″ pancake 60
buttermilk (*Log Cabin*), 4″ pancake 77
sweet grain (*Hungry Jack*), 4″ pancake 67
whole wheat (*Aunt Jemima*), ⅓ cup 142
whole wheat (*Aunt Jemima*), 4″ pancake 83

Pancreas, raw:
beef, fat, 4 oz. 358
beef, medium fat, 4 oz. 321
beef, lean, 4 oz. 160
calf, 4 oz. 183
hog, (hog sweetbreads), 4 oz. 274

Papaw, North American type, fresh:
whole, 1 lb. 289
whole, 1 papaw (3¾″ long, 2″ in diam.) 83
peeled and seeded, 4 oz. 96
peeled and seeded, mashed, 1 cup 213

Papayas, fresh:
whole, 1 lb. 119
whole, 1 papaya (5⅛″ long, 3½″ in diam.) 119
peeled and seeded, 4 oz. 44
peeled and seeded, cubed, 1 cup 55
peeled and seeded, mashed, 1 cup 90

Paprika:
  domestic, ground (all brands), 1 tsp. .7
Parisian style vegetables:
  frozen (*Birds Eye*), 3.3 oz. 30
  frozen (*Stokely-Van Camp*), 3.2 oz. 40
Parsley, fresh:
  whole, 1 lb. 200
  chopped, 1 cup 26
  chopped, 1 tbsp. 2
  1 sprig (about 2½″ long) 4
Parsley flakes:
  ground (all brands), 1 tsp. 4
Parsnips, fresh:
  whole, 1 lb. 293
  whole, boiled, drained, 1 large (9″ long; 2¼″ in diam.) . . .106
  whole, boiled, drained, 1 small (6″ long; 1⅛″ in diam.) 23
  boiled, drained, diced, 1 cup 102
  boiled, drained, mashed, 1 cup 139
Party mix:
  (*Flavor Tree*), 1 oz. 150
Passion fruit, see "Granadillas"
Pasta, plain (spaghetti, vermicelli, linguine, etc.):
  uncooked 8-oz. pkg. 838
  uncooked (*American Beauty*), 2 oz. 210
  uncooked (*Buitoni* High Protein Brand), 2 oz. 210
  uncooked (*Buitoni* Pasta Romana Brand), 2 oz. 210
  uncooked (*La Rosa*), 2 oz. 210
  cooked, firm stage (8–10 minutes), 1 cup 192
  cooked, tender stage (14–20 minutes), 1 cup 155
Pasta, prepared, see individual listings
Pasta sauce, see "Spaghetti sauce"
Pasta shells, frozen:
  baked, in sauce (*Buitoni*), 8 oz. .269
  stuffed, with beef and spinach, tomato sauce (*Stouffer's*),
    9-oz. pkg. 290
  stuffed, with cheese, meat sauce (*Stouffer's*), 9-oz. pkg. . . .320

stuffed, with chicken cheese sauce
   (*Stouffer's*), 9-oz. pkg. 400
stuffed, with ricotta cheese (*Ronzoni*), 15-oz. pkg. 750
stuffed, with sauce (*Buitoni*), 20-oz. pkg. 683
Pastini, dry:
carrot, 8 oz. 840
egg, 8 oz. 868
egg, 1 cup 651
spinach, 8 oz. 836
Pastrami:
(*Danola* Thin Sliced), 1 oz. 35
(*Eckrich* Slender Sliced), 1 slice 35
(*Vienna*), 3½ oz. 303
turkey, see "Turkey pastrami"
Pastry, see individual listings
Pastry sheet:
frozen (*Pepperidge Farm*), 1 sheet 570
Pastry shell:
(*Stella D'Oro*), 1 shell 149
Pâté, canned or in jars:
de foie gras, 1 oz. 131
de foie gras, 1 tbsp. 60
de foie gras, 1 tsp. 18
liver (*Hormel*), 1 tbsp. 33
liver (*Sell's*), 1 tbsp. 45
liver, with herbs (*Le Parfait*), 1 oz. 73
liver, with truffles (*Le Parfait*), 1 oz. 73
Patty shell:
frozen (*Pepperidge Farm*), 1 shell 240
Peach brandy:
(*Bols*), 1 fl. oz. 100
(*DuBouchett*), 1 fl. oz. 88
(*Garnier*), 1 fl. oz. 86
(*Hiram Walker*), 1 fl. oz. 88
(*Old Mr. Boston*—70 proof), 1 fl. oz. 100
(*Old Mr. Boston* Connoisseur—42 proof), 1 fl. oz. 75

Peach butter:
  (*Smucker's*), 1 tbsp. 45
Peach drink:
  canned (*Hi-C*), 6 fl. oz. 90
Peach flavored bourbon:
  (*Old Mr. Boston*), 1 fl. oz. 100
Peach liqueur:
  (*Bols*), 1 fl. oz. 96
  (*Dolfi*), 1 fl. oz. 103
  (*DuBouchett*), 1 fl. oz. 67
  (*Hiram Walker*), 1 fl. oz. 79
Peach nectar, canned:
  (*Del Monte*), 6 fl. oz. 100
  (*Heart's Delight*), 6 fl. oz. 100
Peach pie, see "Pies, frozen" and "Pies, snack"
Peach pie filling:
  canned (*Comstock*), ⅓ cup 100
Peach turnover:
  frozen (*Pepperidge Farm*), 1 piece 320
Peaches:
  fresh:
    whole, 1 lb. 150
    peeled, 1 peach (2¾" in diam.) 58
    peeled, 1 peach (2½" in diam.) 38
    pared, 1 peach (2¾" in diam.) 51
    pared, 1 peach (2½" in diam.) 33
    pared, diced, 1 cup 70
    pared, sliced, 1 cup 65
  canned:
    diced, with liquid (*Del Monte Fruit Cup*), 5-oz. can 110
    in water, with liquid, 8 oz. 70
    in water, with liquid, halves or slices, 1 cup 76
    in water, with liquid, slices (*Libby's*), ½ cup ...29
    in water, 1 peach half and 2 tbsp. liquid 28
    in juice, with liquid, 8 oz. 102
    in juice, 2 peach halves and 2 tbsp. juice 45

in syrup, halves or slices (*Del Monte*), ½ cup 85
in syrup, halves with liquid (*Libby's*), ½ cup 95
in syrup, halves with liquid (*Stokely-Van Camp*), ½ cup ..95
in syrup, slices with liquid (*Libby's*), ½ cup 92
in syrup, slices with liquid (*Stokely-Van Camp*), ½ cup ..90
in syrup, spiced, with liquid (*Del Monte*), 7¼ oz. 150
dehydrated (nuggets):
   uncooked, 8 oz. 771
   uncooked, 1 cup 340
   cooked, sweetened, with liquid, 8 oz. 275
   cooked, sweetened, with liquid, 1 cup 351
dried:
   (*Del Monte*), 1 oz. 70
   (*Sunsweet*), ½ cup 216
   freeze-dried (*Mountain House*), ½ cup 100
   halves, uncooked, 8 oz. 594
   halves, uncooked, 1 cup 419
   halves, uncooked, 10 large halves 380
   halves, cooked, sweetened, with liquid, 8 oz. 270
   halves, cooked, sweetened, with liquid, 1 cup 321
   halves, cooked, unsweetened, with liquid, 8 oz. 186
   halves, cooked, unsweetened, with liquid, 1 cup 205
frozen, sliced, sweetened, thawed, 1 cup 220
frozen (*Birds Eye* Quick Thaw), 5 oz. 130

Peanut butter:
creamy or smooth:
   (*Bama*), 1 tbsp. 100
   (*Jif*), 1 tbsp. 95
   (*Peter Pan*), 1 tbsp. 95
   (*Planters*), 1 tbsp. 95
   (*Skippy/Skippy* Old Fashioned), 1 tbsp. 95
   (*Smucker's*), 1 tbsp. 90
   (*Teddie*), 1 tbsp. 100
   (*Velvet*), 1 tbsp. 97
crunchy or chunk:
   (*Bama*), 1 tbsp. 100

(*Jif*), 1 tbsp. 95
(*Peter Pan*), 1 tbsp. 95
(*Planters*), 1 tbsp. 95
(*Skippy/Skippy Old Fashioned*), 1 tbsp. 95
(*Smucker's*), 1 tbsp. 90
natural (*Elam's*), 1 tbsp. 102
natural (*Smucker's*), 1 tbsp. 103
Peanut butter caramel dessert topping:
(*Smucker's*), 1 tbsp. 75
Peanut butter with grape jelly:
(*Smucker's Goober Grape*), ½ oz. 63
Peanut crunch:
bar (*Sahadi*), ¾-oz. bar 110
in jars (*Sahadi*), 1.2-oz. piece 170
Peanut flour, defatted:
8 oz. 842
1 cup 223
Peanut oil, see "Oils, cooking or salad"
Peanut spread:
4 oz. 685
1 tbsp. 84
Peanuts:
raw, shelled, 4 oz. 640
chocolate-coated, see "Candy"
cocktail (*Planters*), 1 oz. 170
dry-roasted (*Flavor House*), 1 oz. 180
dry-roasted (*Planters*), 1 oz. 160
old-fashioned (*Planters*), 1 oz. 170
redskin, Virginia (*Planters*), 1 oz. 170
roasted, in shell, 1 lb. 1,769
roasted, in shell, 10 peanuts 105
roasted, shelled, 4 oz. 660
roasted, shelled, halves, 1 cup 842
roasted, shelled, chopped, 1 cup 838
roasted, shelled, chopped, 1 tbsp. 52
salted, in shell (*Frito-Lay's*), 1 oz. 160

salted (*Frito-Lay's*), 1 oz. 170
Spanish (*Frito-Lay's*), 1 oz. 170
Spanish (*Planters*), 1 oz. 170
Spanish, dry-roasted (*Planters*), 1 oz. 160
unsalted (*Planters*), 1 oz. 170
Pea pods, Chinese:
raw, 1 lb. 228
frozen (*La Choy*), ½ pkg. 35
Pear-apple juice:
(*Tree Top*), 6 fl. oz. 75
Pear-grape juice:
(*Tree Top*), 6 fl. oz. 83
Pear nectar, canned:
(*Del Monte*), 6 fl. oz. 110
(*Heart's Delight*), 6 fl. oz. 100
Pears:
fresh:
whole, 1 lb. 252
sliced or cubed, 1 cup 101
Bartlett, whole, 1 pear (3½″ long, 2½″ in diam.) 100
bosc, whole, 1 pear (3¼″ long, 2½″ in diam.) 86
D'Anjou, whole, 1 pear (3″ long, 3″ in diam.) 122
canned:
in water, with liquid, 8 oz. 73
in water, with liquid, 1 cup 78
in water, 1 pear half and 1 tbsp. liquid 14
in juice, with liquid, 8 oz. 105
in heavy syrup, with liquid, 8 oz. 173
in heavy syrup, with liquid, 1 cup 194
in heavy syrup, 1 pear half and 1 tbsp. liquid 36
Bartlett, in water, with liquid (*Libby's*), ½ cup 36
Bartlett, in syrup, with liquid (*Libby's*), ½ cup 94
Bartlett, in syrup, with liquid (*Del Monte*), ½ cup 80
Bartlett, in syrup, halves, with liquid
(*Stokely-Van Camp*), ½ cup 105

Bartlett, in syrup, slices, with liquid
   (*Stokely-Van Camp*), ½ cup 100
dried:
   uncooked, halves, 8 oz. 608
   uncooked, halves, 1 cup 482
   uncooked, 10 pear halves 469
   cooked, sweetened, halves, 8 oz. 343
   cooked, sweetened, halves, 1 cup 423
   cooked, unsweetened, halves, with liquid, 8 oz. 286
   cooked, unsweetened, halves, with liquid, 1 cup 321
   (*Del Monte*), 1 oz. 75
   (*Sunsweet*), ½ cup 208
   freeze-dried (*Mountain House*), 1 oz. 100
Pears, candied:
1 oz. 86
Pears, prickly, see "Prickly pears"
Peas, black-eyed, see "Cowpeas"
Peas, crowder:
frozen (*Southland*), 3.2 oz. 120
Peas, field:
frozen, with snap peas (*Southland*), 3.3 oz. 120
Peas, green, immature:
fresh:
   raw, in pods, 1 lb. 145
   raw, shelled, 8 oz. 191
   raw, shelled, 1 cup 122
   boiled, drained, 8 oz. 160
   boiled, drained, 1 cup 114
canned (Alaska—early, or June peas):
   (*Del Monte*), ½ cup 55
   (*Stokely-Van Camp*), ½ cup 60
   small (*April Showers*), ½ cup 60
   small (*Kounty Kist/Lindy*), ½ cup 70
   small (*Le Sueur*), ½ cup 55
   small (*Minnesota Valley*), ½ cup 55
   with onions (*Green Giant*), ½ cup 60

canned (sweet—sweet wrinkled or sugar peas):
  (*Green Giant*), ½ cup 55
  (*Kounty Kist/Lindy*), ½ cup 65
  (*Stokely-Van Camp*), ½ cup 60
  small (*Del Monte*), ½ cup 50
  small (*Green Giant Sweetlets*), ½ cup 50
  small (*Le Sueur*), ½ cup 50
  with onions (*Green Giant*), ½ cup 55
canned:
  (*Libby's*), ½ cup 60
  puree (*Cellu*), ½ cup 70
  seasoned (*Del Monte*), ½ cup 60
  and carrots, see "Peas and carrots"
frozen:
  (*Kounty Kist/Lindy*), ½ cup 60
  (*Seabrook Farms*), 3.3 oz. 80
  (*Stokely-Van Camp*), 3.3 oz. 70
  in butter sauce (*Le Sueur*), ½ cup 75
  in cream sauce (*Birds Eye*), 2.6 oz. 130
  early, small (*Green Giant*), ½ cup 50
  early, in butter sauce (*Le Sueur*), ½ cup 75
  small (*Birds Eye* Tender Tiny Peas), 3.3 oz. 60
  small (*Hanover* Petit Pois), 3.2 oz. 65
  small (*Seabrook Farms* Petite), 3.3 oz. 60
  sweet (*Birds Eye*), 3.3 oz. 80
  sweet, in butter sauce (*Green Giant*), ½ cup 75
  and carrots, see "Peas and carrots"
  and cauliflower, with cream sauce (*Birds Eye*), 3.3 oz. . . .120
  and onions and carrots, in butter sauce
    (*Le Sueur*), ½ cup 80
  pea pods and water chestnuts, in sauce (*Le Sueur*), ½ cup . . .90
  and pearl onions (*Birds Eye*), 3.3 oz. 70
  pea shells, and corn (*Birds Eye* Blue Ribbon), 3.3 oz. . . .130
  pea shells and mushrooms (*Birds Eye* Blue Ribbon),
    3.3 oz. 130
  and potatoes, in cream sauce (*Birds Eye*), 2.6 oz. 140
  with sliced mushrooms (*Birds Eye*), 3.3 oz. 70

Peas, mature seeds, dry:
   whole, uncooked, 8 oz. 771
   whole, uncooked, 1 cup 680
   split, without seed coat, uncooked, 8 oz. 790
   split, without seed coat, uncooked, 1 cup 696
   split, without seed coat, cooked, 8 oz. 261
   split, without seed coat, cooked, 1 cup 230
Peas and carrots:
   canned:
     (*Del Monte*), ½ cup 50
     (*Libby's*), ½ cup 52
     (*Stokely-Van Camp*), ½ cup 50
   frozen:
     (*Birds Eye*), 3.3 oz. 60
     (*Kounty Kist/Lindy*), ½ cup 45
     (*Stokely-Van Camp*), 3.3 oz. 50
Pea soup, see "Soup, canned" "Soup, frozen" and "Soup
mix"
Pecan pie, see "Pies, frozen" and "Pies, snack"
Pecans:
   in shell, 1 lb. 1,652
   in shell, 10 oversize nuts 299
   in shell, 10 extra-large nuts 277
   in shell, 10 large nuts 236
   shelled, 1 lb. 3,116
   shelled, 1 oz. 195
   shelled, 1 cup 742
   shelled, 10 mammoth nuts 124
   shelled, 10 jumbo nuts 96
   shelled, 10 large nuts 62
   shelled, chopped, 1 cup 811
   shelled, chopped, 1 tbsp. 52
   shelled, ground, 1 cup 653
   dry-roasted (*Planters*), 1 oz. 190
Pecans, in syrup, dessert topping:
   (*Smucker's*), 1 tbsp. 65

Pepper:
black, ground (all brands), 1 tsp. 9
chili, ground (all brands), 1 tsp. 9
red, ground (all brands), 1 tsp. 9
white, ground (all brands), 1 tsp. 9
seasoned (*French's*), 1 tsp. 8
seasoned (*Lawry's*), 1 tsp. 8
Pepper, hot chili, green (immature):
raw, whole, 1 lb. 123
raw, without seeds 42
canned, pods, with liquid, 4 oz. 28
canned, whole (*Old El Paso*), 4-oz. can 24
chili sauce, canned, 4 oz. 23
chili sauce, canned, 1 cup 49
Pepper, hot chili, red (mature):
raw, whole, 1 lb. 405
raw, pods with seeds, 4 oz. 105
raw, pods, without seeds, 4 oz. 74
dried pods, 1 oz. 91
dried pods, 1 tbsp. 26
chili sauce, canned, 4 oz. 24
chili sauce, canned, 1 cup 51
powder, see "Chili powder"
Pepper, jalapeño:
whole, canned (*Old El Paso*), 10-oz. can 90
Pepper Oriental:
canned:
(*Chun King*—Divider Pak), ¼ of pkg. 70
beef (*La Choy*), ¾ cup 90
beef (*La Choy*—Bi-Pack), ¾ cup 70
frozen:
beef (*Chung King* Pouched Entree), ½ of pkg. 80
steak (*Chun King* Stir Fry), ⅕ of pkg. 185
steak, with rice (*Stouffer's*), 10½-oz. pkg. 350
Pepper Oriental dinner:
canned, steak (*La Choy* Dinner), ¾ cup 220

frozen (*Chun King*), 1 dinner 310
frozen, beef (*Chun King*), 11-oz. pkg. 310
frozen, beef (*La Choy*), 1 dinner 250
Peppers, stuffed:
canned (*Joan of Arc*), ½ cup 102
green, frozen, in creole sauce
  (*Green Giant* Baked Entree), 7-oz. pkg. 200
green, frozen, with beef, in tomato sauce (*Stouffer's*),
  15½-oz. pkg. 450
Peppers, sweet, green:
fresh:
  raw, whole, 1 lb. 82
  raw, cored and seeded, 4 oz. 25
  raw, 1 pepper fancy grade (3¾" long, 3" in diam.) 36
  raw, 1 pepper No. 1 grade (2¾" long, 2½" in diam.) 16
  raw, chopped or diced, 1 cup 33
  raw, cut in strips, 1 cup 22
  raw, sliced, 1 cup 18
  raw, 1 ring (3" in diam., ¼" thick) 2
  boiled, drained, 1 pepper fancy grade
    (3¾" long, 3" in diam.) 29
  boiled, drained, 1 pepper No. 1 grade
    (2¾" long, 2½" in diam.) 13
  boiled, drained, strips, 1 cup 24
  boiled, drained, 4 oz. 21
frozen:
  diced (*Southland*), 2 oz. 10
  and onions (*Southland*), 2 oz. 15
  red and green, see "Peppers, sweet, red"
Peppers, sweet, red:
fresh:
  raw, whole, 1 lb. 112
  raw, cored and seeded, 4 oz. 35
  raw, 1 pepper fancy grade (3¾" long, 3" in diam.) 51
  raw, 1 pepper No. 1 grade (2¾" long, 2½" in diam.) 23
  raw, chopped or diced, 1 cup 47

raw, cut in strips, 1 cup 31
raw, 1 ring (3″ in diam., ¼″ thick) 3
canned, see "Pimentos"
frozen, red and green, cut (*Southland*), 2 oz. 15
frozen, red and green, and onions (*Southland*), 2 oz. 20
Peppered loaf:
(*Oscar Mayer*), 1-oz. slice 40
Peppermint extract:
pure (*Burton's*), 1 tsp. 12
pure (*Ehlers*), 1 tsp. 24
imitation (*Durkee*), 1 tsp. 15
Peppermint flavored vodka:
(*Old Mr. Boston*), 1 fl. oz. 90
Peppermint schnapps:
(*DuBouchett*—48 proof), 1 fl. oz. 70
(*DuBouchett*—60 proof), 1 fl. oz. 85
(*Garnier*), 1 fl. oz. 83
(*Hiram Walker*), 1 fl. oz. 80
(*Old Mr. Boston*—60 proof), 1 fl. oz. 78
(*Old Mr. Boston* Connoisseur—42 proof), 1 fl. oz. 60
Pepperoni:
(*Hormel*), 1 oz. 150
(*Swift*), 1 oz. 150
Pepperoni pizza, see "Pizza, frozen"
Perch:
raw:
white, whole, 1 lb. 193
white, meat only, 4 oz. 134
yellow, whole, 1 lb. 161
yellow, meat only, 4 oz. 103
frozen, batter-fried (*Van de Kamp's*), 4¾ oz., or 2 pieces 290
frozen, breaded (*Taste O' Sea*), 1 portion 100
Perch, ocean, see "Ocean perch"
Perch dinner:
frozen, fried (*Taste O' Sea*), 9-oz. pkg. 400

Persimmons, fresh:
  Japanese, or kaki, with seeds, 1 lb. .286
  Japanese, or kaki, seedless, whole, 1 lb. 293
  Japanese, or kaki, seedless, trimmed, 4 oz. 87
  Japanese, or kaki, seedless, 1 average (2½″ in diam.) 129
  native, whole, 1 lb. 472
  native, trimmed and seeded, 4 oz. 144
  native, 1 average 31
(*Peter Heering*) liqueur:
  1 fl. oz. 80
Pheasant, raw:
  whole, ready to cook, 1 lb. 596
  meat only, 4 oz. 184
Piccalilli relish:
  (*Crosse & Blackwell*), 1 tbsp. 26
  green tomato (*Heinz*), 1 tbsp. 19
Pickerel, chain, raw:
  whole, 1 lb. 194
  meat only, 4 oz. 95
Pickle loaf:
  (*Eckrich*), 1-oz. slice 85
  (*Eckrich Smorgas Pac*), 1 slice 85
  (*Hormel*), 1-oz. slice 71
  beef (*Eckrich Smorgas Pac*), 1 slice 65
Pickle and pimento loaf:
  (*Oscar Mayer*), 1-oz. slice 65
Pickle relish:
  sour, 4 oz. 22
  sour, 1 tbsp. 3
  sweet:
    4 oz. 132
    1 cup 338
    1 tbsp. 21
    (*Crosse & Blackwell*), 1 tbsp. .26
    (*Heinz*), 1 tbsp. 20

Pickles, chowchow (with cauliflower):
sour, 4 oz. 33
sour, 1 cup 70
sweet, 4 oz. 132
sweet, 1 cup 284
Pickles, cucumber:
dill:
 whole (*Bond's Flavor-Pack* Dills), 1 pickle 1
 whole (*Bond's Fresh-Pack* Dills), 1 pickle 2
 whole (*Bond's Fresh-Pack* Kosher Dills), 1 pickle 2
 whole (*Claussen* Kosher), 1 pickle 7
 whole (*Heinz* Fresh Kosher Baby Dills), 1 pickle 2
 whole (*Heinz* Fresh Kosher Dills), 1 pickle 5
 whole (*Heinz* Genuine Dills), 1 pickle 10
 whole (*Heinz* Processed Dills), 1 pickle 2
 whole (*L & S* Dills), 1 pickle 1
 whole (*L & S* Fresh-Pack Kosher Dills), 1 pickle 2
 spears (*Bond's* Fresh-Pack Dills), 1 piece 2
 spears (*Bond's* Fresh-Pack Kosher Dills), 1 piece 2
 slices (*Crosse & Blackwell* Kosher Dills), 1 tbsp. 2
 slices (*Heinz* Hamburger), 3 slices .1
fresh, bread and butter:
 8 oz. 166
 2 crosscut slices (1½″ in diam., ¼″ thick) 11
 crosscut slices, 1 cup 124
sour:
 8 oz. 23
 1 large (4″ long, 1¾″ in diam.) 14
 1 medium (3¾″ long, 1¼″ in diam.) 7
 whole (*Heinz* Sour Gherkins), 1 pickle 4
sweet:
 whole (*Bond's* Gherkins), 1 pickle 19
 whole (*Heinz* Gherkins), 1 pickle 20
 whole (*Heinz* Midget Gherkins), 1 pickle 5
 whole (*Heinz* Sweet Pickles), 1 pickle 40
 whole (*L & S* Sweet Pickles), 1 pickle 19

chopped, see ''Pickle relish''
pieces (*Heinz* Mixed), 3 pieces 23
slices (*Crosse & Blackwell* Fresh Cucumber Slices),
   1 tbsp. 15
slices (*Crosse & Blackwell* Sweet Chips), 1 tbsp. 17
slices (*Fannings* Bread & Butter Pickles), 1 oz. 13
slices (*Heinz* Candied Krink-L-Chips), 3 pieces 33
slices (*Heinz* Fresh Cucumber Slices), 3 pieces 12
slices (*Heinz* Sweet Pickle Chips), 3 pieces 15
sliced lengthwise, 1 spear (4¼″ long) 29
spears (*Crosse & Blackwell* Fresh Cucumber Spears),
   1 piece 28
spears (*Heinz* Sweet Pickle Spears), 1 piece 16
sticks (*Heinz* Sweet Pickle Sticks), 1 piece 16
strips (*Heinz* Candied Dill Strips), 1 piece 30
and sour (*Claussen*), 1 slice 3
Pickled herring, see ''Herring, pickled''
Picnic loaf:
  (*Oscar Mayer*), 1-oz. slice 65
Pie crust:
  frozen:
    (*Mrs. Smith's*), ⅙ of 8″ crust 129
    (*Mrs. Smith's*), ⅙ of 9″ crust 233
    deep bottom crust (*Pepperidge Farm*), ⅙ of crust 172
    shallow bottom crust (*Pepperidge Farm*), ⅙ of crust 147
    top crust (*Pepperidge Farm*), ⅙ of crust 127
  mix*:
    made with water, 11.3 oz.
      (yield from 10-oz. pkg. mix) 1,485
    made with water, 9″ shell 675
    (*Betty Crocker*), ¹⁄₁₆ of pkg. 120
    (*Flako*), ⅙ of 9″ crust 260
    (*Pillsbury*), ⅙ of 2-crust pie 290
    sticks (*Betty Crocker*), ⅛ of stick 120
    sticks (*Pillsbury*), ⅙ of 2-crust pie 290

*Prepared according to directions on container

Pie fillings, see individual listings and "Pudding mix"
Pie tarts, see individual listings
Pies, frozen (see also "Pies, snack"):
  apple:
    (*Banquet*), ⅙ of 20-oz. pie 240
    (*Morton*), ⅙ of 24-oz. pie 290
    (*Mrs. Smith's*), ⅙ of 26-oz. pie 295
    (*Sara Lee*), ⅙ of 31-oz. pie 421
    Dutch apple (*Mrs. Smith's*), ⅙ of 26-oz. pie 312
    Dutch apple (*Sara Lee*), ⅙ of 30-oz. pie 391
    lattice crust (*Christopher Edwards* Bak'd For You),
      ⅙ of 38-oz. pie 528
    natural juice (*Mrs. Smith's*), ⅙ of 26-oz. pie 477
    tart apple (*Mrs. Smith's*), ⅙ of 26-oz. pie 250
  banana cream:
    (*Banquet*), ⅙ of 14-oz. pie 172
    (*Morton*), ⅙ of 14-oz. pie 160
    (*Mrs. Smith's Light*), ⅙ of 14-oz. pie 220
  blueberry:
    (*Banquet*), ⅙ of 20-oz. pie 253
    (*Morton*), ⅙ of 24-oz. pie 280
    (*Mrs. Smith's*), ⅙ of 26-oz. pie 292
    (*Sara Lee*), ⅙ of 31-oz. pie 404
    natural juice (*Mrs. Smith's*), ⅙ of 37-oz. pie 404
  Boston cream (*Mrs. Smith's*), ⅙ of 20-oz. pie 327
  Boston cream cake, see "Cakes, frozen"
  cheesecake:
    plain (*Sara Lee*), ⅙ of 17-oz. cake 240
    plain (*Sara Lee*—small), ⅓ of 10-oz. cake 287
    cherry (*Sara Lee*), ⅙ of 19-oz. cake 214
    French, plain (*Sara Lee*), ⅛ of 23½-oz. cake 274
    French, strawberry (*Sara Lee*), ⅛ of 26-oz. cake 258
    strawberry (*Sara Lee*) ⅙ of 19-oz. cake 214
  cherry:
    (*Banquet*), ⅙ of 20-oz. pie 228
    (*Morton*), ⅙ of 24-oz. pie 300
    (*Mrs. Smith's*), ⅙ of 26-oz. pie 312

(*Sara Lee*), ⅙ of 31-oz. pie 385
natural juice (*Mrs. Smith's*), ⅙ of 37-oz. pie 478
chocolate cream:
  (*Banquet*), ⅙ of 14-oz. pie 178
  (*Morton*), ⅙ of 14-oz. pie 180
  (*Mrs. Smith's* Light), ⅙ of 14-oz. pie 250
  Bavarian (*Sara Lee*), ⅙ of 22½-oz. pie 380
  meringue, condensed (*Christopher Edwards*),
    ⅙ of 38-oz. pie 485
coconut:
  cream (*Banquet*), ⅙ of 14-oz. pie 174
  cream (*Morton*), ⅙ of 14-oz. pie 170
  cream (*Mrs. Smith's* Light), ⅙ of 14-oz. pie 230
  custard (*Banquet*), ⅙ of 20-oz. pie 203
  custard (*Mrs. Smith's*), ⅙ of 25-oz. pie 265
custard, egg (*Mrs. Smith's*), ⅙ of 25-oz. pie 243
lemon:
  (*Mrs. Smith's*), ⅙ of 26-oz. pie 343
  cream (*Banquet*), ⅙ of 14-oz. pie 172
  cream (*Morton*), ⅙ of 14-oz. pie 160
  krunch (*Mrs. Smith's*), ⅙ of 26-oz. pie 380
  meringue (*Mrs. Smith's*), ⅙ of 20-oz. pie 260
  meringue, condensed (*Christopher Edwards*),
    ⅙ of 34-oz. pie 504
  yogurt (*Mrs. Smith's*), ⅙ of 16-oz. pie 200
mincemeat:
  (*Banquet*), ⅙ of 20-oz. pie 252
  (*Morton*), ⅙ of 24-oz. pie 310
  (*Mrs. Smith's*), ⅙ of 26-oz. pie 333
peach:
  (*Banquet*), ⅙ of 20-oz. pie 219
  (*Morton*), ⅙ of 24-oz. pie 280
  (*Mrs. Smith's*), ⅙ of 26-oz. pie 298
  (*Sara Lee*), ⅙ of 31-oz. pie 432
  natural juice (*Mrs. Smith's*), ⅙ of 37-oz. pie 462
Neapolitan cream (*Morton*), ⅙ of 16-oz. pie 190

pecan:
  (*Mrs. Smith's*), ⅙ of 24-oz. pie .430
  southern (*Christopher Edwards* Bak'd For You),
    ⅙ of 32-oz. pie 597
pineapple (*Mrs. Smith's*), ⅙ of 26-oz. pie 300
pumpkin:
  (*Banquet*), ⅙ of 20-oz. pie 206
  (*Morton*), ⅙ of 24-oz. pie 230
  (*Mrs. Smith's*), ⅙ of 25-oz. pie 240
  (*Sara Lee*), ⅙ of 45-oz. pie 473
strawberry:
  cream (*Banquet*), ⅙ of 14-oz. pie 169
  cream (*Morton*), ⅙ of 16-oz. pie 180
  yogurt (*Mrs. Smith's*), ⅙ of 16-oz. pie 200
strawberry-rhubarb:
  (*Mrs. Smith's*), ⅙ of 26-oz. pie 315
  natural juice (*Mrs. Smith's*), ⅙ of 37-oz. pie 448
Pies, mix*:
banana cream (*Jell-O*), ⅙ of 8″ pie, without crust 110
Boston cream (*Betty Crocker*), ⅛ pie or pkg. 260
cheesecake:
  (*Jell-O*), ⅛ of 8″ pie 300
  (*Royal*), ⅛ of pie or pkg. 230
  creamy (*Pillsbury* No Bake), ⅙ of pie or pkg. 410
chocolate cream (*Pillsbury* No Bake), ⅙ of pie or pkg. . . .410
coconut cream (*Jell-O*), ⅙ of 8″ pie, without crust 110
lemon (*Jell-O*), ⅙ of 9″ pie, without crust 180
lemon chiffon (*Pillsbury* No Bake), ⅙ of pie or pkg. 330
vanilla marble (*Pillsbury* No Bake), ⅙ of pie or pkg. 390
Pies, snack:
apple:
  (*Drake's*), 1 pie 230
  (*Hostess*), 4½-oz. piece 400
  (*Tastykake*), 4-oz. pkg. 348
  French (*Tastykake*), 4¼-oz. pkg. 405

*Prepared according to directions on container

berry (*Hostess*), 4½-oz. piece 400
blueberry (*Hostess*), 4½-oz. piece 390
blueberry (*Tastykake*), 4-oz. pkg. 366
cherry:
   (*Drake's*), 1 pie 230
   (*Hostess*), 4½-oz. piece 420
   (*Tastykake*), 4-oz. pkg. 381
lemon:
   (*Drake's*), 2-oz. piece 200
   (*Hostess*), 4½-oz. piece 420
   (*Tastykake*), 4-oz. pkg. 370
peach (*Hostess*), 4½-oz. piece 400
peach (*Tastykake*), 4-oz. pkg. 349
pecan (*Frito-Lay's*), 3-oz. pkg. 350

Pies, snack, frozen:
apple (*Morton*), 8-oz. piece 590
apple, Dutch (*Morton*), 7¾-oz. piece 600
banana cream (*Morton*), 3½-oz. piece 250
blueberry (*Morton*), 8-oz. piece 580
cheesecake:
   cherry (*Morton*), 6-oz. piece 460
   cream (*Morton*), 6-oz. piece 480
   pineapple (*Morton*), 6-oz. piece 460
   strawberry (*Morton*), 6-oz. piece 470
cherry (*Morton*), 8-oz. piece 590
chocolate cream (*Morton*), 3½-oz. piece 270
coconut cream (*Morton*), 3½-oz. piece 270
coconut custard (*Morton*), 6½-oz. piece 370
lemon cream (*Morton*), 3½-oz. piece 250
peach (*Morton*), 8-oz. piece 590

Pigeon peas:
raw, immature seeds in pods, 1 lb. 207
dry, 4 oz. 388

Pignolias, see "Pine nuts"

Pigs' feet, pickled:
4 oz. 227

Pike, raw:
  blue, whole, 1 lb. 180
  blue, meat only, 4 oz. 102
  northern, whole, 1 lb. 104
  northern, meat only, 4 oz. 100
  walleye, whole, 1 lb. 240
  walleye, meat only, 4 oz. 106
Pili nuts:
  in shell, 1 lb. 546
  shelled, 4 oz. 763
Pimentos:
  canned, with liquid, 4-oz. can or jar 31
  canned, drained, 1 average 10
Piña colada cocktail mix:
  bottled (*Holland House*), 1 fl. oz. 60
  instant (*Holland House*), 1 packet 66
Pineapple:
  fresh:
    whole, 1 lb. 123
    trimmed, 4 oz. 59
    diced, 1 cup 81
    sliced, 1 slice (3½″ in diam., ¾″ thick) 44
  candied:
    4-oz. container 357
    8-oz. container 717
    1 oz. 90
  canned:
    in water, with liquid, 8 oz. 89
    in water, tidbits, with liquid, 1 cup 96
    in juice, with liquid, 8 oz. 132
    in juice, 1 slice with 2 tbsp. juice 71
    in juice, with liquid, chunks, crushed, or slices
      (*Del Monte*), ½ cup 70
    in juice, with liquid, chunks or crushed (*Dole*), ½ cup ...70
    in syrup, with liquid, chunks, crushed, or slices
      (*Del Monte*), ½ cup 95

in syrup, with liquid, chunks, crushed, or slices (*Dole*),
  ½ cup 95
in heavy syrup, with liquid, 8 oz. 168
in heavy syrup, with liquid, chunks, crushed, or tidbits,
  1 cup 189
in heavy syrup, 1 large slice
  or 8 chunks and 2¼ tbsp. syrup 78
in heavy syrup, 1 medium slice
  or 4 chunks and 1¼ tbsp. syrup 43
freeze-dried (*Mountain House*), .85 oz. 90
frozen, chunks, sweetened, 8 oz. 193
frozen, chunks, sweetened, 1 cup 208
Pineapple dessert topping:
  (*Smucker's*), 1 tbsp. 65
Pineapple extract:
  imitation (*Ehlers*), 1 tsp. 14
Pineapple flavoring:
  pure (*Burton's*), 1 tsp. 12
  imitation (*Durkee*), 1 tsp. 6
Pineapple-grapefruit drink:
  canned (*Del Monte*), 6 fl. oz. 90
  dairy pack (*Tropicana*), 6 fl. oz. 70
Pineapple-grapefruit juice:
  canned (*Del Monte*), 6 fl. oz. 90
  canned (*Texsun*), 6 fl. oz. 91
Pineapple juice:
  canned:
    (*Del Monte*), 6 fl. oz. 100
    (*Dole*), 6 fl. oz. 100
    (*Heinz*), 6 fl. oz. 100
    (*Texsun*), 6 fl. oz. 97
  frozen* (*Minute Maid*), 6 fl. oz. 92
Pineapple-orange drink:
  canned (*Del Monte*), 6 fl. oz. 90

*Prepared according to directions on container

Pineapple-orange juice:
    canned (*Del Monte*), 6 fl. oz. 90
    frozen* (*Minute Maid*), 6 fl. oz. 94
Pineapple pie, see "Pies, frozen"
Pineapple pie filling:
    canned (*Comstock*), ⅓ cup 100
Pineapple-pink grapefruit drink:
    canned (*Del Monte*), 6 fl. oz. 90
Pineapple-pink grapefruit juice:
    canned (*Del Monte*), 6 fl. oz. 90
    canned (*Dole*), 6 fl. oz. 100
Pine nuts:
    pignolias, shelled, 4 oz. 629
    pinons, in shell, 1 lb. 1,671
    pinons, shelled, 4 oz. 724
(*Pink Carousel*) wine:
    4 fl. oz. 167
Pink squirrel cocktail mix:
    instant (*Holland House*), 1 packet 69
Pistachio nuts:
    in shell, 1 lb. 1,347
    shelled, 4 oz. 674
    shelled, 1 cup 743
    shelled, chopped, 1 tbsp. 53
    (*Frito-Lay's*), 1 oz. 180
    dry-roasted (*Planters*), 1 oz. 170
Pitangas (Surinam cherries), raw:
    whole, 1 lb. 187
    whole, 2 average 5
    pitted, 1 cup 87
Pizza, frozen*:
    Canadian bacon (*Totino's* Party Pizza), 1 pie 740
    cheese:
       (*Buitoni*), 14-oz. pie 896

*Prepared according to directions on container

(*Buitoni* Instant Pizza), 12-oz. pkg. 830
(*Celeste*), 7-oz. pie 490
(*Celeste*), 19-oz. pie 1,280
(*Celeste* Sicilian Style), 20-oz. pie 1,316
(*Jeno's*), 13-oz. pie 840
(*Jeno's* Deluxe), 20-oz. pie 1,470
(*La Pizzeria*), 10¾-oz. pie 624
(*La Pizzeria*), 20-oz. pie 1,160
(*La Pizzeria* Thick Crust), 18½-oz. pie 1,223
(*Totino's* Classic), 1 pie 1,500
(*Totino's* Extra Cheese), 1 pie 1,120
(*Totino's* Party Pizza), 1 pie 740
on bagel (*Lender's*), 2-oz. piece 140
on French bread (*Stouffer's*), 10¼-oz. pkg. 660
combination:
(*Celeste* Deluxe), 9-oz. pie 596
(*Celeste* Deluxe), 23½-oz. pie 1,468
(*Celeste* Deluxe Sicilian Style), 26-oz. pie 1,700
(*Jeno's* Deluxe), 23-oz. pie 1,680
(*La Pizzeria*), 13½-oz. pie 834
(*La Pizzeria*), 24½-oz. pie 1,526
(*Van de Kamp's*), 23½-oz. pie 1,240
on bagel (*Lender's Works*), 2¾-oz. piece 170
on French bread (*Stouffer's* Deluxe), 12⅜-oz. pkg. 800
hamburger:
(*Jeno's*), 13½-oz. pie 880
(*Totino's* Party Pizza), 1 pie 880
on French bread (*Stouffer's*), 12¼-oz. pkg. 800
mushroom, on bagel (*Lender's*), 2⅕-oz. piece 150
mushroom, on French bread (*Stouffer's*), 12-oz. pkg. 680
onion, on bagel (*Lender's*), 2⅕-oz. piece 140
pepperoni:
(*Celeste*), 7¼-oz. pie 528
(*Celeste*), 20-oz. pie 1,424
(*Jeno's*), 13-oz. pie 900
(*La Pizzeria*), 21-oz. pie 1,308

(*Totino's* Deep Crust), 1 pie 1,800
(*Totino's* Extra Pepperoni), 1 pie 1,080
(*Totino's* Party Pizza), 1 pie 860
(*Van de Kamp's*), 22-oz. pie 1,480
on French bread (*Stouffer's*), 11¼-oz. pkg. 820
and mushroom (*Totino's* Classic), 1 pie 1,530
sausage:
(*Celeste*), 8-oz. pie 562
(*Celeste*), 22-oz. pie 1,500
(*Celeste* Sicilian Style), 24-oz. pie 1,596
(*Jeno's*), 13½-oz. pie 900
(*Jeno's* Deluxe), 21-oz. pie 1,500
(*La Pizzeria*), 13-oz. pie 860
(*La Pizzeria*), 23-oz. pie 1,507
(*Totino's* Extra Sausage), 1 pie 1,140
(*Totino's* Party Pizza), 1 pie 880
on French bread (*Stouffer's*), 12-oz. pkg. 840
sausage and mushroom:
(*Celeste*), 9-oz. pie 570
(*Celeste*), 24-oz. pie 1,516
(*Totino's* Classic), 1 pie 1,530
(*Totino's* Deep Crust), 1 pie 1,800
on French bread (*Stouffer's*), 12½-oz. pkg. 790
sausage and pepperoni:
(*Totino's* Classic), 1 pie 1,590
(*Totino's* Deep Crust), 1 pie 1,740
(*Totino's* Extra Sausage and Pepperoni), 1 pie 1,160
Pizza, mix, dry:
regular (*Jeno's*), 6¾ oz. 420
cheese (*Jeno's*), 7⅛ oz. 420
pepperoni (*Jeno's*), 8 oz. 530
sausage (*Jeno's*), 7⅛ oz. 510
Pizza rolls:
cheeseburger (*Jeno's*), ½-oz. roll 45
pepperoni and cheese (*Jeno's*), ½-oz. roll 43
sausage and cheese (*Jeno's*), ½-oz. roll 43
shrimp and cheese (*Jeno's*), ½-oz. roll 37

Pizza sauce:
  canned (*Buitoni*), 4 oz. 92
  canned (*Contadina*), 4 oz. 65
Pizza seasoning:
  (*French's*), 1 tsp. 4
Plantains (baking bananas):
  whole, with skin, 1 lb. 389
  peeled, 4 oz. 135
  1 banana (11″ long, 1⅞″ in diam.) 313
Plum fruit roll:
  dried, sweetened (*Grocer's Choice*), 1 oz. 90
  dried, sweetened (*Sahadi*), 1 oz. 90
Plums:
  fresh:
    damson, whole, 1 lb. 272
    damson, whole, 10 plums (1″ in diam.) 66
    damson, with pits, 1 cup 87
    damson, pitted, 4 oz. 75
    damson, pitted, halves, 1 cup 112
    Japanese or hybrid, whole, 1 lb. 205
    Japanese or hybrid, whole, 1 plum (2⅛″ in diam.) 32
    Japanese or hybrid, pitted, 4 oz. 55
    Japanese or hybrid, pitted, halves, 1 cup 89
    Japanese or hybrid, pitted, sliced or diced, 1 cup 79
    prune type, whole, 1 lb. 320
    prune type, whole, 1 plum (1½″ in diam.) 21
    prune type, pitted, 4 oz. 85
    prune type, pitted, halves, 1 cup 124
  canned:
    greengage, in water, with liquid, 8 oz. 72
    purple, in water, with liquid, 8 oz. 99
    purple, in water, with liquid, 1 cup 114
    purple, in water, 3 plums and 2 tbsp. liquid 44
    purple, in syrup, with liquid (*Del Monte*), ½ cup 95
    purple, in syrup, with liquid
      (*Stokely-Van Camp*), ½ cup. 120
    purple, in heavy syrup, with liquid, 8 oz. 179

248

purple, in heavy syrup, with liquid, 1 cup 214
purple, in heavy syrup, 3 plums and 2¾ tbsp. liquid 110
freeze-dried (*Mountain House*), 1 oz. 100
Pohas, see "Ground cherries"
Poke shoots (pokeberry):
raw, 1 lb. 104
boiled, drained, 8 oz. 46
boiled, drained, 1 cup 33
Polish sausage, see "Kielbasa"
Pollack:
raw, drawn, 1 lb. 194
raw, fillets, 1 lb. 431
frozen, fillets (*Taste O'Sea*), 16-oz. pkg. 360
Pollack dinner:
frozen, fried (*Taste O' Sea*), 1 dinner 390
Polynesian style dinner:
frozen (*Swanson TV Brand*), 13-oz. pkg. 490
Pomegranates:
fresh, whole, 1 lb. 160
fresh, whole, 1 average (3⅜" in diam., 2¾" high) 97
Pompano:
raw, whole, 1 lb. 422
raw, meat only, 4 oz. 188
Popcorn:
unpopped, 4 oz. 411
unpopped, 1 cup 742
popped, plain, 2 oz. 219
popped, plain, large-kernel, 1 cup 23
popped, with oil and salt added, 2 oz. 259
popped, with oil and salt added, large-kernel, 1 cup 41
(*Bachman*), 1 oz. 160
(*Belvins*), 1 cup 55
(*Golden Pop*), 1 oz. 160
(*Mary Poppin'*), 1 cup 60
(*Super Pop*), ⅛ cup unpopped 100
(*TV Time*), 1 cup 70

butter flavor (*Wise*), 1 cup 70
caramel-coated, see "Candy"
cheese flavor (*Bachman*), 1 oz. 180
cheese flavor (*Golden Pop*), 1 oz. 150
cheese flavor (*Wise*), 1 cup 90
microwave (*Pillsbury*), 1 cup 60
salted (*Frito-Lay's*), 1 oz. 150
Popover, mix*:
(*Flako*), 1 piece 170
Poppy seeds:
all brands, 1 tsp. 13
Porgy:
raw, whole, 1 lb. 208
raw, meat only, 4 oz. 127
Pork, fresh, retail cuts (see also "Ham" and "Pork, cured"):
Boston butt (shoulder), with bone and skin, lean with fat:
  roasted, 10.2 oz. (yield from 1 lb. raw) 1,024
Boston butt (shoulder), without bone and skin, lean with fat:
  roasted, 10.9 oz. (yield from 1 lb. raw) 1,087
  roasted, 3 pieces (2½″ × 2½″ × ¼″) 300
  roasted, chopped or diced, 1 cup loosely packed 494
  roasted, ground, 1 cup loosely packed 388
Boston butt (shoulder), with bone and skin, lean only
  (trimmed of fat):
  roasted, 8.1 oz. (yield from 1 lb. raw with fat) 559
Boston butt (shoulder), without bone and skin, lean only
  (trimmed of fat):
  roasted, 8.6 oz. (yield from 1 lb. raw with fat) 595
  roasted, chopped or diced, 1 cup loosely packed 342
  roasted, ground, 1 cup loosely packed 268
loin chops, with bone, lean with fat:
  broiled, 8.2 oz. (yield from 1 lb. raw) 911
  broiled, 1 chop (2.7 oz.; 3 chops per lb. raw) 305
  broiled, 1 chop (2 oz.; 4 chops per lb. raw) 227

---

*Prepared according to directions on container

loin chops, without bone, lean with fat:
   broiled, 10.4 oz. (yield from 1 lb. raw) 1,153
   broiled, 4 oz. 411
loin chops, with bone, lean only (trimmed of fat):
   broiled, 5.9 oz. (yield from 1 lb. raw with fat) 454
   broiled, 1 chop (2 oz.; 3 chops per lb. raw with fat) 151
   broiled, 1 chop (1.5 oz.; 4 chops per lb. raw with fat) . . .113
loin chops, without bone, lean only (trimmed of fat):
   broiled, 7.5 oz. (yield from 1 lb. raw with fat) 572
   broiled, 4 oz. 288
loin roast, with bone, lean with fat:
   baked or roasted, 8.6 oz. (yield from 1 lb. raw) 883
loin roast, without bone, lean with fat:
   baked or roasted, 10.9 oz. (yield from 1 lb. raw) 1,115
   baked or roasted, 4 oz. 411
   baked or roasted, 1 piece (2½" × 2½" × ¾") 308
   baked or roasted, chopped or diced,
     1 cup loosely packed 507
loin roast, with bone, lean only (trimmed of fat):
   baked or roasted, 6.9 oz. (yield from 1 lb. raw with fat) . . .495
   baked or roasted, 1 piece (2½" × 2½" × ¾") 216
   baked or roasted, chopped or diced,
     1 cup loosely packed 356
loin roast, without bone, lean only (trimmed of fat):
   baked or roasted, 8.7 oz. (yield from 1 lb. raw with fat) 627
   baked or roasted, 4 oz. 288
   baked or roasted, chopped or diced,
     1 cup loosely packed 356
picnic (shoulder), with bone and skin, lean with fat:
   simmered, 8.4 oz. (yield from 1 lb. raw) 890
picnic (shoulder), without bone and skin, lean with fat:
   simmered, 10.2 oz. (yield from 1 lb. raw) 1,085
   simmered, 4 oz. 424
   simmered, 3 pieces (2½" × 2½" × ¼") 318
   simmered, chopped or diced, 1 cup loosely packed 524
picnic (shoulder), with bone and skin, lean only (trimmed of fat):
   simmered, 6.2 oz. (yield from 1 lb. raw with fat) 373

picnic (shoulder), without bone and skin, lean only
  (trimmed of fat):
    simmered, 7.6 oz. (yield from 1 lb. raw with fat) 456
    simmered, 4 oz. 241
    simmered, 3 pieces (2½″ × 2½″ × ¼″) 180
    simmered, chopped or diced, 1 cup loosely packed 297
spareribs, with bone, lean with fat:
    braised, 6.3 oz. (yield from 1 lb. raw) 792
    braised, 4 oz. 499
Pork, cured, retail shoulder cuts (see also "Bacon" and "Ham"):
Boston butt, with bone and skin, lean with fat:
    baked or roasted, 11 oz. (yield from 1 lb. unbaked) ...1,030
Boston butt, without bone and skin, lean with fat:
    baked or roasted, 11.8 oz. (yield from 1 lb. unbaked) 1,109
    baked or roasted, 4 oz. 374
    baked or roasted, 3 pieces (2½″ × 2½″ × ¼″) 281
    baked or roasted, chopped or diced,
      1 cup loosely packed 462
    baked or roasted, ground, 1 cup loosely packed 363
Boston butt, with bone and skin, lean only
  (trimmed of fat):
    baked or roasted, 9.1 oz.
      (yield from 1 lb. unbaked with fat) 629
Boston butt, without bone and skin, lean only
  (trimmed of fat):
    baked or roasted, 9.8 oz.
      (yield from 1 lb. unbaked with fat) 678
    baked or roasted, 4 oz. 276
    baked or roasted, 3 pieces (2½″ × 2½″ × ¼″) 207
    baked or roasted, chopped or diced,
      1 cup loosely packed 340
    baked or roasted, ground, 1 cup loosely packed 267
picnic, with bone and skin, lean with fat:
    baked or roasted, 9.7 oz. (yield from 1 lb. unbaked) 888
picnic, without bone and skin, lean with fat:
    baked or roasted, 11.8 oz.
      (yield from 1 lb. unbaked) 1,085

baked or roasted, 4 oz. 366
baked or roasted, 3 pieces (2½″ × 2½″ × ¼″) 275
baked or roasted, chopped or diced,
  1 cup loosely packed 452
baked or roasted, ground, 1 cup loosely packed 355
picnic, with bone and skin, lean only (trimmed of fat):
baked or roasted, 6.8 oz.
  (yield from 1 lb. unbaked with fat) 405
picnic, without bone and skin, lean only (trimmed of fat):
baked or roasted, 8.3 oz.
  (yield from 1 lb. unbaked with fat) 496
baked or roasted, 4 oz. 239
baked or roasted, 3 pieces (2½″ × 2½″ × ¼″) 179
baked or roasted, chopped or diced,
  1 cup loosely packed 295
baked or roasted, ground, 1 cup loosely packed 232
Pork and beans, see "Beans, baked"
Pork, canned or refrigerated:
cured, see "Ham"
roast (*Wilson Tender Made*), 8 oz. 354
shoulder (*Wilson Certified*), 8 oz. 558
shoulder (*Wilson Corn King*), 8 oz. 558
sliced, and gravy (*Morton House* Heat 'n Serve), 6¼ oz. . .190
Pork, frozen:
steaks, breaded (*Hormel*), 3 oz. .223
Pork dinner:
loin, frozen (*Swanson TV Brand*), 11¼-oz. pkg. 470
Pork gravy:
mix* (*Durkee*), ½ cup 35
mix (*Durkee Roastin' Bag*), 1½-oz. packet 130
mix* (*French's*), ½ cup 40
Pork, salt, see "Salt pork"
Pork sausage, see "Sausage"
Pork, smoked:
loin (*Eckrich* Slender Smoked), 1 slice 47

*Prepared according to directions on container

Pork rind snack:
   fried (*Baken•Ets*), 1 oz. 140
Pork, sweet and sour, see "Sweet and sour entree"
Port wine:
   (*Hiram Walker Porto Branco*), 2 fl. oz. 92
   (*Partners* Port), 2 fl. oz. 94
   all varieties, domestic (*Gold Seal*), 2 fl. oz. 105
   ruby (*Hiram Walker*), 2 fl. oz. 92
   ruby, domestic (*Italian Swiss Colony* Gold Medal),
     2 fl. oz. 86
   ruby, domestic (*Taylor*), 2 fl. oz. 100
   ruby, imported (*Robertson Bros. & Co.* Black Label),
     2 fl. oz. 92
   ruby, imported (*Sandeman & Co.*), 2 fl. oz. 92
   tawny (*Hiram Walker*), 2 fl. oz. 92
   tawny, domestic (*Taylor*), 2 fl. oz. 96
   tawny, imported (*Sandeman & Co.*), 2 fl. oz. 92
Pot pies, see individual listings
Pot roast seasoning mix:
   onion (*Durkee Roastin' Bag*), 1½-oz. packet 124
   and stew (*Durkee Roastin' Bag*), 1½-oz. packet 125
Potato and cheese pierogies:
   frozen (*Mrs. Paul's*), 5 oz. 300
Potato chips:
   smooth or corrugated surface, 2 oz. 324
   smooth or corrugated surface, 10 chips
     (1/16″ × 1¾″ × 2½″) 114
   (*Bachman*), 1 oz. 150
   (*Cains*), 1 oz. 160
   (*Chipsters*), 1 oz. 130
   (*Kas*), 1 oz. 160
   (*Kitty Clover*), 1 oz. 160
   (*Lay's*), 1 oz. 160
   (*Planters*), 1 oz. 150
   (*Pringle's*), 1 oz. 150
   (*Pringle's* Country Style), 1 oz. 160
   (*Pringle's* Rippled Style), 1 oz. 160

(*Ruffles*), 1 oz. 160
(*Snack Time*), 1 oz. 160
(*Snack Time* Rippled), 1 oz. 160
(*Wise*), 1 oz. 150
(*Wise Light*), 1 oz. 170
(*Wise Ridgies*), 1 oz. 170
barbecue flavor (*Lay's* Bar-B-Q), 1 oz. 160
barbecue flavor (*Wise*), 1 oz. 150
onion and garlic flavor (*Wise*), 1 oz. 150
sour cream and onion flavor (*Lay's*), 1 oz. 160
sour cream and onion flavor (*Wise*), 1 oz. 170
sour cream and onion flavor (*Wise Ridgies*), 1 oz. 170
Potato crisps:
(*Munchos*), 1 oz. 150
Potato flour:
4 oz. 400
Potato pancake:
mix* (*French's*), 1 oz., or 3″ cake 43
mix* (*Tato Mix*), 2¾-oz. serving 132
frozen (*Golden*), 1⅝-oz. pancake 85
Potato pirogen:
frozen (*Golden*), 1¾-oz. pirogen 61
Potato puffs, frozen:
(*Birds Eye Tasti Puffs*), 2.5 oz. 190
(*Ore-Ida Tater Tots*), 10 pieces 168
bacon flavor (*Ore-Ida Tater Tots*), 10 pieces 159
onion flavor (*Ore-Ida Tater Tots*), 10 pieces 163
Potato salad, canned or in jars:
(*Joan of Arc*), ½ cup 159
German (*Read*), 4 oz. 115
Potato soup, see "Soup, canned" and "Soup mix"
Potato sticks:
2 oz. 310
1 cup 190
(*O&C*), 1½ oz. 231

*Prepared according to directions on container

Potatoes, fresh:

raw, whole, 1 lb. 279
raw, peeled, chopped, diced, or sliced, 1 cup 114
baked in skin, 4 oz. 81
baked in skin, 1 long (4¾″ long, 3⅓″ in diam.) 145
boiled in skin, 4 oz. 79
boiled in skin, 1 long (4¾″ long, 2⅓″ in diam.) 173
boiled in skin, 1 round (2½″ in diam.) 104
boiled in skin, diced or sliced, 1 cup 118
boiled, peeled, 4 oz. 74
boiled, peeled, 1 long (4¾″ long, 2⅓″ in diam.) 146
boiled, peeled, 1 round (2½″ in diam.) 88
boiled, peeled, diced or sliced, 1 cup 101
French-fried, 4 oz. 311
French-fried, 10 strips (2″–3½″ long) 137
French-fried, 10 strips (1″–2″ long) 96
fried, 4 oz. 304
fried, 1 cup 456
hash brown, 4 oz. 260
hash brown, 1 cup 355

Potatoes, canned:

with liquid, 8 oz. 100
with liquid, 1 cup 110
white, new (*Del Monte*), ½ cup 45
white, whole (*Hanover*), 4 oz. 48
white, whole (*Stokely-Van Camp*), ½ cup 50
white, sliced (*Hanover*), 4 oz. 50
au gratin, with bacon (*Hormel*), 7½-oz. can 234
hashed, with beef (*Dinty Moore*), 7½-oz. can 255
scalloped, with ham (*Hormel*), 7½-oz. can 253

Potatoes, dehydrated:

mashed (*Borden Country Store*), ⅓ cup flakes 70
mashed, with bacon bits (*Borden Country Store*),
  ½ pkg. flakes 70
mashed, with chives (*Borden Country Store*), ½ pkg. flakes ...70
mashed, with onion (*Borden Country Store*), ½ pkg. flakes ...70
mashed, with parsley (*Borden Country Store*), ½ pkg. flakes ...70

Potatoes, frozen:

whole, small, boiled (*Seabrook Farms*), 3.5 oz. 70
whole, small, peeled (*Birds Eye*), 3.2 oz. 60
whole, small, peeled (*Ore-Ida*), 3 average 45
au gratin (*Green Giant* Bake 'n Serve), ½ cup . . . . , ...195
au gratin (*Stouffer's*), 3¹³⁄₁₆ oz. 135
bites (*Birds Eye Tiny Taters*), 3.2 oz. 200
in butter sauce (*Ore-Ida* Southern Style), ½ cup 70
in butter sauce, shoestring (*Green Giant*), ½ cup 155
in butter sauce, sliced (*Green Giant*), ½ cup 105
in butter sauce, with onion (*Ore-Ida* Southern Style), ½ cup 71
fried (*Heinz* Self-Sizzling Fries), 17 pieces 156
fried (*Ore-Ida* Crispers), 17 pieces 245
fried (*Ore-Ida* Country Style Dinner Fries), 10 pieces 145
fried (*Ore-Ida* Golden Fries), 17 pieces 106
fried, cottage fries (*Birds Eye*), 2.8 oz. 120
fried, cottage fries (*Ore-Ida*), 17 pieces 136
fried, crinkle cut (*Birds Eye*), 3 oz. 110
fried, crinkle cut (*Heinz* Self-Sizzling), 17 pieces 163
fried, crinkle cut (*Ore-Ida* Golden Crinkles), 17 pieces 107
fried, crinkle cut (*Ore-Ida* Pixie Crinkles), 25 pieces 74
fried, crinkle cut (*Stokely-Van Camp*), 3 oz. 120
fried, crinkle cut or french, 7 oz. (yield from 9 oz. pkg.) . .434
fried, crinkle cut or french, 10 strips (3½–4″ long unheated) . . .172
fried, crinkle cut or french, 10 strips (2″–3½″ long unheated) . .110
fried, crinkle cut or french, 10 strips (1″–2″ long) 77
fried, french (*Birds Eye*), 3 oz. 110
fried, french (*Birds Eye Tasti Fries*), 2.5 oz. 140
fried, shoestring (*Birds Eye*), 3.3 oz. 140
fried, shoestring (*Hanover* Julienne), 3.2 oz. 130
fried, shoestring (*Heinz* Self-Sizzling), 25 pieces 104
fried, shoestring (*Ore-Ida*), 25 pieces 73
fried, steak fries (*Birds Eye*), 3 oz. 110
hash brown, 1 cup 347
hash brown (*Birds Eye*), 4 oz. 70
hash brown (*Hanover*), 3.2 oz. 100
hash brown (*Hanover* Potato Medley), 3.2 oz. 90

hash brown O'Brien (*Ore-Ida*), ½ cup 41
hash brown, shredded (*Birds Eye*), 3 oz. 60
hash brown, shredded (*Ore-Ida*), ½ patty 63
hash brown (*Ore-Ida* Southern Style), ½ cup 50
and peas, creamed (*Stouffer's*), 10-oz. pkg. 280
puffs, see "Potato puffs"
scalloped (*Stouffer's*), 4 oz. 126
Potatoes, mashed, see "Potatoes, dehydrated" and "Potatoes, mix"
Potatoes, mix*
au gratin (*Betty Crocker*), ½ cup 150
au gratin, tangy (*French's* Casserole), ½ cup 150
creamed (*Betty Crocker*—oven method), ½ cup 160
creamed (*Betty Crocker*—saucepan method), ½ cup 160
creamed (*Betty Crocker* Potatoes 'N Cream), ½ cup 140
hash brown (*Betty Crocker*), ½ cup 130
julienne (*Betty Crocker*), ½ cup 150
mashed (*American Beauty*), ½ cup 140
mashed (*Betty Crocker* Potato Buds), ½ cup 130
mashed (*French's Big Tate*), ½ cup 140
mashed (*French's* Idaho), ½ cup 120
mashed (*Hungry Jack* Flakes), ½ cup 140
scalloped (*Betty Crocker*), ½ cup 150
scalloped (*French's* Casserole), ½ cup 160
scalloped, with cheese (*French's* Casserole), ½ cup 160
with sour cream and chives (*Betty Crocker*), ½ cup 140
with sour cream and chives (*French's* Casserole), ½ cup ..170
Potatoes, stuffed:
frozen, with cheese flavor topping (*Green Giant* Entree),
   5 oz. 240
frozen, with sour cream and chives (*Green Giant* Entree),
   5 oz. 230
Potatoes, sweet, see "Sweet potatoes"
Pouilly-Fumé wine:
(*B & G*), 4 fl. oz. 80
Poultry, see individual listings

*Prepared according to directions on container

Praline liqueur:
  (*Hiram Walker*), 1 fl. oz. 68
Preserves:
  all flavors (*Crosse & Blackwell*), 1 tbsp. 59
  all flavors (*Kraft*), 1 tsp. 16
  all flavors (*Ma Brown*), 1 tbsp. 51
  all flavors (*Smucker's*), 1 tbsp. 53
  all flavors, except apricot, peach, pear, and plum
    (*Bama*), 1 tbsp. 54
  apricot, peach, pear, and plum (*Bama*), 1 tbsp. 51
  grape (*Welch's*), 1 tbsp. 53
  strawberry (*Welch's*), 1 tbsp. 53
  wild blueberry (*Reese*), 1 tbsp. 55
  wild strawberry (*Reese*), 1 tbsp. 55
Pretzels:
  all varieties (*Quinlan*), 1 oz. 109
  bite size:
    (*Bachman B's*), 1 piece 8
    (*Bachman Nutzels*), 1 piece 7
    (*Old London Pretz-L Nuggets*), 1 oz. 110
    (*Wise Pretz-L Nuggets*), 1 oz. .110
  logs (*Bachman's*), 1 piece 18
  mini size (*Old London Mini Pretz-Ls*), 1 oz. 110
  mini size (*Wise Mini Pretz-Ls*), 1 oz. 110
  (*Mr. Salty Veri-Thin*), 9 oz., or 5 pieces 100
  rings:
    (*Bachman Beers*), 1 piece 56
    (*Bachman* Medium), 1 piece 20
    (*Bachman* Teeny), 1 piece 11
    (*Bachman Thin*), 1 piece 18
    (*Mr. Salty* Pretzelettes), 1 oz., or 17 pieces 110
    (*Rold Gold*), 1 oz. 110
  rods (*Bachman's*), 1 piece 50
  rods (*Rold Gold*), 1 oz. 110
  sticks:
    (*Bachman's*), 1 piece 3
    (*Mr. Salty Veri-Thin*), 1 oz. or 94 sticks 100

(*Rold Gold*), 1 oz. 110
twists (*Rold Gold*), 1 oz. 110
Prickly pears:
raw, whole, 1 lb. 84
peeled and seeded, 4 oz. 48
Prune juice, canned or bottled:
(*Del Monte*), 6 fl. oz. 120
(*Heinz*), 6 fl. oz. 130
(*Mott's*), 6 fl. oz. 140
(*Sunsweet*), 6 fl. oz. 140
with prune pulp (*Mott's*), 6 fl. oz. 120
Prune nectar:
bottled (*Mott's*), 6 fl. oz. 100
Prunes, canned:
stewed, with pits (*Del Monte*), ½ cup 115
Prunes, dehydrated (nugget type):
uncooked, 8 oz. 780
uncooked, 1 cup 344
cooked, sweetened, with liquid, 8 oz. 408
cooked, sweetened, with liquid, 1 cup 504
Prunes, dried:
uncooked:
whole, with pits, extra-large (up to 43 per lb.), 8 oz. ...509
whole, with pits, extra-large (up to 43 per lb.),
10 prunes 274
whole, with pits, large (up to 53 per lb.), 8 oz. 501
whole, with pits, large (up to 53 per lb.), 10 prunes 215
whole, with pits, medium (up to 67 per lb.), 8 oz. 498
whole, with pits, medium (up to 67 per lb.), 10 prunes 164
whole, pitted, 8 oz. 579
whole, pitted, 1 cup 459
whole, pitted, 10 prunes 260
chopped or ground, 1 cup loosely packed 408
chopped or ground, 1 cup packed 663
with pits (*Del Monte*), 1 oz. 60
with pits (*Del Monte* Moist-Pak), 1 oz. 60
with pits (*Sunsweet*), 1 oz. 60

pitted (*Del Monte*), 1 oz. 70
cooked:
   with pits, unsweetened, with liquid, cold, 8 oz. 230
   with pits, unsweetened, with liquid, cold, 1 cup 253
   with pits, sweetened, with liquid, cold, 8 oz. 332
   with pits, sweetened, with liquid, cold, 1 cup 409
Pudding, rennin, see "Rennin dessert"
Pudding (see also "Pudding mix"):
banana (*Del Monte Pudding Cup*), 5-oz. container 180
banana (*Hunt's Snack Pack*), 5-oz. container 180
butterscotch:
   (*Del Monte Pudding Cup*), 5-oz. container 180
   (*Hunt's Snack Pack*), 5-oz. container 170
   (*Rich's*), 3-oz. container 133
   (*Swiss Miss*), 1 container 150
chocolate:
   (*Betty Crocker RTS*), ½ cup 180
   (*Del Monte Pudding Cup*), 5-oz. container 190
   (*Hunt's Snack Pack*), 5-oz. container 180
   (*Rich's*), 3-oz. container 140
   (*Swiss Miss*), 1 container 160
   (*Swiss Miss* Double Rich), 1 container 160
   dark (*Rich's*), 3-oz. container 140
   dark (*Swiss Miss*), 4¼-oz. container 180
   German (*Hunt's Snack Pack*), 5-oz. container 170
   malt (*Swiss Miss*), 1 container 150
chocolate fudge:
   (*Betty Crocker RTS*), ½ cup 180
   (*Del Monte Pudding Cup*), 5-oz. container 190
   (*Hunt's Snack Pack*), 5-oz. container 180
chocolate marshmallow (*Hunt's Snack Pack*), 5-oz.
   container 170
chocolate sundae (*Swiss Miss*), 1 container 170
custard (*Swiss Miss*), 4-oz. container 160
custard, chocolate (*Swiss Miss*), 1 container 150
custard, egg (*Swiss Miss*), 1 container 160
lemon (*Hunt's Snack Pack*), 5-oz. container 150

plum (*Crosse & Blackwell*), 4 oz. .340
plum (*Richardson & Robbins*), ½ cup 300
rice pudding:
    (*Betty Crocker RTS*), ½ cup 150
    (*Hunt's Snack Pack*), 5-oz. container 190
    (*Swiss Miss*), 1 container 150
tapioca:
    (*Betty Crocker RTS*), ½ cup 150
    (*Hunt's Snack Pack*), 5-oz. container 140
    (*Swiss Miss*), 1 container 130
vanilla:
    (*Betty Crocker RTS*), ½ cup 190
    (*Del Monte Pudding Cup*), 5-oz. container 190
    (*Hunt's Snack Pack*), 5-oz. container 180
    (*Rich's*), 3-oz. container 130
    (*Swiss Miss*), 1 container 150
    sundae (*Swiss Miss*), 1 container 170
Pudding, frozen:
    (*Good Humor* Bullwinkle Stix), 2½-fl.-oz. bar 120
Pudding mix*:
banana:
    (*Royal*), ½ cup 160
    cream (*Jell-O*), ⅙ of 8″ pie, without crust 100
    cream (*Jell-O* Instant), ½ cup 170
butter pecan (*Jell-O* Instant), ½ cup 170
butterscotch:
    (*Jell-O*), ½ cup 170
    (*Jell-O* Instant), ½ cup 170
    (*My-T-Fine*), ½ cup 143
    (*Royal*), ½ cup 160
    (*Royal* Instant), ½ cup 180
chocolate:
    (*Jell-O*), ½ cup 170
    (*Jell-O* Instant), ½ cup 180
    (*My-T-Fine*), ½ cup 133

*Prepared according to directions on container

(*Royal*), ½ cup 180
(*Royal* Instant), ½ cup 190
dark (*Royal Dark 'N Sweet*), ½ cup 180
dark (*Royal Dark 'N Sweet* Instant), ½ cup 190
milk (*Jell-O*), ½ cup 170
chocolate almond (*My-T-Fine*), ½ cup 169
chocolate fudge:
    (*Jell-O*), ½ cup 170
    (*Jell-O* Instant), ½ cup 180
    (*My-T-Fine*), ½ cup 151
coconut:
    (*Royal* Instant), ½ cup 170
    cream (*Jell-O*), ⅙ of 8″ pie, without crust ....
    cream (*Jell-O* Instant), ½ cup 180
    coffee (*Royal* Instant), ½ cup 180
custard (*Royal*), ½ cup 150
custard, golden egg (*Jell-O Americana*), ½ cup 160
flan (*Royal*), ½ cup 150
lemon:
    (*Jell-O*), ⅙ of 9″ pie, without crust 170
    (*Jell-O* Instant), ½ cup 180
    (*My-T-Fine*), ½ cup 164
    (*Royal*), ½ cup 160
    (*Royal* Instant), ½ cup 180
lime, key (*Royal*), ½ cup 160
pineapple cream (*Jell-O* Instant), ½ cup 170
pistachio (*Jell-O* Instant), ½ cup 180
pistachio (*Royal* Instant), ½ cup 170
rice pudding (*Jell-O Americana*), ½ cup 170
tapioca:
    chocolate (*Jell-O Americana*), ½ cup 160
    chocolate (*Royal*), ½ cup 180
    vanilla (*Jell-O Americana*), ½ cup 160
    vanilla (*My-T-Fine*), ½ cup 130
    vanilla (*Royal*), ½ cup 160
vanilla:
    (*Jell-O*), ½ cup 160
    (*Jell-O* Instant), ½ cup 180

   (*My-T-Fine*), ½ cup 133
   (*Royal*), ½ cup 160
   (*Royal* Instant), ½ cup 180
   French (*Jell-O*), ½ cup 170
   French (*Jell-O* Instant), ½ cup 170
Pumpkin:
   fresh, raw, whole, 1 lb. 83
   fresh, raw, pulp only, 4 oz. 30
   (*Del Monte*), ½ cup 25
   (*Joan of Arc*), 4 oz. 45
   (*Libby's*), ½ cup 43
   (*Stokely-Van Camp*), ½ cup 40
Pumpkin pie, see "Pies, frozen"
Pumpkin pie filling:
   canned (*Comstock*), 4½ oz. 150
   canned (*Stokely-Van Camp*), ⅓ cup 117
Pumpkin seed kernels, dry:
   whole, weighed in hull, 4 oz. 464
   hulled, 4 oz. 627
   hulled, 1 cup 774
Punch:
   all flavors, canned (*Hawaiian Punch*), 6 fl. oz. 90
   all flavors, frozen* (*Hawaiian Punch*), 6 fl. oz. 90
   fruit, bottled (*Welch's*), 6 fl. oz. 100
   fruit, dairy pack (*Hood*), 6 fl. oz. 75
   fruit, dairy pack (*Tropicana*), 6 fl. oz. 70
   fruit, mix* (*Cramores*), 6 fl. oz. 68
   fruit, mix* (*Hi-C*), 6 fl. oz. 76
   fruit, mix* (*Wyler's*), 6 fl. oz. 68
   fruit, Florida, canned (*Hi-C*), 6 fl. oz. 95
   fruit, tropical, mix* (*Kool-Aid*), 6 fl. oz. 75
   red, mix* (*Hawaiian Punch*), 6 fl. oz. 75
Purslane leaves:
   fresh, raw, whole, with stems, 1 lb. 95
   fresh, boiled, drained, 1 cup 27

*Prepared according to directions on container

Q

Quail, raw:
  whole, ready-to-cook, 1 lb. 686
  meat and skin only, 4 oz. 196
  giblets, 2 oz. 100
Quince:
  fresh, whole, 1 lb. 158
  fresh, peeled and seeded, 4 oz. 65

R

uncooked, ½-oz. pkg. 40
uncooked, whole, 1 cup loosely packed 419
uncooked, whole, 1 cup packed 477
uncooked, whole, 1 tbsp. 26
uncooked, chopped, 1 cup loosely packed 390
uncooked, chopped, 1 cup packed 549
uncooked, ground, 1 cup loosely packed 578
uncooked, ground, 1 cup packed 780
cooked, sweetened, with liquid, 1 cup 628
golden seedless (*Del Monte*), 1 oz. 87
golden seedless (*Sun•Maid*), 1 oz. 83
golden seedless (*Sun•Maid*), ½ cup 250
muscat (*Del Monte*), 1 oz. 83
seedless (*Del Monte*), 1 oz. 87
seedless (*Sun•Maid*), 1 oz. 83
seedless (*Sun•Maid*), ½ cup 250
freeze-dried (*Mountain House*), 82 oz. 80

Raspberries:
  fresh:
    black, 1 lb. 331
    black, 1 cup 98
    red, 1 lb. 259
    red, 1 pint 185
    red, 1 cup 70
  canned:
    black, in water, with liquid, 8 oz. 116
    red, in water, with liquid, 8 oz. 80
    red, in water, with liquid, 1 cup 85
  frozen:
    red (*Birds Eye* Quick Thaw), 5 oz. 150
    red, in syrup (*Stokely-Van Camp*), 5 oz. 160

Raspberry brandy:
  (*Hiram Walker*), 1 fl. oz. 88

Raspberry drink:
  mix* (*Kool-Aid*), 6 fl. oz. 68

*Prepared according to directions on container

black, mix* (*Cramores*), 6 fl. oz. 68
Raspberry extract:
pure (*Burton's*), 1 tsp. 8
imitation (*Burton's*), 1 tsp. 10
imitation (*Ehlers*), 1 tsp. 14
Raspberry fruit roll:
dried, sweetened (*Grocer's Choice*), 1 oz. 90
dried, sweetened (*Sahadi*), 1 oz. 90
Raspberry liqueur:
(*Dolfi*), 1 fl. oz. 78
(*DuBouchett*), 1 fl. oz. 56
Raspberry pie tart:
frozen (*Pepperidge Farm*), 1 piece 320
Raspberry turnover:
frozen (*Pepperidge Farm*), 1 piece 340
Ratatouille:
frozen (*Stouffer's*), 10-oz. pkg. 120
Ravioli:
canned:
    beef, in meat sauce (*Franco-American*), 7½ oz. 220
    cheese (*Buitoni*), 15-oz. can 408
    meat (*Buitoni*), 15-oz. can 448
frozen:
    cheese (*Buitoni*), 15-oz. pkg. 1,192
    cheese, Parmigiana (*Buitoni*), 12-oz. pkg. 452
    cheese, round (*Buitoni*), 11-oz. pkg. 912
    meat (*Buitoni*), 15-oz. pkg. 1,280
    meat Parmigiana (*Buitoni*), 12-oz. pkg. 581
Raviolios:
beef, in meat sauce, canned (*Franco-American*), 7½ oz. 220
(*Red Carousel*) wine:
4 fl. oz. 139
Red and gray snapper:
raw, whole, 1 lb. 219
raw, meat only, 4 oz. 106

---

*Prepared according to directions on container

Red horse, silver:
    raw, drawn, 1 lb. 204
    raw, meat only, 4 oz. 111
Red pepper, see "Pepper, sweet, red"
Redfish, see "Drum, red" and "Ocean perch, Atlantic"
Reindeer:
    raw, lean meat only, 4 oz. 144
Relish, see individual listings
Relish spread:
    (*Mrs. Filbert's*), 1 tbsp. 80
Rennin dessert, mix:
    chocolate, dry form, 2-oz. pkg. 221
    chocolate, prepared with milk, 1 cup 260
    vanilla, caramel, or fruit flavor, dry form, 1½-oz. pkg. ...165
    vanilla, caramel, or fruit flavor,
      prepared with milk, 1 cup 238
Rhine wine:
    domestic (*Gold Seal*), 4 fl. oz. 108
    domestic (*Italian Swiss Colony*), 4 fl. oz. 86
    domestic (*Taylor*), 4 fl. oz. 92
Rhubarb:
    fresh:
      raw, with leaves, 1 lb. 33
      raw, well trimmed, 1 lb. 62
      raw, diced, 1 cup 20
      cooked, sweetened, 1 cup 381
    frozen, sweetened, cooked with added sugar, 1 cup 386
Rice, plain:
    brown:
      cooked (*River Brand*), ½ cup 110
      cooked (*Uncle Ben's*), ½ cup 100
    white:
      cooked (*Carolina*), ½ cup 90
      cooked (*Comet*), ½ cup 102
      cooked (*River*), ½ cup 100
      cooked (*Success*), ½ cup 110
      cooked (*Uncle Ben's* Converted), ½ cup 97

parboiled (*Comet*), ½ cup 90
precooked (*Minute Rice*), ½ cup 90
precooked (*Uncle Ben's* Quick), ½ cup 89
Rice, flavored:
beef flavor, mix*:
  (*Comet*), ½ cup 100
  (*Uncle Ben's* British Style), ½ cup 141
  with vermicelli (*Carolina bake-it-easy*), ½ cup 100
  with vermicelli (*Minute Rice* Rib Roast), ½ cup 150
  with vermicelli (*Rice-A-Roni*), ½ cup 160
  with broccoli in cheese sauce, frozen (*Green Giant*),
  ½ cup 125
brown and wild rice, mix* (*Comet*), ½ cup 100
brown and wild rice, mix* (*Uncle Ben's*), ½ cup 150
with cheese flavor sauce and vermicelli, mix*
  (*Rice-A-Roni*), ½ cup 145
chicken flavor, mix*:
  (*Comet*), ½ cup 100
  (*Uncle Ben's* French Style), ½ cup 144
  with vermicelli (*Carolina bake-it-easy*), ½ cup 100
  with vermicelli (*Minute Rice* Drumstick), ½ cup 150
  with vermicelli (*Rice-A-Roni*), ½ cup 160
curry, mix* (*Uncle Ben's*), ½ cup 106
French style, frozen (*Birds Eye*), 3.6 oz. 120
fried, Chinese:
  canned (*La Choy*), ¾ cup 190
  mix* (*Durkee* Seasoning Mix), ½ cup 108
  mix* (*Minute Rice*), ½ cup 160
  with meat, frozen (*La Choy*), ¾ cup 140
  pork, frozen (*Chun King*), ½ pkg. 180
  stir-fry (*Chun King*), ⅕ pkg. 130
  with vermicelli, mix* (*Rice-A-Roni*), ½ cup 187
herb and butter flavor, with vermicelli, mix*
  (*Carolina bake-it-easy*) ½ cup 100

Prepared according to directions on container

Italian style, frozen (*Birds Eye*), 3.6 oz. 130
long grain and wild rice:
    frozen (*Green Giant*), ½ cup 110
    mix* (*Comet*), ½ cup 100
    mix* (*Carolina*), ½ cup 90
    mix* (*Minute Rice*), ½ cup 150
    mix* (*Uncle Ben's*), ½ cup 113
    mix* (*Uncle Ben's* Fast), ½ cup 127
Oriental style:
    fried, see "fried, Chinese," above
    frozen (*Birds Eye*), 3.6 oz. 130
    mix* (*Hamburger Helper*—8-oz. pkg.) ⅕ pkg. 340
    mix* (*Hamburger Helper*—6½-oz. pkg.), ⅕ pkg. 300
paella, mix* (*R.M. Quigg's*), 4½ oz. 153
with peas and mushrooms, frozen (*Birds Eye*), 2.3 oz. 110
with peas and mushrooms, frozen
    (*Green Giant* Rice Medley), ½ cup 100
with peppers and parsley, frozen
    (*Green Giant* Rice Verdi), ½ cup 135
pilaf:
    frozen (*Green Giant* Rice Pilaf), ½ cup 115
    mix* (*Uncle Ben's* Greek Style), ½ cup 144
    with vermicelli, mix* (*Carolina bake-it-easy*), ½ cup ...100
Spanish:
    canned (*Comstock*), 7½ oz. 130
    canned (*Heinz*), 7½-oz. can 170
    canned (*Libby's*), ½ cup 60
    canned (*Old El Paso*), 4 oz. 97
    canned (*Stokely-Van Camp*), ½ cup 85
    frozen (*Birds Eye*), 3.6 oz. 120
    mix* (*Durkee* Seasoning Mix), ½ cup 137
    mix* (*Minute Rice*), ½ cup 150
    with vermicelli, mix* (*Rice-A-Roni*), ½ cup 118
turkey flavor, with vermicelli, mix* (*Rice-A-Roni*), ½ cup 182

*Prepared according to directions on container

Rice, wild:
  raw, 8 oz. 801
  raw, 1 cup 565
  with vermicelli, mix* (*Rice-A-Roni*), ½ cup 134
Rice bran:
  4 oz. 313
Rice cereal, see "Cereals, ready-to-eat"
Rice noodles, see "Noodles, rice"
Rice polish:
  4 oz. 301
  stirred, spooned into cup, 1 cup 278
Rice pudding, see "Pudding" and "Pudding mix"
Rock and rum liqueur:
  (*DuBouchett*), 1 fl. oz. 77
Rock and rye liqueur:
  (*DuBouchett*—60 proof), 1 fl. oz. 78
  (*DuBouchett*—70 proof), 1 fl. oz. 86
  (*Garnier*), 1 fl. oz. 83
  (*Hiram Walker*), 1 fl. oz. 88
  (*Old Mr. Boston*—48 proof), 1 fl. oz. 72
  (*Old Mr. Boston*—60 proof), 1 fl. oz. 94
Rockfish fillets:
  raw, meat only, 1 lb. 440
  oven steamed, with onions, 13 oz. (yield from 1 lb. raw) ...396
  oven steamed, with onions, 4 oz. 121
  oven steamed, with onions, 1 fillet (7″ × 3⅜″ × ⅝″) 123
Roe (see also "Caviar"):
  raw, carp, cod, haddock, herring, pike or shad, 4 oz. 148
  baked or broiled with butter, cod and shad, 4 oz. 144
  canned, with liquid, cod, haddock, and herring, 4 oz. 135
Rolls and buns:
  brown and serve:
    (*Taystee*), 1 piece 83
    (*Wonder* Half & Half), 1 piece 80

*Prepared according to directions on container

(*Wonder* Home Bake), 1 piece 85
with buttermilk (*Wonder*), 1 piece 85
club (*Pepperidge Farm*), 1 piece 120
crescent (*Pepperidge Farm* Butter Crescent), 1 piece 130
deli style (*Arnold* Deli Twist), 1 piece 110
deli style (*Pepperidge Farm*), 1 piece 180
dinner:
    (*Arnold*), 1 piece 60
    (*Arnold* Party Rolls), 1 piece 55
    (*Home Pride*), 1 piece 90
    (*Pepperidge Farm*), 1 piece 65
    (*Pepperidge Farm* Golden Twist), 1 piece 120
    (*Pepperidge Farm* Hearth), 1 piece 60
    (*Pepperidge Farm* Old Fashioned), 1 piece 37
    (*Pepperidge Farm* Party Rolls), 1 piece 35
    (*Wonder*), 1 piece 105
finger (*Pepperidge Farm*), 1 piece 60
frankfurter or hot dog:
    (*Arnold*), 1 piece 110
    (*Pepperidge Farm*), 1 piece 120
    (*Taystee*), 1 piece 120
    (*Wonder*), 1 piece 160
French:
    (*Pepperidge Farm*—4-pack), 1 piece 230
    (*Pepperidge Farm*—9-pack), 1 piece 110
    brown and serve (*Francisco*), 1 piece 90
    brown and serve (*Pepperidge Farm*—large), ½ roll 200
    brown and serve (*Pepperidge Farm*—small), ½ roll 130
    brown and serve (*Wonder*), 1 piece 85
    sweet, brown and serve (*Francisco*), 6" roll 240
    sweet, brown and serve (*Francisco*), 3" roll 100
gem style, brown and serve (*Wonder*), 1 piece 85
hamburger:
    (*Arnold*), 1 piece 110
    (*Pepperidge Farm*), 1 piece 110
    (*Taystee*), 1 piece 120
    (*Wonder*), 1 piece 160

hoagie, or submarine, see "Bread, French or Vienna"
kaiser (*Francisco*), 1 piece 180
kaiser and hoagie (*Wonder*), ½ roll 230
pan roll (*Wonder*), 1 piece 105
parkerhouse (*Pepperidge Farm*), 1 piece 60
sandwich:
   (*Arnold*), 1 piece 130
   (*Pepperidge Farm*), 1 piece 140
   soft (*Arnold*), 1 piece 110
   wheat (*Oroweat*), 1 piece 200
sesame seed (*Pepperidge Farm* Buns), 1 piece 120
sesame seed (*Pepperidge Farm* Sesame Crisp), 1 piece 70
variety (*Francisco*), 1 piece 100
Rolls and buns, frozen:
croissant (*Sara Lee*), 1 piece 109
dinner (*Sara Lee* Party Rolls), 1 piece 55
Parker House (*Sara Lee*), 1 piece 73
sesame seed (*Sara Lee*), 1 piece 55
Rolls and buns, mix*:
(*Pillsbury* Hot Rolls), 1 piece 95
Rolls and buns, refrigerator:
(*Butterflake*), 1 piece 110
crescent (*Ballard*), 1 piece 95
crescent (*Pillsbury*), 1 piece 100
dinner, wheat (*Pillsbury* Bakery Style), 1 piece 90
dinner, white (*Pillsbury* Bakery Style), 1 piece 90
frankfurter wrap (*Pillsbury Wiener Wrap*), 1 piece 60
frankfurter wrap, cheese (*Pillsbury Wiener Wrap*), 1 piece 60
Rolls and buns, sweet:
apple crunch, frozen (*Sara Lee*), 1-oz. piece 102
caramel pecan, frozen (*Sara Lee*), 1.3-oz. piece 154
caramel, sticky, frozen (*Sara Lee*), 1.1-oz. piece 118
cinnamon:
   frozen (*Sara Lee*), .9-oz. piece 100

*Prepared according to directions on container

iced, refrigerator (*Ballard*), 1 piece* 100
iced, refrigerator (*Hungry Jack Butter Tastin'*), 1 piece* ..145
iced, refrigerator (*Pillsbury*), 1 piece* 115
frozen, honey (*Morton*), 2.3-oz. piece 230
frozen, honey (*Sara Lee*), 1-oz. piece 112
frozen, honey, mini (*Morton*), 1.3-oz. piece 130
danish pastry, see "Danish pastry"

Romaine, see "Lettuce"
Root beer, see "Soft drinks and mixers"
Rose apples:
raw, whole, 1 lb. 170
raw, trimmed and seeded, 4 oz. 64
Rose extract:
pure (*Burton's*), 1 tsp. 9
Rosé wine:
domestic (*Italian Swiss Colony*), 4 fl. oz. 86
domestic (*Taylor*), 4 fl. oz. 92
imported (*Cruse & Fils Frères* Vin Rosé), 4 fl. oz. 96
Rosemary leaves:
ground (all brands), 1 tsp. 5
Rotelle alla Romana:
with sauce, frozen (*Ronzoni*), 15-oz. pkg. 480
Rotini, canned:
in tomato sauce (*Franco-American*), 7½ oz. 200
and meatballs, in tomato sauce
(*Franco-American*), 7¼ oz. 230
Rum, see "Liquor, pure distilled"
Rum extract:
imitation (*Burton's*), 1 tsp. 11
imitation (*Durkee*), 1 tsp. 14
Rum flavoring:
pure (*Ehlers*), 1 tsp. 19
Rutabagas:
fresh:
raw, without tops, 1 lb. 177

*Prepared according to directions on container

raw, trimmed, 4 oz. 52
raw, diced, 1 cup 64
boiled, drained, cubes or slices, 1 cup 60
boiled, drained, mashed, 1 cup 84
frozen (*Southland*), 4 oz. 50
Rye, see "Bread," "Flour," etc.
Rye wafers, see "Crackers"

S

Sable, smoked:
  flesh only (*Vita*), 2 oz. 74
Sablefish:
  raw, whole, 1 lb. 362
  raw, meat only, 4 oz. 216
Safflower oil, see "Oils, cooking or salad"
Safflower seed kernels:
  dry, 1 oz. 174
Safflower seed meal:
  partially defatted, 4 oz. 405
Sage:
  ground (all brands), 1 tsp. 4
Saint-John's-bread flour, see "Flour, carob"
Salad, see individual listings ("Chicken," "Potato," etc.)
Salad dressings:
  avocado goddess, bottled (*Marie's Specialty Brands*), 1 tbsp. . 96
  bacon, creamy, bottled (*Seven Seas*), 1 tbsp. 60
  blue cheese:
    bottled (*Marie's Specialty Brands*), 1 tbsp. 100
    bottled (*Roka*), 1 tbsp. 60
    chunky, bottled (*Kraft*), 1 tbsp. 70
    chunky, bottled (*Seven Seas*), 1 tbsp. 70
    chunky, bottled (*Wish-Bone*), 1 tbsp. 70
    mix* (*Good Seasons*), 1 tbsp. 90
    mix* (*Good Seasons Thick 'n Creamy*), 1 tbsp. 80

*Prepared according to directions on container

bottled (*Bennett's*), 1 tbsp. 60
bottled (*Hellmann's Spin Blend*), 1 tbsp. 55
bottled (*Mrs. Filberts*), 1 tbsp. 70
bottled (*Saffola*), 1 tbsp. 56
bottled (*Seven Seas Capri*), 1 tbsp. 70
buttermilk:
   bottled (*Kraft*), 1 tbsp. 80
   farm style, mix* (*Good Seasons*), 1 tbsp. 60
   ranch style, bottled (*Marie's Specialty Brands*), 1 tbsp. ...105
   and chive, bottled (*Kraft*), 1 tbsp. 80
   and green pepper, bottled (*Kraft*), 1 tbsp. 70
Caesar, bottled:
   (*Hain*), 1 tbsp. 63
   (*Kraft*), 1 tbsp. 70
   (*Lawry's*), 1 tbsp. 70
   (*Pfeiffer*), 1 tbsp. 70
   (*Seven Seas*), 1 tbsp. 60
   (*Seven Seas Viva*), 1 tbsp. 60
   (*Wish-Bone*), 1 tbsp. 80
Canadian, bottled (*Lawry's*), 1 tbsp. 72
cheese-garlic, mix* (*Good Seasons*), 1 tbsp. 90
cheese-Italian, mix* (*Good Seasons*), 1 tbsp. 90
coleslaw, bottled (*Kraft*), 1 tbsp. 70
cucumber, bottled (*Kraft*), 1 tbsp. 70
cucumber, creamy, bottled (*Wish-Bone*), 1 tbsp. 80
farm style, mix* (*Good Seasons*), 1 tbsp. 50
French:
   bottled (*Bennett's*), 1 tbsp. 60
   bottled (*Catalina*), 1 tbsp. 70
   bottled (*Kraft*), 1 tbsp. 60
   bottled (*Lawry's*), 1 tbsp. 60
   bottled (*Lawry's San Francisco*), 1 tbsp. 53
   bottled (*Pfeiffer*), 1 tbsp. 55
   bottled (*Saffola*), 1 tbsp. 54

Prepared according to directions on container

bottled (*Seven Seas* Family Style), 1 tbsp. 60
bottled (*Wish-Bone* DeLuxe), 1 tbsp. 60
bottled (*Wish-Bone* Sweet 'n Spicy), 1 tbsp. 60
creamy, bottled (*Hain*), 1 tbsp. 63
creamy, bottled (*Seven Seas*), 1 tbsp. 60
mix* (*Good Seasons*), 1 tbsp. 80
mix* (*Good Seasons* Old Fashion), 1 tbsp. 80
mix* (*Good Seasons* Riviera), 1 tbsp. 90
mix* (*Good Seasons Thick 'n Creamy*), 1 tbsp. 75
garlic:
  creamy, bottled (*Wish-Bone*), 1 tbsp. 80
  French, bottled (*Wish-Bone*), 1 tbsp. 60
  mix* (*Good Seasons*), 1 tbsp. 80
green goddess:
  bottled (*Lawry's*), 1 tbsp. 59
  bottled (*Seven Seas*), 1 tbsp. 60
  bottled (*Wish-Bone*), 1 tbsp. 70
Hawaiian, bottled (*Lawry's*), 1 tbsp. 77
herbs and spices, bottled (*Seven Seas*), 1 tbsp. 60
Italian:
  bottled (*Bennett's*), 1 tbsp. 60
  bottled (*Hain*), 1 tbsp. 64
  bottled (*Kraft Golden Blend*), 1 tbsp. 70
  bottled (*Kraft Zesty*), 1 tbsp. 80
  bottled (*Lawry's*), 1 tbsp. 80
  bottled (*Pfeiffer* Chef), 1 tbsp. 60
  bottled (*Saffola*), 1 tbsp. 50
  bottled (*Seven Seas* Family Style), 1 tbsp. 70
  bottled (*Seven Seas Viva*), 1 tbsp. 70
  bottled (*Wish-Bone*), 1 tbsp. 80
  bottled (*Wish-Bone* Robusto), 1 tbsp. 80
  with cheese, bottled (*Marie's Specialty Brands*), 1 tbsp. 62
  with cheese, bottled (*Wish-Bone*), 1 tbsp. 60
  creamy, bottled (*Seven Seas*), 1 tbsp. 70

Prepared according to directions on container

279

creamy, bottled (*Wish-Bone*), 1 tbsp. 80
garlic, bottled (*Marie's Specialty Brands*), 1 tbsp. 100
with sour cream, bottled (*Kraft*), 1 tbsp. 50
mix* (*Good Seasons*), 1 tbsp. 80
mix* (*Good Seasons* Mild), 1 tbsp. 90
mix* (*Good Seasons Thick 'n Creamy*), 1 tbsp. 85
mayonnaise, see "Mayonnaise"
mayonnaise type (imitation), bottled:
(*Bama*), 1 tbsp. 50
(*Bennett's*), 1 tbsp. 40
(*Mrs. Filberts*), 1 tbsp. 40
(*Miracle Whip*), 1 tbsp. 70
(*Saffola*), 1 tbsp. 59
eggless (*Hain*), 1 tbsp. 85
oil and vinegar, bottled (*Hain*), 1 tbsp. 90
oil and vinegar, bottled (*Kraft*), 1 tbsp. 70
onion, bottled (*Wish-Bone* California Onion), 1 tbsp. 80
onion, mix* (*Good Seasons*), 1 tbsp. 80
onion and chives, bottled (*Kraft*), 1 tbsp. 70
red wine vinegar and oil (*Seven Seas Viva*), 1 tbsp. 60
Roquefort
bottled (*Marie's Specialty Brands*), 1 tbsp. 105
Russian, bottled:
(*Bennett's*), 1 tbsp. 70
(*Hain*), 1 tbsp. 66
(*Kraft*), 1 tbsp. 60
(*Marie's Specialty Brands*), 1 tbsp. 88
(*Pfeiffer*), 1 tbsp. 65
(*Wish-Bone*), 1 tbsp. 50
creamy (*Seven Seas*), 1 tbsp. 80
sesame, creamy, bottled (*Sahadi*), 1 tbsp. 60
sesame, spice, bottled (*Sahadi*), 1 tbsp. 80
Thousand Island:
bottled (*Hain*), 1 tbsp. 55

*Prepared according to directions on container

bottled (*Kraft*), 1 tbsp. 70
bottled (*Lawry's*), 1 tbsp. 69
bottled (*Marie's Specialty Brands*), 1 tbsp. 88
bottled (*Pfeiffer*), 1 tbsp. 65
bottled (*Seven Seas*), 1 tbsp. 50
bottled (*Wish-Bone*), 1 tbsp. 70
mix* (*Good Seasons Thick 'n Creamy*), 1 tbsp. 75
Salad dressing seasoning:
(*Durkee*), 1 tsp. 4
(*French's* Salad Lift), 1 tsp. 6
with cheese (*Durkee*), 1 tsp. 10
Salami:
dry:
roll, 8¼-oz. 1,053
roll, 1 slice (1¾″ in diam., ⅛″ thick) 23
sliced, 4-oz. pkg. 509
sliced, 1 slice (3⅛″ in diam., ¹⁄₁₆″ thick) 45
cooked:
8-oz. pkg. 706
1 slice (4½″ in diam.; about 1 oz.) 88
1 slice (4″ in diam.; about ¾ oz.) 68
beef (*Vienna*), 3½ oz. 278
beer (*Oscar Mayer*), .8-oz. slice 55
cotto:
(*Hormel*), 1-oz. slice 66
(*Oscar Mayer*), .8-oz. slice 50
beef (*Oscar Mayer*), .8-oz. slice 50
Danish, cocktail (*Reese* Sticks), 1 oz. 128
Genoa (*Hormel*), 1 oz., or about 5 slices 126
Genoa (*Swift*), 1 oz. 120
hard:
(*Hormel*), 1 oz., or about 5 slices 117
(*Oscar Mayer*), 1 oz., or about 3 slices 105
(*Swift*), 1 oz. 110

*Prepared according to directions on container

party (*Hormel*), 1 oz., or about 4 slices 94
Salami, turkey, see "Turkey salami"
Salisbury steak:
canned; and mushroom gravy
(*Morton House* Heat 'n Serve), 4⅙ oz. 160
frozen:
(*Howard Johnson's*), 4½ oz. 273
(*Morton* Boil-in-Bag), 5-oz. pkg. 150
(*Morton Country Table* Entree), 10¼-oz. pkg. 500
(*Swanson Hungry-Man* Entree), 12½-oz. pkg. 640
with crinkle cut potatoes (*Swanson TV Brand* Entree),
5½-oz. pkg. 370
with gravy (*Banquet Cookin' Bag*), 5-oz. pkg. 246
with gravy (*Green Giant* Baked Entree), 7-oz. pkg. 290
with gravy (*Morton*), 8 oz. 240
gravy and (*Banquet Buffet Suppers*), 32-oz. pkg. 1,454
with onion gravy (*Stouffer's*), 12-oz. pkg. 500
with tomato sauce (*Green Giant* Entree), 9-oz. pkg. 390
Salisbury steak dinner, frozen:
(*Banquet*), 11-oz. pkg. 390
(*Banquet Man Pleaser*), 19-oz. pkg. 873
(*Morton*), 11-oz. pkg. 290
(*Morton Country Table*), 15-oz. pkg. 500
(*Morton* King Size), 19-oz. pkg. 780
(*Swanson*), 16-oz. pkg. 490
(*Swanson Hungry-Man*), 17-oz. pkg. 870
(*Swanson TV Brand*), 11½-oz. pkg. 500
Salmon:
fresh:
Atlantic, raw, whole, 1 lb. 640
Atlantic, raw, meat only, 4 oz. 240
chinook (king), raw, steak, 1 lb. 886
chinook (king), raw, meat only, 4 oz. 252
pink (humpback), raw, steak, 1 lb. 475
pink (humpback), raw, meat only, 4 oz. 135
broiled or baked with butter, meat only, 4 oz. 207
broiled or baked with butter, 1 steak (6¾″ × 2½″) 232

canned:

Atlantic, with liquid, 4 oz. 447

blueback (*Icy Point*), 3¾-oz. can 181

blueback (*Icy Point*), 7¾-oz. can 376

chinook (king), with liquid, 7¾-oz. can 462

chinook (king), with liquid, 4 oz. 238

chum, with liquid, 7¾-oz. can 306

chum, with liquid, 4 oz. 158

coho, or silver, with liquid, 7¾-oz. can 337

coho, or silver, with liquid, 4 oz. 174

coho steak (*Icy Point*), 3¾-oz. can 162

pink (*Del Monte*), 7¾-oz. can 310

pink (*Icy Point*), 7¾-oz. can 310

pink (*Pink Beauty*), 7¾-oz. can 310

red (*Icy Point*), 15½-oz. can 775

red sockeye (*Del Monte*), 7¾-oz. can 340

red sockeye (*Pillar Rock*), 3¾-oz. can 181

red sockeye (*Pillar Rock*), 7¾-oz. can 376

red sockeye (*Pillar Rock*), 15½-oz. can 775

Salmon, smoked:

flesh only (*Vita*), 2 oz. 100

lox, Nova (*Vita*), 2 oz. 122

lox, regular (*Vita*), 2 oz. 112

Salsify, fresh:

freshly harvested, raw, without tops, 1 lb. 51

stored, raw, without tops, 1 lb. 324

freshly harvested, boiled, drained, cubed, 1 cup 16

stored, boiled, drained, cubed, 1 cup 94

Salt, flavored, see individual listings

Salt, table:

1 lb. 0

1 cup 0

Salt pork:

raw, with skin, 1 lb. 3,410

raw, without skin, 1 oz. 222

Salt sticks, see "Bread sticks"

Sancerre wine:
(*B & G*), 4 fl. oz. 80
Sand dab:
raw, whole, 1 lb. 118
raw, meat only, 4 oz. 89
Sandwich spread:
(*Bama*), 1 tbsp. 45
(*Bennett's*), 1 tbsp. 45
(*Best Foods*), 1 tbsp. 60
(*Hellman's*), 1 tbsp. 60
(*Kraft*), 1 tbsp. 50
(*Mrs. Filberts*), 1 tbsp. 50
meat (*Oscar Mayer*), ½ oz. 33
Sapodillas:
whole, 1 lb. 323
peeled and seeded, 4 oz. 101
Sapotes (marmalade plums):
whole, 1 lb. 431
peeled and seeded, 4 oz. 143
Sardines:
Atlantic, canned:
in oil, 4 oz. 353
in oil, drained, 3¼ oz. (yield from 3¾-oz. can with oil) . . .187
in oil, with liquid, 3¾-oz. can 330
in oil, 1 fish (3½″ long, 1½″ wide) 41
in oil, 1 fish (3″ long, ½″ wide) 24
in oil, 1 fish (2⅔″ long, ½″ wide) 10
Pacific:
raw, meat only, 4 oz. 181
canned, in mustard sauce (*Underwood*), 3¾-oz. can 197
canned, in oil (*Crown*), 3¾-oz. can, drained 192
canned, in oil (*King Oscar*), 3¾-oz. can, drained 205
canned, in oil (*Underwood*), 3¾-oz. can, drained 233
canned, in tomato sauce (*Del Monte*), 7½-oz. can 330
canned, in tomato sauce (*Underwood*), 3¾-oz. can 169
Sauce, see individual listings

Sauce, all-purpose:
  canned (*Ronzoni*), 4 oz. 80
Sauerkraut, canned or in jars:
  (*Claussen*), ½ cup drained 15
  (*Del Monte*), ½ cup 25
  (*Libby's*—canned), ½ cup 21
  (*Libby's*—in jars), ½ cup 19
  (*Stokely-Van Camp* Bavarian Style), ½ cup 30
  chopped (*Stokely-Van Camp*), ½ cup 20
  shredded (*Stokely-Van Camp*), ½ cup 20
Sauerkraut juice:
  canned, 15-fl. oz. can 45
  canned, 1 cup 24
Sauerkraut pierogies:
  frozen (*Mrs. Paul's*), 5 oz. 310
Sauger:
  raw, whole, 1 lb. 133
  raw, meat only, 4 oz. 95
Sausages:
  beef (*Swift Premium*), 1 sausage, cooked 85
  beef, Polish (*Vienna*), 3½ oz. 280
  blood (pudding), 4 oz. 447
  blood (pudding), 1 slice (2¼″ in diam., ⅛″ thick) 32
  brown and serve, before browning:
    8-oz. pkg. (8–9 patties or 10–11 links) 892
    1 link (3⅞″ long, ⅝″ in diam.) 83
    1 patty (2⅜″ × 1⅞″ × ½″) 111
  brown and serve, browned:
    6.3 oz. (yield from 8-oz. pkg. before browning) 760
    1 link (3⅞″ long, ⅝″ in diam. before browning) 72
    1 patty (2⅜″ × 1⅞″ × ½″ before browning) 97
    4 oz. 479
  country style, 4 oz. 391
  Polish, see "Kielbasa"
  pork:
    raw, 8-oz. pkg. (4 patties or 8 links) 1,130
    raw, 2.4-oz. piece (3″ long, 1¼″ in diam.) 339

285

raw, 2-oz. patty (3⅞″ in diam., ¼″ thick) 284
raw, 1-oz. link (4″ long, ⅞″ in diam.) 141
cooked, 3.8 oz. (yield from 8-oz. pkg. raw) 509
cooked, 1 piece (yield from 2.4-oz. piece raw) 152
cooked, 1 patty (yield from 2-oz. patty raw) 129
cooked, 1 link (yield from 1-oz. link raw) 62
cooked, 4 oz. 543
canned, with liquid, 8-oz. can (about 14 links) 942
canned, drained, 5.7 oz. (yield from 8-oz.
  can with liquid) 617
canned, drained, 1 link (3″ long, ½″ in diam.) 46
and beef, chopped, 4 oz. 383
(*Hormel* Brown 'n Serve), 1 sausage 78
(*Hormel Little Sizzlers*), 1 sausage, cooked 67
(*Oscar Mayer*), 1 patty, cooked 125
(*Oscar Mayer Little Friers*), 1 sausage, cooked 80
(*Swift Bacon 'N Sausage*), 1 sausage, cooked 70
(*Swift Premium* Brown 'N Serve), 1 sausage, cooked 75
(*Swift Kountry Kured*), 1 sausage, cooked 85
(*Wilson Certified*), 1-lb. pkg. 2,100
(*Wilson Corn King*), 1-lb. pkg. 2,100
(*Wilson* Western Style), 1 patty 140
roll (*Oscar Mayer*), 1 oz., cooked 109
roll, smoked (*Hormel*), 1 oz. 98
scrapple, 16-oz. loaf (4½″ × 2¾″ × 2⅛″) 975
scrapple, 1 slice (2¾″ × 2⅛″ × ¼″; ¹⁄₁₈ of 16-oz. loaf) ...54
scrapple, 4 oz. 244
smoked (see also ''country style,'' above):
(*Eckrich* Skinless Links—12-oz. pkg.), 1 link 115
(*Eckrich* Skinless Links—1-lb. pkg.), 1 link 190
(*Eckrich Smok-Y-Links*), 1 link 85
(*Eckrich* Smoked Sausage), 1 oz. 105
(*Hormel Range Brand Wranglers*), 1 link 175
(*Hormel* Smokies), 1 link 93
(*Kahn's Big Red Smoky*), 1 link 175
(*Kahn's* Smoked Sausage), 1 oz. 91
(*Oscar Mayer* Little Smokies), ⅓-oz. link 32

(*Oscar Mayer* Smoked Breakfast Sausages), .7-oz. link ...68
(*Oscar Mayer* Smokie Links), 1½-oz. link 135
(*Vienna*), 3½-oz. 276
(*Wilson Certified*), 1-lb. pkg. 1,525
(*Wilson Corn King*), 1-lb. pkg. 1,525
beef (*Eckrich Smok-Y-Links*), 1 link 75
beef (*Eckrich* Smoked Sausage), 1 oz. 95
beef (*Hormel Wranglers*), 1 link 156
cheese (*Oscar Mayer* Cheese Smokies), 1½-oz. link 140
souse, 6-oz. pkg. (about 6 slices) 308
souse, 1-oz. slice 51
souse, 4 oz. 205
Vienna:
   (*Armour Star*), 3 sausages 150
   (*Wilson's Certified*), 3 sausages 144
   barbecue (*Libby's*), 3 sausages 154
   beef broth (*Libby's*), 3 sausages 138
Sausage and peppers:
   frozen (*Buitoni*), 15-oz. pkg. 618
Sausage rolls, dried:
   (*Cow-Boy Jo's* Beef Jerky), ¼-oz. pkg. 24
   (*Cow-Boy Jo's* Beef Sausage), ⅝-oz. pkg. 81
   (*Cow-Boy Jo's Smok-O-Roni* Beef Sausage), ¼-oz. pkg. ...42
   (*Frito-Lay's* Smoked Beef Polish Sausage), 1-oz. pkg. 70
   (*Lowrey's* Pickled Hot Sausage), 1¼-oz. pkg. 110
   (*Lowrey's* Pickled Polish Sausage), ⅝-oz. pkg. 50
Sausage sandwich:
   frozen (*Stouffer's* Italian), 8¼-oz. pkg. 470
Sausage, summer, see "Summer sausage"
Sauterne table wine:
   (*Gold Seal*), 4 fl. oz. 116
   dry (*Gold Seal*), 4 fl. oz. 108
   dry (*Taylor*), 4 fl. oz. 108
Sauternes wine:
   (*B & G*), 2 fl. oz. 64
   (*Château Voigny*), 2 fl. oz. 64

Savory:
　ground (all brands), 1 tsp. 5
Scallions, see "Onions, young green"
Scallop crepes:
　frozen (*Mrs. Paul's*), 5½-oz. crepe 220
Scallop dinner:
　frozen, fried (*Taste O' Sea*), 8-oz. pkg. 380
Scallops, bay and sea:
　fresh:
　　raw, meat only, 4 oz. 92
　　steamed, meat only, 4 oz. 127
　frozen:
　　batter-fried (*Mrs. Paul's*), 7-oz. pkg. 400
　　with butter and cheese (*Mrs. Paul's*), 7-oz. pkg. 260
　　country seasoned (*Van de Kamp's*), 3½ oz. 270
　　fried (*Mrs. Paul's*), 7-oz. pkg. 420
　　fried (*Mrs. Paul's*), 12-oz. pkg. 720
Scallops and shrimp mariner:
　frozen, with rice (*Stouffer's*), 10¼-oz. pkg. 400
Scrapple, see "Sausages"
Screwdriver cocktail:
　vodka (*Old Mr. Boston*—25 proof), 1 fl. oz. 39
Screwdriver cocktail mix:
　instant (*Holland House*), 1 packet 69
Scrod:
　frozen, baked, stuffed (*Gorton*), 9½-oz. pkg. 420
Scrod dinner:
　frozen, batter-fried (*Taste O' Sea Batter Dipt*),
　　8¾-oz. pkg. 500
Scup, see "Porgy"
Sea bass, white:
　raw, meat only, 4 oz. 109
Seafood cocktail sauce, see "Cocktail seafood sauce"
Seafood croquettes:
　frozen (*Mrs. Paul's*), 3-oz. cake 180
Seafood platter:
　frozen, combination (*Mrs. Paul's*), 9-oz. pkg. 510

Seafood platter dinner:
frozen (*Taste O'Sea*), 9-oz. pkg. 520
Seafood seasoning:
(*French's*), 1 tsp. 2
Seasoned coating mix:
for chicken:
(*Shake 'n Bake*), 1 packet 279
barbecue style (*Shake 'n Bake*), 1 packet 366
crispy country mild (*Shake 'n Bake*), 1 packet 318
Italian flavor (*Shake 'n Bake*), 1 packet 286
for fish (*Shake 'n Bake*), 1 packet 226
for hamburger (*Shake 'n Bake*), 1 packet 163
for pork (*Shake 'n Bake*), 1 packet 260
for pork and ribs, barbecue style (*Shake 'n Bake*),
1 packet 290
Seasoned salt:
(*French's*), 1 tsp. 2
(*Lawry's*), 1 tsp. 1
Seasoning, see individual listings
Sesame buds:
(*Flavor Tree*), 1 oz. 160
with garlic (*Flavor Tree*), 1 oz. 160
Sesame butter:
(*Hain*), 1 tbsp. 90
Sesame chips:
(*Flavor Tree*), 1 oz. 160
Sesame coconut crunch:
(*Flavor Tree*), 1 oz. 140
Sesame honey crunch:
(*Flavor Tree*), 1 oz. 140
Sesame nut mix:
(*Planters*), 1 oz. 160
Sesame oil, see "Oils, cooking or salad"
Sesame paste, see "Tahini"
Sesame seeds, dry:
whole, 4 oz. 639
hulled, 4 oz. 660

hulled, 1 cup 873
hulled, 1 tbsp. 47
all brands, 1 tsp. 9
Shad:
fresh:
raw, whole, 1 lb. 370
raw, meat only, 4 oz. 193
baked, fillets, with butter and bacon, 4 oz. 228
canned, with liquid, 4 oz. 172
Shad gizzard:
raw, meat only, 4 oz. 227
Shad roe, see "Roe"
Shallots, raw:
with skin, 1 oz. 18
peeled, 1 oz. 20
peeled, chopped, 1 tbsp. 7
Sheefish, see "Inconnu"
Sheepshead, Atlantic:
raw, whole, 1 lb. 159
raw, meat only, 4 oz. 128
Shells, pasta, see "Pasta shells"
Sherbet:
fruit flavors (*Meadow Gold*), ½ cup 120
lime (*Foremost*), ½ cup 110
orange, 1 cup 259
orange (*Foremost*), ½ cup 110
orange (*Hood*), ½ cup 110
pineapple (*Foremost*), ½ cup 110
rainbow (*Foremost*), ½ cup 110
raspberry (*Foremost*), ½ cup 110
strawberry (*Foremost*), ½ cup 100
Sherbet bar:
fudge (*Fudgsicle*), 2½ fl. oz. 110
Sherry wine:
(*Hiram Walker* Armada Cream), 2 fl. oz. 82
domestic (*Gold Seal* Private Reserve New York State),
2 fl. oz. 93

290

domestic (*Taylor* New York State), 2 fl. oz. 88
domestic (*Taylor* New York State Cream), 2 fl. oz. 100
imported (*Williams & Humbert* Dry Sack), 2 fl. oz. 80
dry (*Hiram Walker* Cocktail), 2 fl. oz. 70
dry, domestic (*Gold Seal* Private Reserve New York State
   Cocktail), 2 fl. oz. 81
dry, domestic (*Taylor* New York State Pale Dry Cocktail),
   2 fl. oz. 76
dry, imported (*Sandeman* Cocktail), 2 fl. oz. 72

Shortbread, see "Cookies"

Shortening:
vegetable, 8 oz. 2,005
vegetable, 1 cup 1,768
vegetable, 1 tbsp. 111
(*Bake Rite*), 1 tbsp. 91
(*Crisco*), 1 tbsp. 110
(*Fluffo*), 1 tbsp. 110
(*Hi Tone*), 1 tbsp. 120
(*Light Spry*), 1 tbsp. 93
(*Snowdrift*), 1 tbsp. 110

Shrimp:
fresh:
   raw, whole, in shell, 1 lb. 285
   raw, shelled and cleaned, 4 oz. 103
   breaded, french-fried, 4 oz. 255
canned or in jars:
   with liquid, 8 oz. 182
   drained or dry pack, 8 oz. 263
   drained, 1 cup
     (22 large, 40 medium, or 76 small shrimp) 148
   drained, 10 large shrimp (about 3¼″ long) 67
   drained, 10 medium shrimp (about 2½″ long) 37
   drained, 10 small shrimp (about 2″ long) 17
   (*Blue Gulf/High Sea/Louisiana*), 4 oz. 116
frozen:
   batter-fried (*Booth*), 3 oz., or 5–6 shrimp 193

batter-fried (*Booth* Heat 'n Serve),
   3 oz., or 5–7 shrimp 265
breaded (*Booth* Heat 'n Serve), 4 oz., or 7–9 shrimp ...296
breaded (*Booth* Ready to Fry), 4 oz., or 7–9 shrimp 160
breaded (*Gorton 1836*), 4 oz. 190
cakes (*Mrs. Paul's*), 3-oz. cake 150
croquettes, with Newburg sauce (*Howard Johnson's*),
   12-oz. pkg. 478
fried (*Mrs. Paul's*), 6-oz. pkg. 340
fritters, batter-fried (*Mrs. Paul's*), 7¾-oz. pkg. 480
sticks (*Gorton*), 5 sticks 200
sticks, batter-fried (*Booth*), 3¼-oz., or 4 sticks 210
sticks, fried (*Mrs. Paul's*), 3.2 oz., or 4 sticks 190
sticks, fried (*Mrs. Paul's* Family Size), 3 oz. or 4 sticks ...190

Shrimp chow mein, see "Chow mein"
Shrimp cocktail:
with sauce (*Sau-Sea*), 4-oz. jar 112
with sauce (*Sau-Sea*), 6-oz. jar 121
Shrimp crepes:
frozen (*Mrs. Paul's*), 5½-oz. crepe 250
Shrimp dinner, frozen:
(*Van de Kamp's*), 10-oz. pkg. 370
Chinese (*La Choy*), 11-oz. pkg. 325
fried (*Taste O'Sea*), 7-oz. pkg. 350
patty, fried (*Taste O' Sea*), 1 dinner* 390
Shrimp marinara:
frozen (*Buitoni*), 17-oz. pkg. 486
Shrimp Newburg:
frozen (*Stouffer's*), 6½-oz. pkg. 300
Shrimp paste:
canned, 1 oz. 51
canned, 1 tsp. 13
Shrimp puff pastry:
frozen (*Durkee*), 1 piece 44

*Prepared according to directions on container

Shrimp scampi:
   frozen (*Gorton*), ½ pkg. 200
Sip 'n slim cocktail mix:
   bottled (*Holland House*), 1 fl. oz. 9
Siscowet, see "Lake trout"
Skate (Raja fish):
   raw, meat only, 4 oz. 111
Sloe gin liqueur:
   (*Bols*), 1 fl. oz. 85
   (*Dolfi Prunelle*), 1 fl. oz. 114
   (*DuBouchett*—48 proof), 1 fl. oz. 68
   (*DuBouchett*—60 proof), 1 fl. oz. 71
   (*Garnier*), 1 fl. oz. 83
   (*Hiram Walker*), 1 fl. oz. 66
   (*Old Mr. Boston*—70 proof), 1 fl. oz. 76
   (*Old Mr. Boston* Connoisseur—42 proof), 1 fl. oz. 50
Sloppy hot dog seasoning mix:
   dry (*French's*), 1½-oz. packet 160
Sloppy joe:
   canned:
      (*Hormel* Short Order), 7½-oz. can 344
      (*Morton House*), 5 oz. 240
      beef (*Libby's*), 8 oz. 370
      pork (*Libby's*), 8 oz. 315
   frozen (*Morton* Boil-in-Bag), 5-oz. pkg. 210
   frozen, with tomato sauce and beef
      (*Green Giant Toast Toppers*), 5 oz. 160
Sloppy joe seasoning mix:
   dry (*Durkee*), 1½-oz. packet 118
   dry (*French's*), 1½-oz. packet 128
   dry (*McCormick/Schilling*), 1⁵⁄₁₆-oz. packet 102
   dry, pizza flavor (*Durkee*), 1-oz. packet 99
Smelt, Atlantic, jack, or bay:
   raw, whole, 1 lb. 244
   raw, meat only, 4 oz. 111
   canned, with liquid, 8 oz. 454
Smelt, eulachon, see "Eulachon"

Snack cracker chips:
  (*Skittle Chips*), 1 oz. 140
Snack sticks:
  (*Lil' Loaf*), 1 oz. 140
  (*Twigs*), 1 oz. 140
Snack crisps:
  (*O & C Snackin' Crisp*), 1 oz. 155
Snails:
  raw, meat only, 4 oz. 103
  raw, giant African, meat only, 4 oz. 83
Snapper, see "Red and gray snapper"
Snow peas, see "Pea pods, Chinese"
Soft drinks and mixers:
  birch beer (*Canada Dry*), 8 fl. oz. 110
  bitter lemon (*Canada Dry*), 8 fl. oz. 100
  bitter lemon (*Schweppes*), 8 fl. oz. 88
  blended flavors:
    (*Canada Dry* Purple Passion), 8 fl. oz. 120
    (*Canada Dry* Tahitian Treat), 8 fl. oz. 130
    (*Shasta* Fruit Punch), 8 fl. oz. 112
  (*Bubble-Up*), 8 fl. oz. 97
  (*Canada Dry* Cactus Cooler), 8 fl. oz. 120
  (*Canada Dry* Hi Spot), 8 fl. oz. 100
  (*Canada Dry* Rooti), 8 fl. oz. 110
  (*Canada Dry* Vostok), 8 fl. oz. 90
  cherry:
    (*Fanta*), 8 fl. oz. 117
    black (*Shasta*), 8 fl. oz. 105
    wild (*Canada Dry*), 8 fl. oz. 130
  chocolate (*Yoo-Hoo*), 9 fl. oz. 170
  club soda (all brands), 8 fl. oz. 0
  coconut shake (*Yoo-Hoo*), 9½-fl. oz. 150
  cola:
    12-fl. oz. can or bottle 144
    (*Canada Dry* Jamaican Cola), 8 fl. oz. 110
    (*Coca-Cola*), 8 fl. oz. 96
    (*Pepsi Cola*), 8 fl. oz. 104

(*Royal Crown*), 8 fl. oz. 109
(*Shasta*), 8 fl. oz. 95
cherry flavored (*Shasta*), 8 fl. oz. 90
Collins mixer:
    12-fl.-oz. can or bottle 171
    (*Canada Dry*), 8 fl. oz. 80
cream:
    12-fl.-oz. can or bottle 160
    (*Canada Dry* Vanilla), 8 fl. oz. 130
    (*Shasta*), 8 fl. oz. 100
(*Dr Pepper*), 8 fl. oz. 94
fruit punch, see "blended flavors," above
ginger ale:
    pale dry or golden, 12-fl.-oz. can or bottle 113
    (*Canada Dry*), 8 fl. oz. 90
    (*Canada Dry* Golden), 8 fl. oz. 100
    (*Schweppes*), 8 fl. oz. 88
    (*Shasta*), 8 fl. oz. 78
grape:
    (*Canada Dry* Concord), 8 fl. oz. 130
    (*Crush*), 8 fl. oz. 119
    (*Shasta*), 8 fl. oz. 115
grapefruit (*Shasta*), 8 fl. oz. 105
grapefruit (*Wink*), 8 fl. oz. 120
half and half mixer (*Canada Dry*), 8 fl. oz. 110
lemon, bitter, see "bitter lemon," above
lemonade (*Shasta*), 8 fl. oz. 95
lemon-lime (*Shasta*), 8 fl. oz. 93
lime (*Canada Dry*), 8 fl. oz. 130
(*Mello Yello*), 8 fl. oz. 116
orange:
    (*Canada Dry* Sunripe), 8 fl. oz. 130
    (*Crush*), 8 fl. oz. 114
    (*Shasta*), 8 fl. oz. 115
pineapple (*Canada Dry*), 8 fl. oz. 110
quinine water, see "tonic water," below

root beer:
    12-fl.-oz. can or bottle 152
    (*Canada Dry* Barrelhead), 8 fl. oz. 110
    (*Dads*), 8 fl. oz. 105
    (*Hires*), 8 fl. oz. 100
    (*Shasta*), 8 fl. oz. 100
    (*Schweppes* Rondo), 8 fl. oz. 102
    (*7-Up*), 8 fl. oz. 97
    (*Squirt*), 8 fl. oz. 105
strawberry:
    (*Canada Dry* California), 8 fl. oz. 120
    (*Shasta*), 8 fl. oz. 95
    shake (*Yoo-Hoo*), 9½ fl. oz. 150
tonic water:
    12-fl.-oz. can or bottle 113
    (*Canada Dry*), 8 fl. oz. 90
    (*Schweppes*), 8 fl. oz. 88
vanilla shake (*Yoo-Hoo*), 9½ fl. oz. 150
whiskey sour mix (*Canada Dry*), 8 fl. oz. 90
Sole:
raw, whole, 1 lb. 118
raw, meat only (fillets), 4 oz. 90
frozen:
    batter fried (*Van de Kamp's*), 4¾ oz.,
      or 2 pieces 280
    fillets (*Taste O'Sea*), 16-oz. pkg. 360
    with lemon butter (*Gorton*), ½ pkg. 200
    with lemon butter (*Mrs. Paul's*), 9-oz. pkg. 320
Sole dinner:
frozen, fried (*Taste O' Sea*), 9-oz. pkg. 330
Sorghum grain:
    4 oz. 378
Sorghum syrup, see "Syrups"
Sorrel, see "Dock"
Soup greens:
    (*Durkee*), 2½-oz. jar 216

Soups, canned:
  asparagus, cream of:
    cond.* (*Campbell's*), 10 oz. 100
    cond.** (*Campbell's*), 10 oz. 200
  bean:
    with bacon, cond.* (*Campbell's*), 10 oz. 190
    with ham, old-fashioned (*Campbell's* Chunky), 9½ oz. ...260
    with ham, old-fashioned
        (*Campbell's* Chunky—Individual), 11-oz. can 300
    with hot dog, cond.* (*Campbell's*), 10 oz. 210
    old-fashioned, semicond.*** (*Campbell's* Soup for One),
        11⅝ oz. 210
  bean, black, cond.* (*Campbell's*), 10 oz. 130
  bean, black, with sherry (*Crosse & Blackwell*), 13-oz. can ...160
  beef:
    (*Campbell's* Chunky), 9½ oz. 190
    (*Campbell's* Chunky—Individual), 10¾-oz. can 220
    cond.* (*Campbell's*), 10 oz. 100
    broth or bouillon, cond.* (*Campbell's*), 10 oz. 35
    broth (*College Inn*), 1 cup 18
    broth (*Swanson*), 6¾ oz. 20
    cabbage (*Manischewitz*), 8 oz. 125
    consommé, cond.* (*Campbell's*), 10 oz. 45
    noodle, cond.* (*Campbell's*), 10 oz. 90
  borscht:
    (*Manischewitz*), 8 oz. 72
    (*Mother's*), 1 cup 90
    egg-enriched (*Mother's*), 1 cup 124
  celery, cream of:
    cond.* (*Campbell's*), 10 oz. 110
    cond.** (*Campbell's*), 10 oz. 210
  cheddar cheese, cond.* (*Campbell's*), 10 oz. 180
  chicken:
    (*Campbell's* Chunky), 9½ oz. 200

---

*Prepared with 5 oz. soup and 5 oz. water
**Prepared with 5 oz. soup and 5 oz. whole milk
***Prepared with 7¾ oz. soup and 3⅞ oz. water

(*Campbell's* Chunky—Individual), 10¾-oz. can 230
(*Progresso* Homestyle), 8 fl. oz. 70
alphabet, cond.* (*Campbell's*), 10 oz. 110
barley (*Manischewitz*), 8 oz. 168
broth (*College Inn*), 1 cup 35
broth (*Swanson*), 6¾ oz. 25
broth, cond.* (*Campbell's*), 10 oz. 50
cream of, cond.* (*Campbell's*), 10 oz. 140
cream of, cond.** (*Campbell's*), 10 oz. 240
and dumplings, cond.* (*Campbell's*), 10 oz. 120
golden, and noodles, semicond.***
   (*Campbell's* Soup for One) 11⅝ oz. 120
gumbo, cond.* (*Campbell's*), 10 oz. 70
with meatballs (*Progresso Chickarina*), 8 fl. oz. 100
noodle (*Manischewitz*), 8 oz. 91
noodle, cond.* (*Campbell's*), 10 oz. 90
noodle, O-shape, cond.* (*Campbell's* NoodleO's), 10 oz. 90
noodle stars, cond.* (*Campbell's*), 10 oz. 80
rice (*Campbell's* Chunky), 9½ oz. 160
rice (*Manischewitz*), 8 oz. 95
rice, cond.* (*Campbell's*), 10 oz. 80
vegetable (*Campbell's* Chunky), 9½ oz. 190
vegetable (*Manischewitz*), 8 oz. 109
vegetable, cond.* (*Campbell's*), 10 oz. 90
chili beef:
   (*Campbell's* Chunky), 9¾ oz. 260
   (*Campbell's* Chunky—Individual), 11-oz. can 300
   cond.* (*Campbell's*), 10 oz. 190
clam chowder:
   (*Progresso*), 1 cup 100
   Manhattan (*Campbell's* Chunky), 9½ oz. 160
   Manhattan (*Crosse & Blackwell*), 13-oz. can 100
   Manhattan, cond.* (*Campbell's*), 10 oz. 100
   Manhattan, cond.* (*Doxsee*), 6 oz. 48

*Prepared with 5 oz. soup and 5 oz. water
**Prepared with 5 oz. soup and 5 oz. whole milk
***Prepared with 7¾ oz. soup and 3⅞ oz. water

Manhattan, cond.* (*Snow's*), ⅞ cup 70
New England (*Crosse & Blackwell*), 13-oz. can 180
New England, cond.* (*Campbell's*), 10 oz. 100
New England, cond.** (*Campbell's*), 10 oz. 200
New England, cond.** (*Snow's*), ⅞ cup 130
New England, semicond.*** (*Campbell's* Soup for One),
   11⅝ oz. 125
New England, semicond.† (*Campbell's* Soup for One),
   11⅝ oz. 200
corn chowder, New England, cond.** (*Snow's*), ⅞ cup ...140
crab, a la Maryland (*Crosse & Blackwell*), 13-oz. can 100
escarole, in chicken broth (*Progresso*), 8 fl. oz. 25
fish chowder, New England, cond.** (*Snow's*), ⅞ cup 130
gazpacho (*Crosse & Blackwell*), 13-oz. can 60
green pea, see "pea," below
lentil (*Progresso*), 8 fl. oz. 150
lentil, with ham (*Crosse & Blackwell*), 13-oz. can 160
macaroni and bean (*Progresso*), 8 fl. oz. 170
Madrilene consommé, clear (*Crosse & Blackwell*),
   13-oz. can 50
Madrilene consommé, red (*Crosse & Blackwell*),
   13-oz. can 60
meatball alphabet, cond.* (*Campbell's*), 10 oz. 140
minestrone:
   (*Campbell's* Chunky), 9½ oz. 160
   (*Crosse & Blackwell*), 13-oz. can 180
   (*Progresso*), 8 fl. oz. 130
   cond.* (*Campbell's*), 10 oz. 110
mushroom:
   barley (*Manischewitz*), 8 oz. 145
   cream of, cond.* (*Campbell's*), 10 oz. 150
   cream of, cond.** (*Campbell's*), 10 oz. 250
   cream of, bisque (*Crosse & Blackwell*), 13-oz. can 180

---

*Prepared with 5 oz. soup and 5 oz. water
**Prepared with 5 oz. soup and 5 oz. whole milk
***Prepared with 7¾ oz. soup and 3⅞ oz. water
†Prepared with 7¾ oz. soup and 3⅞ oz. whole milk

cream of, with wine, semicond.***
   (*Campbell's* Soup for One) 11¼ oz. 160
   golden, cond.* (*Campbell's*), 10 oz. 110
noodle, curly, with chicken, cond.* (*Campbell's*), 10 oz. 100
noodle and ground beef, cond.* (*Campbell's*), 10 oz. 110
onion:
   cond.* (*Campbell's*), 10 oz. 80
   cream of, cond.‡ (*Campbell's*), 10 oz. 180
oyster stew:
   (*Chicken of the Sea*), 8 oz. 163
   cond.* (*Campbell's*), 10 oz. 70
   cond.** (*Campbell's*), 10 oz. 170
pea:
   green, cond.* (*Campbell's*), 10 oz. 180
   green, split (*Progresso*), 8 fl. oz. 180
   split (*Manischewitz*), 8 oz. 265
   split, with ham (*Campbell's* Chunky), 9½ oz. 220
   split, with ham and bacon, cond.* (*Campbell's*), 10 oz. 210
pepperpot, cond.* (*Campbell's*), 10 oz. 130
potato, cream of:
   cond.* (*Campbell's*), 10 oz. 90
   cond.** (*Campbell's*), 10 oz. 190
   cond.‡ (*Campbell's*), 10 oz. 140
seafood chowder, New England, cond.** (*Snow's*), ⅞ cup ...130
shav (*Manischewitz*), 8 oz. 11
Scotch broth, cond.* (*Campbell's*), 10 oz. 100
shrimp, cream of:
   (*Crosse & Blackwell*), 13-oz. can 180
   cond.* (*Campbell's*), 10 oz. 110
   cond.** (*Campbell's*), 10 oz. 210
sirloin burger (*Campbell's* Chunky), 9½ oz. 210
sirloin burger (*Campbell's* Chunky—Individual),
   10¾-oz. can 230

---

*Prepared with 5 oz. soup and 5 oz. water
**Prepared with 5 oz. soup and 5 oz. whole milk
***Prepared with 7¾ oz. soup and 3⅞ oz. water
‡Prepared with 5 oz. soup, 2½ oz. water, and 2½ oz. whole milk.

steak and potato (*Campbell's* Chunky), 9½ oz. 190
tomato:
  (*Manischewitz*), 8 oz. 127
  (*Progresso*), 8 fl. oz. 110
  cond.* (*Campbell's*), 10 oz. 110
  cond.** (*Campbell's*), 10 oz. 210
  semicond.*** (*Campbell's* Royale Soup for One),
    11⅝ oz. 180
  beef, noodle, O-shaped, cond.* (*Campbell's* NoodleO's),
    10 oz. 160
  bisque, cond.* (*Campbell's*), 10 oz. 140
  rice, old-fashioned, cond.* (*Campbell's*), 10 oz. 130
turkey:
  (*Campbell's* Chunky), 9¼ oz. 160
  noodle, cond.* (*Campbell's*), 10 oz. 80
  vegetable, cond.* (*Campbell's*), 10 oz. 90
turtle, mock (*Stegner's*), 10½-oz. can 212
turtle, mock (*Stegner's*), 15-oz. can 302
vegetable:
  (*Campbell's* Chunky), 9½ oz. 140
  (*Campbell's* Chunky—Individual), 10¾-oz. can 150
  (*Manischewitz*), 8 oz. 125
  cond.* (*Campbell's*), 10 oz. 100
  semicond.*** (*Campbell's* Old World Soup for One),
    11⅝ oz. 125
  and beef, stockpot, cond.* (*Campbell's*), 10 oz. 120
  beef, cond.* (*Campbell's*), 10 oz. 90
  beef, old-fashioned (*Campbell's* Chunky), 9½ oz. 160
  golden, with O-shaped noodles, cond.*
    (*Campbell's* NoodleO's) 10 oz. .90
  old-fashioned, cond.* (*Campbell's*), 10 oz. 90
  vegetarian, cond.* (*Campbell's*), 10 oz. 90
vichyssoise, cream of (*Crosse & Blackwell*), 13-oz. can . . .140

*Prepared with 5 oz. soup and 5 oz. water
**Prepared with 5 oz. soup and 5 oz. whole milk
***Prepared with 7¾ oz. soup and 3⅞ oz. water

Soup, frozen:

clam chowder, New England (*Stouffer's*), 8-oz. pkg. 200
oyster stew:
    cond., 8 oz. 232
    diluted with equal part whole milk, 1 cup 197
pea, green, with ham, cond., 8 oz. 257
pea, green, with ham, diluted with equal part water, 1 cup ..134
pea, split, with ham (*Stouffer's*), 8¼-oz. pkg. 190
potato, cream of:
    cond., 8 oz. 197
    diluted with equal part whole milk, 1 cup 179
shrimp, cream of:
    cond., 8 oz. 302
    diluted with equal part whole milk, 1 cup 233
spinach, cream of (*Stouffer's*), 8-oz. pkg. 230
won ton chicken (*La Choy*), ½ pkg. 50

Soup mix*:

alphabet (*Golden Grain*), 8 fl. oz. 55
asparagus (*Knorr*), 6 fl. oz. 45
beef, and beef flavor:
    barley (*Knorr*), 6 fl. oz. 45
    bouillon, see "Bouillon"
    broth, see "broth," below
    mushroom (*Lipton*), 8 oz. can 40
    noodle (*Knorr Swiss*), 6 fl. oz. 25
    noodle (*Lipton Cup-a-Soup*), 6 fl. oz. 35
    noodle (*Nestlé Souptime*), 6 fl. oz. 30
    noodle, beef flavor, see "noodle," below
    onion (*Lipton*), 8 fl. oz. 40
bouillon, see "Bouillon"
broth:
    beef (*Carmel*), 1 tsp. 12
    beef (*Herb-Ox*), 6 fl. oz. 8
    beef (*Maggi* Broth & Seasoning), 1 tsp. 27

*Prepared according to directions on container

beef (*MBT*), 6 fl. oz. 14
chicken (*Carmel*), 1 tsp. 12
chicken (*Lipton Cup-a-Broth*), 6 fl. oz. 25
chicken (*Maggi* Broth & Seasoning), 1 tsp. 29
chicken (*MBT*), 6 fl. oz. 12
onion (*Carmel*), 1 tsp. 12
onion (*Maggi* Broth & Seasoning), 1 tsp. 28
onion (*MBT*), 6 fl. oz. 16
vegetable (*Maggi* Broth & Seasoning), 1 tsp. 27
vegetable (*MBT*), 6 fl. oz. 12
chicken, and chicken flavor:
  bouillon, see "Bouillon"
  broth, see "broth," above
  cream of (*Knorr Swiss*), 6 fl. oz. .80
  cream of (*Lipton Cup-a-Soup*), 6 fl. oz. 80
  cream of (*Nestlé Souptime*), 6 fl. oz. 100
  creamy (*Hain* Old Fashion Naturals), 8 fl. oz. 224
  hearty (*Lipton Country Style Cup-a-Soup*), 6 fl. oz. 70
  noodle (*Golden Grain*), 6 fl. oz. .34
  noodle (*Knorr*), 6 fl. oz. 45
  noodle (*Knorr Swiss*), 6 fl. oz. 20
  noodle (*Nestlé Souptime*), 6 fl. oz. 30
  noodle, chicken flavor, see "noodle," below
  noodle, with meat (*Lipton*), 8 fl. oz. 50
  noodle, with meat (*Lipton Cup-a-Soup*), 6 fl. oz. 45
  noodle ripples (*Lipton*), 8 fl. oz. .80
  rice (*Lipton*), 8 fl. oz. 60
  rice, with white meat (*Lipton Cup-a-Soup*), 6 fl. oz. 45
  supreme (*Lipton Country Style Cup-a-Soup*), 6 fl. oz. . . .100
  vegetable, with white meat
    (*Lipton Cup-a-Soup*), 6 fl. oz. .40
green pea, see "pea," below
leek (*Knorr*), 6 fl. oz. 50
minestrone (*Golden Grain*), 8 fl. oz. 66
minestrone (*Knorr*), 6 fl. oz. 50
mushroom:
  (*Carmel*), 1 tsp. 12

(*Knorr*), 6 fl. oz. 50
(*Nestlé Souptime*), 6 fl. oz. 80
cream of (*Hain* Old Fashion Naturals), 8 fl. oz. 275
cream of (*Lipton Cup-a-Soup*), 6 fl. oz. 80
Napoli (*Knorr*), 6 fl. oz. 40
noodle:
    beef (*Cup O'Noodles*), 2½-oz. packet* 343
    beef (*Cup O'Noodles* Twin Pack), 1.2-oz. packet* 151
    beef flavor (*Lipton Cup-a-Soup*), 6 fl. oz. 50
    beef flavor (*Lipton Lots-a-Noodles Cup-a-Soup*),
      7 fl. oz. 120
    beef onion (*Cup O'Noodles*), 2½-oz. packet* 323
    beef onion (*Cup O'Noodles* Twin Pack), 1.2-oz. packet* ..158
    chicken (*Cup O'Noodles*), 2½-oz. packet* 343
    chicken (*Cup O'Noodles* Twin Pack), 1.2-oz. packet* ...155
    chicken flavor (*Lipton Cup-a-Soup*), 7 fl. oz. 130
    with real chicken broth (*Lipton*), 8 fl. oz. 60
    with real chicken broth
      (*Lipton Cup-a-Soup* Giggle Noodle), 6 fl. oz. 40
    with real chicken broth (*Lipton* Giggle Noodle), 8 fl. oz. ...80
    oriental style (*Lipton Cup-a-Soup*), 7 fl. oz. 130
    pork (*Cup O'Noodles*), 2½-oz. packet* 331
    rings (*Lipton Cup-a-Soup*), 6 fl. oz. 50
    rings (*Lipton* Ring-O), 8 fl. oz. 60
    shrimp (*Cup O'Noodles*), 2½-oz. packet* 336
    vegetable, garden (*Lipton Cup-a-Soup*), 7 fl. oz. 130
onion:
    (*Golden Grain*), 8 fl. oz. 33
    (*Knorr* Soup-Dip), 6 fl. oz. 30
    (*Knorr Swiss*), 6 fl. oz. 45
    (*Lipton*) 8 fl. oz. 35
    (*Lipton Cup-a-Soup*), 6 fl. oz. 30
    (*Nestlé Souptime* French Onion), 6 fl. oz. 20
    beefy (*Lipton*), 8 fl. oz. 30
    broth, see "broth," above

*Prepared according to directions on container

mushroom (*Lipton*), 8 fl. oz. 35
zesty (*Hain* Old Fashion Naturals), 8 fl. oz. 220
oxtail (*Knorr*), 6 fl. oz. 50
pea:
   green (*Knorr*), 6 fl. oz. 55
   green (*Knorr Swiss*), 6 fl. oz. 65
   green (*Lipton Cup-a-Soup*), 6 fl. oz. 120
   green (*Nestlé Souptime*), 6 fl. oz. 70
   split, savory (*Hain* Old Fashion Naturals), 8 fl. oz. 257
   virginia (*Lipton Country Style Cup-a-Soup*), 6 fl. oz. . . .140
potato (*Knorr Swiss*), 6 fl. oz. 70
tomato:
   (*Knorr Swiss*), 6 fl. oz. 70
   (*Lipton Cup-a-Soup*), 6 fl. oz. .80
   (*Nestlé Souptime*), 6 fl. oz. 70
   tangy (*Hain* Old Fashion Naturals), 8 fl. oz. 264
vegetable:
   (*Knorr*), 6 fl. oz. 25
   (*Knorr Swiss*), 6 fl. oz. 75
   alphabet (*Lipton*), 8 fl. oz. 40
   beef (*Lipton*), 8 fl. oz. 50
   beef (*Lipton Cup-a-Soup*), 6 fl. oz. 50
   bouillon, see "Bouillon"
   broth, see "broth," above
   country (*Lipton*), 8 fl. oz. 80
   cream of (*Nestlé Souptime*), 6 fl. oz. 80
   harvest (*Lipton Country Style Cup-a-Soup*), 6 fl. oz. 100
   hearty (*Hain* Old Fashion Naturals), 8 fl. oz. 147
   spring vegetable (*Lipton Cup-a-Soup*), 6 fl. oz. 40
Sour cream, see "Cream, sour"
Sour cream sauce mix*:
   (*Durkee*), ½ cup 160
   (*French's*), 2½ tbsp. 60
   (*McCormick/Schilling*), ½ cup .146

*Prepared according to directions on container

Soursop, raw:
whole, 1 lb. 200
peeled and seeded, 4 oz. 74
pureed, 1 cup 146
Souse, see "Sausages"
(Southern Comfort):
1 fl. oz. 120
Soybean curd (tofu):
4 oz. 82
1 piece (2½″ × 2¾″ × 1″) 86
Soybean flour, see "Flour"
Soybean "milk":
fluid, 4 oz. 37
powder, 4 oz. 486
dry *(Worthington Soyamel*—regular), 1 oz. 140
dry *(Worthington Soyamel*—fortified), 1 oz. 140
dry *(Worthington Soyamel*—low-fat), 1 oz. 110
Soybean oil, see "Oils, cooking or salad"
Soybean protein:
4 oz. 365
Soybean proteinate:
4 oz. 354
Soybean seeds, immature:
raw, in pods, 1 lb. 322
raw, shelled, 1 lb. 608
boiled, drained, 4 oz. 135
canned, drained, 8 oz. 234
canned, with liquid, 8 oz. 170
Soybean seeds, mature, dry:
uncooked, 8 oz. 914
uncooked, 1 cup 846
cooked, 8 oz. 295
cooked, 1 cup 234
Soybean sprouts, see "Bean sprouts"
Soybeans, fermented:
natto, 4 oz. 190
miso (with cereal), 4 oz. 194

Soy nuts:
   (*Flavor Tree* Peanuts), 1 oz. 150
   (*Planters*), 1 oz. 130
   roasted, all varieties (*Malt-O-Meal*), 1 oz. 140
Soy sauce:
   1 cup 197
   1 tbsp. 12
   (*Chun King*), 1 tbsp. 6
   (*Kikkoman*), 1 tbsp. 12
   (*La Choy*), 1 tbsp. 8
Spaghetti, plain, see "Pasta, plain"
Spaghetti, canned:
   and beef (*Hormel* Short Order), 7½-oz. can 242
   with franks, in tomato sauce (*Heinz*), 1 cup 280
   in meat sauce (*Franco-American*), 7¾-oz. 220
   in meat sauce (*Heinz*), 8 oz. 170
   with meatballs:
      (*Buitoni*), 15-oz. can 456
      (*Hormel* Short Order), 7½-oz. can 211
      (*Libby's*), 1 cup 206
      in tomato sauce (*Franco-American*), 7¼-oz. 210
   with tomato sauce and cheese (*Franco-American*), 7 oz. 170
   with tomato sauce and cheese (*Heinz*), 1 cup 160
   rings, with meatballs in tomato sauce
      (*Franco-American* SpaghettiOs) 7⅜ oz. 210
   rings, in tomato and cheese sauce
      (*Franco-American* SpaghettiOs), 7⅜ oz. 160
   twists, with meatballs (*Buitoni*), 15-oz. can 456
   twists, with sauce (*Buitoni*), 15-oz. can 320
Spaghetti, frozen:
   and meat casserole (*Morton*), 8-oz. pkg. 220
   with meat sauce (*Stouffer's*), 14-oz. pkg. 445
   with meat sauce, casserole (*Banquet*), 8-oz. pkg. 311
   and meatballs, with tomato sauce
      (*Banquet Buffet Suppers*), 32-oz. pkg. 1,084
   and meatballs, with tomato sauce
      (*Green Giant* Baked Entree), 9-oz. pkg. 280

in tomato sauce, with veal (*Swanson TV Brand* Entree)
   8¼-oz. pkg. 290

Spaghetti mix:
  (*Kraft* American Style), 1 cup* 270
  (*Kraft* Tangy Italian Style), 1 cup* 270
  dry (*Hamburger Helper*), ⅕ pkg. 150
  with meat* (*Hamburger Helper*), ⅕ pkg. 330
  with meat sauce (*Kraft*), ¾ cup 250
  and sauce (*Mug•O•Lunch*), 1 pouch* 160

Spaghetti dinner, frozen:
  and meatballs (*Morton*), 11-oz. pkg. 360
  and meatballs (*Swanson Hungry-Man*), 18½-oz. pkg. 660
  and meatballs (*Swanson TV Brand*), 12½-oz. pkg. 410

Spaghetti sauce:
  canned (*Hunt's Prima Salsa*), 4 oz.* 110
  mix* (*Durkee*), ½ cup 45
  mix* (*French's* Homemade Style), ½ cup 97
  mix* (*McCormick/Schilling*), ½ cup 53
  mix* (*Spatini*), ½ cup 80
  Italian, canned (*Contadina* Cookbook Sauces), ½ cup 80
  Italian, mix, dry (*Durkee* Simmer Sauce), 1¾-oz. pkg. 144
  Italian style, mix* (*French's*), ½ cup 80
  marinara, canned (*Buitoni*), 4 oz. 88
  marinara, canned (*Ronzoni*), 4 oz. 80
  meat, canned (*Ronzoni*), 4 oz. 80
  meat flavor, canned (*Buitoni*), 4 oz. 120
  meat flavor, canned (*Hunt's Prima Salsa*), 4 oz. 120
  meatless, canned (*Buitoni*), 4 oz. 92
  mushroom, canned (*Buitoni*), 4 oz. 88
  with mushrooms, canned (*Hunt's Prima Salsa*), 4 oz. 110
  with mushrooms, mix* (*Durkee*), ½ cup 40
  with mushrooms, mix* (*French's*), ½ cup 80

Spanish mackerel:
  raw, whole, 1 lb. 490
  raw, meat only, 4 oz. 202

Prepared according to directions on container

Spanish rice, see "Rice, flavored"
Sparerib sauce mix:
   (*Durkee Roastin' Bag*), 1.9-oz. pkg. 162
Spinach:
  fresh:
    raw, whole, 1 lb. 85
    raw, trimmed, packaged, 1 lb. 118
    raw, trimmed, leaves, 1 cup 9
    raw, trimmed, chopped, 1 cup 14
    boiled, drained, leaves, 1 cup 41
  canned:
    drained, 8 oz. 55
    drained, 1 cup 49
    with liquid, 8 oz. 43
    with liquid, 1 cup 44
    (*Del Monte*), ½ cup 23
    (*Libby's*), ½ cup 23
    puree (*Cellu*), ½ cup 50
  frozen:
    leaf or chopped (*Birds Eye*), 3.3 oz. 20
    leaf or chopped (*Seabrook Farms*), 3.3 oz. 25
    leaf or chopped (*Stokely-Van Camp*), 3.3 oz. 25
    in butter sauce (*Green Giant*), ½ cup 45
    creamed (*Birds Eye*), 3 oz. 60
    creamed (*Green Giant*), ½ cup 95
    creamed (*Stouffer's*), 3 oz. 127
Spinach, New Zealand, see "New Zealand spinach"
Spinach crepes:
  frozen (*Stouffer's*), 9½-oz. pkg. 415
Spinach soufflé:
  frozen (*Stouffer's*), 12-oz. pkg. 405
Spiny lobster, see "Crayfish"
Spleen, raw:
  beef or calf, 4 oz. 118
  hog, 4 oz. 122
  lamb, 4 oz. 131

Spot:
  fresh, raw, fillets, 4 oz. 248
  fresh, baked, fillets, 4 oz. 335
Spreads, see individual listings
Spring roll (see also "Egg roll"):
  frozen (*Royal Dragon*), 1½-oz. roll 106
  cocktail, frozen (*Royal Dragon*), ½-oz. roll 40
Squab (pigeon), raw:
  whole, dressed, 1 lb. 569
  meat only, 4 oz. 162
  light meat only, 4 oz. 143
Squash, summer, fresh:
  white and pale green, scallop varieties:
    raw, whole, 1 lb. 93
    raw, trimmed, 8 oz. 48
    raw, cubed, diced, or sliced, 1 cup 27
    boiled, drained, 8 oz. 37
    boiled, drained, sliced, 1 cup 29
    boiled, drained, cubed or diced, 1 cup 34
    boiled, drained, mashed, 1 cup 38
  yellow, crookneck, or straightneck:
    raw, whole, 1 lb. 89
    raw, trimmed, 8 oz. 46
    raw, cubed, diced, or sliced, 1 cup 26
    boiled, drained, 8 oz. 34
    boiled, drained, cubed or diced, 1 cup 32
    boiled, drained, mashed, 1 cup 36
    boiled, drained, sliced, 1 cup 27
  zucchini or cocozelle (Italian marrow type), green:
    raw, whole, 1 lb. 73
    raw, trimmed, 8 oz. 39
    raw, cubed, diced, or sliced, 1 cup 22
    boiled, drained, 8 oz. 27
    boiled, drained, cubed or diced, 1 cup 25
    boiled, drained, mashed, 1 cup 29
    boiled, drained, sliced, 1 cup 22

Squash, winter, fresh:
  acorn:
    raw, whole, 1 lb. 152
    raw, whole, 1 squash (4⅓″ long, 4″ in diam.) 190
    raw, cavity cleaned, ½ squash 97
    baked, 8 oz. 125
    baked, ½ squash 86
    baked, mashed, 1 cup 113
    boiled, 8 oz. 77
    boiled, mashed, 1 cup 83
  butternut:
    raw, whole, 1 lb. 171
    baked, 8 oz. 154
    baked, mashed, 1 cup 139
    boiled, 8 oz. 93
    boiled, mashed, 1 cup 100
  hubbard:
    raw, whole, 1 lb. 117
    baked, 8 oz. 114
    baked, mashed, 1 cup 103
    boiled, 8 oz. 68
    boiled, cubed or diced, 1 cup 71
    boiled, mashed, 1 cup 74
Squash, canned:
  puree (*Cellu*), ½ cup 50
  zucchini, in tomato sauce (*Del Monte*), ½ cup 30
Squash, frozen:
  (*Stokely-Van Camp*), 3 oz. 30
  cooked (*Birds Eye*), 4 oz. 45
  butternut (*Southland*), 4 oz. 60
  crookneck (*Seabrook Farms*), 3.3 oz. 20
  crookneck (*Southland*), 3.3 oz. 20
  crookneck, with onions (*Southland*), 3.2 oz. 20
  summer, in cheese sauce (*Green Giant*), ½ cup 60
  summer, sliced (*Birds Eye*), 3.3 oz. 18

zucchini:

    (*Birds Eye*), 3.3 oz. 16

    (*Seabrook Farms*), 3.5 oz. 18

    sliced (*Southland*), 3.2 oz. 15

    sticks, light batter-fried (*Mrs. Paul's*), 3 oz. 180

Squash seed kernels:

    dry, 4 oz. 630

Squid:

    raw, meat only, 4 oz. 95

Stew, see individual listings

Stew vegetables, see "Vegetables, mixed"

Stock base (see also "Bouillon"):

    beef flavor (*French's*), 1 tsp. 8

    chicken flavor (*French's*), 1 tsp. 8

Stomach, pork:

    scalded, 4 oz. 173

Strawberries:

    fresh:

        whole, with caps and stems, 1 lb. 161

        whole, capped, trimmed, 1 lb. 168

        whole, 1 cup 55

    canned:

        in water, with liquid, 8 oz. 50

        in water, with liquid, 1 cup 53

    freeze-dried (*Mountain House*), 1 oz. 90

    frozen:

        (*Birds Eye* Quick Thaw), 5 oz. 120

        whole (*Birds Eye*), 4 oz. 80

        whole, without syrup (*Stokely-Van Camp*), 5 oz. 60

        whole, in syrup (*Stokely-Van Camp*), 4 oz. 110

        halves (*Birds Eye*), 5.3 oz. 180

        halves, in syrup (*Stokely-Van Camp*), 5 oz. 160

Strawberry dessert topping:

    (*Kraft*), 1 tbsp. 45

    (*Smucker's*), 1 tbsp. 60

Strawberry drink:
  canned (*Borden Frosted*), 1 can 270
  canned (*Hi-C*), 6 fl. oz. 89
  mix*:
    (*Cramores*), 6 fl. oz. 68
    (*Hi-C*), 6 fl. oz. 76
    (*Kool-Aid*), 6 fl. oz. 68
    (*Wyler's*), 6 fl. oz. 70
Strawberry extract:
  pure (*Burton's*), 1 tsp. 10
  imitation (*Durkee*), 1 tsp. 12
  imitation (*Ehlers*), 1 tsp. 16
Strawberry flavored drink mix:
  (*Nestlé Quik*), 2 tsp. 90
  (*Ovaltine*), .54 oz. 60
Strawberry fruit roll:
  dried, sweetened (*Grocer's Choice*), 1 oz. 100
  dried, sweetened (*Sahadi*), 1 oz. 100
Strawberry liqueur:
  (*Hiram Walker*), 1 fl. oz. 76
  wild (*Dolfi* Fraise des Bois), 1 fl. oz. 88
Strawberry Margarita cocktail mix:
  instant (*Holland House*), 1 packet 62
Strawberry pie, see "Pies, frozen"
Strawberry sting cocktail mix:
  bottled (*Holland House*), 1 fl. oz. 35
  instant (*Holland House*), 1 packet 74
Stroganoff sauce mix*:
  (*French's*), ½ cup 165
Stroganoff seasoning mix:
  (*Durkee*), 1¼-oz. packet 90
  (*French's*), 1 packet 55
  (*McCormick/Schilling*), 1½-oz. packet 113
Stuffing, see "Bread stuffing"

---

*Prepared according to directions on container

Sturgeon:
  fresh, raw, meat only, 4 oz. 107
  fresh, steamed, meat only, 4 oz. 181
Sturgeon roe, see "Caviar"
Sturgeon, smoked:
  4 oz. 169
Succotash (corn and lima beans):
  canned:
    whole kernel (*Libby's*), ½ cup 78
    whole kernel (*Stokely-Van Camp*), ½ cup 85
    cream style (*Libby's*), ½ cup 96
  frozen:
    (*Birds Eye*), 3.3 oz. 90
    (*Hanover*), 3.2 oz. 95
    (*Stokely-Van Camp*), 3.3 oz. 60
Sucker, carp:
  raw, whole, 1 lb. 196
  raw, meat only, 4 oz. 126
Sucker, white and mullet:
  raw, whole, 1 lb. 203
  raw, meat only (fillets), 4 oz. 118
Suet (beef kidney fat):
  raw, 1 oz. 242
Sugar, beet or cane:
  brown:
    1 lb. 1,692
    1 cup loosely packed 541
    1 cup firm-packed 821
    1 tbsp. firm packed 52
  granulated:
    1 lb. 1,746
    1 cup 770
    1 tbsp. 46
    1 tsp. 15
    1 cube (½″) 10

1 lump (1⅛″ × ¾″ × 5⁄16″) 19
1 packet 23
powdered (confectioners'):
  1 lb. 1,746
  1 cup unsifted 462
  1 cup sifted 385
  1 tbsp. stirred 31
Sugar, cinnamon, see "Cinnamon sugar"
Sugar, maple:
  1 lb. 1,579
  1 piece (1¾″ × 1¼″ × ½″) or 1 oz. 99
Sugar apples (sweetsop):
  whole, 1 lb. 192
  peeled and seeded, 4 oz. 107
  peeled and seeded, 1 cup 235
Sugar substitute:
  (*Sprinkle Sweet*), ⅛ tsp. 2
Sukiyaki:
  canned (*La Choy*—Bi-Pack), ¾ cup 75
  canned (*La Choy* Dinner), ¾ cup 210
  with flank steak, frozen (*Chun King* Stir Fry),
  ⅕ of pkg.* 280
  with round steak, frozen (*Chun King* Stir Fry),
  ⅕ of pkg.* 220
Summer sausage:
  (*Hormel* Buffet Thuringer), 1 oz. 95
  (*Hormel Old Smokehouse* Thuringer), 1 oz. 99
  (*Hormel* Summer Sausage), 1-oz. slice 90
  (*Oscar Mayer* Summer Sausage), .8-oz. slice 75
  (*Swift*), 1 oz. 90
  beef (*Oscar Mayer* Summer Sausage), .8-oz. slice 68
Summer sausage, turkey, see "Turkey summer sausage"
Sunflower seed flour, see "Flour"
Sunflower seed kernels:
  dry, in hull, 1 lb. 1,371

*Prepared according to directions on container

dry, in hull, 1 cup 257
dry, hulled, 4 oz. 635
dry, hulled, 1 cup 812
(*Frito-Lay's*), 1 oz. 180
dry roasted (*Flavor House*), 1 oz. 180
dry roasted (*Planters*), 1 oz. 160
unsalted (*Planters*), 1 oz. 170
and sesames (*Flavor Tree*), 1 oz. 158

Surinam cherries, see "Pitangas"

Swamp cabbage:
raw, whole, 1 lb. 107
raw, trimmed, 1 lb. 132
boiled, drained, 8 oz. 48

Sweet and sour dressing:
(*Bennett's*), 1 tbsp. 70

Sweet and sour entree, frozen:
(*Chun King* Stir Fry), ⅕ of pkg.* 270
with ham (*Chun King* Stir Fry), ⅕ of pkg.* 440
with lean pork (*Chun King* Stir Fry), ⅕ of pkg.* 460
pork (*Chun King* Pouched Entree), 6 oz. 200
pork (*La Choy*), ⅔ cup 180

Sweet and sour sauce:
canned (*Contadina* Cookbook Sauces), ½ cup 120
in jars (*La Choy*), ½ cup 262
mix* (*Durkee*), ½ cup 115
mix* (*French's*), ½ cup 55

Sweet bread, see "Bread, sweet, mix"

Sweetbreads:
beef (yearlings), raw, 1 lb. 939
beef (yearlings), braised, 4 oz. 365
calf, raw, 1 lb. 426
calf, braised, 4 oz. 192
hog, see "Pancreas"
lamb, raw, 1 lb. 426
lamb, braised, 4 oz. 200

Prepared according to directions on container

Sweet potatoes:

  fresh:

    raw, all varieties, whole, 1 lb. 419

    raw, firm-fleshed (Jersey type), whole, 1 lb. 375

    raw, firm-fleshed (Jersey type), without skin, 8 oz. 232

    raw, firm-fleshed (Jersey type), pared,

      1 potato (5″ long) 165

    raw, soft-fleshed (Puerto Rico type), whole, 1 lb. 430

    raw, soft-fleshed (Puerto Rico type),

      without skin, 8 oz. 266

    raw, soft-fleshed (Puerto Rico type), pared,

      1 potato (5″ long) 190

    baked, in skin, 8 oz. 250

    baked, in skin, 1 potato (5″ long, 2″ in diam.) 161

    boiled, without skin, 8 oz. 259

    boiled, in skin, 8 oz. 217

    boiled, in skin, 1 potato (5″ long, 2″ in diam.) 172

    boiled, in skin, sliced, 1 cup 181

    boiled, in skin, mashed, 1 cup 291

  candied:

    4 oz. 191

    1 piece (2½″ long, 2″ in diam.) .176

  canned:

    vacuum pack, 8 oz. 245

    vacuum pack, 1 piece (2¾″ long, 1″ in diam.) 43

    vacuum pack, pieces, 1 cup 216

    vacuum pack, mashed, 1 cup 275

    whole, in heavy syrup (*Royal Prince* Yams), 4 oz. 147

    cut, in light syrup (*Princella*), 4 oz. 105

    in orange-pineapple sauce (*Royal Prince* Yams), 4 oz. 180

  dehydrated:

    flakes, dry form, 4 oz. 432

    flakes, dry form, 1 cup 455

    flakes, instant (*Royal Prince*), 2 oz. dry 222

    flakes, prepared with water, 8 oz. 216

    flakes, prepared with water, 1 cup 242

frozen:
    candied, orange or yellow (*Mrs. Paul's*), 4 oz. 180
    candied, with apples (*Mrs. Paul's* Sweets 'n Apples),
       4 oz. 150
    candied, with apples (*Stouffer's*), 5 oz. 160
    glazed (*Green Giant*), ½ cup 170
Sweetsop, see "Sugar apples"
Swiss chard, see "Chard, Swiss"
Swiss steak dinner:
    frozen (*Swanson TV Brand*), 10-oz. pkg. 350
Swiss steak gravy:
    mix* (*Durkee*), ½ cup 23
Swiss steak sauce:
    canned (*Contadina* Cookbook Sauces), ½ cup 40
Swiss steak seasoning mix:
    (*Durkee*), ½ cup* 23
    dry (*Durkee Roastin' Bag*), 1½-oz. packet 115
    dry (*McCormick/Schilling*), 1-oz. packet 44
Swordfish:
    fresh:
       raw, meat only, 1 lb. 535
       broiled with butter, 10.1 oz. (yield from 1 lb. raw) 499
       broiled with butter, 4 oz. 186
       broiled with butter, 1 piece (4½″ × 2⅛″ × ⅞″) 237
    canned:
       with liquid, 8 oz. 116
Syrups, see individual listings

---

*Prepared according to directions on container

T

Food and Measure   *Calories*

Taco sauce:
(*Gebhardt*), 1 tsp. 3
(*Old El Paso*), 1 tsp. 3
(*Ortega*), 1 tbsp. 21
Taco seasoning mix:
dry (*Durkee*), 1⅛-oz. packet 67
dry (*French's*), 1¾-oz. packet 120
dry (*McCormick/Schilling*), 1¼-oz. packet 61
Taco shell:
(*Ortega*), 1 shell* 50
Taffy, see "Candy"
Tahini:
(*Sahadi*), 2 tbsp., or 1 oz. 190
Tamales, canned or in jars:
(*Armour Star*), 1 tamale* 92
(*Austex*), 2-oz. tamale 112
(*Gebhardt*), 2-oz. tamale 134
(*Hormel*—5-oz. can), 1 tamale* 72
(*Hormel* Short Order), 7½-oz. can 271
(*Old El Paso*), 2-oz. tamale 117
beef, with sauce (*Derby*), 2.2-oz. tamale 92
Tamarinds:
fresh, whole, 1 lb. 520
fresh, shelled and seeded, 4 oz. 271

Prepared according to directions on container

Tangelo juice, fresh:
1 cup 101
juice from 1 large tangelo (2¾″ in diam.) 47
juice from 1 medium tangelo (2⁹⁄₁₆″ in diam.) 39
juice from 1 small tangelo (2¼″ in diam.) 28
Tangerine drink:
canned (*Hi-C*), 6 fl. oz. 90
Tangerine juice:
fresh, 1 cup 106
canned:
unsweetened, 6-fl.-oz. can 80
unsweetened, 1 cup 106
sweetened, 6-fl.-oz. can 94
sweetened, 1 cup 125
frozen*, sweetened (*Minute Maid*), 6 fl. oz. 85
Tangerine liqueur:
(*Dolfi*), 1 fl. oz. 97
Tangerines, fresh (Dancy variety):
whole, 1 lb. 154
whole, 1 large tangerine (2½″ in diam.) 46
whole, 1 medium tangerine (2⅜″ in diam.) 39
whole, 1 small tangerine (2¼″ in diam.) 33
sections, without membranes, 1 cup 90
Taro:
corms and tubers, whole, 1 lb. 373
corms and tubers, without skin, 4 oz. 111
leaves and stems, 1 lb. 181
Tarragon:
all brands, 1 tsp. 5
Tart shell:
frozen (*Pepperidge Farm*), 1 shell 90
Tartar sauce:
1 cup 1,221
1 tbsp. 74

Prepared according to directions on container

(*Bama*), 1 tbsp. 80
(*Bennett's*), 1 tbsp. 70
(*Best Foods*), 1 tbsp. 70
(*Kraft*), 1 tbsp. 80
(*Hellmann's*), 1 tbsp. 70
(*Mrs. Filberts*), 1 tbsp. 80
mix (*Mrs. Paul's Create A Sauce*), ½ packet 22
mix* (*Van de Kamp's*), ½ oz. 80
Tautog (blackfish):
raw, whole, 1 lb. 149
raw, meat only, 4 oz. 101
Tavern nuts:
(*Planters*), 1 oz. 170
Tea:
regular, loose or bags*:
(*Bigelow Constant Comment*), 6 fl. oz. 1
(*Lipton*), 8 fl. oz. 2
(*Tender Leaf*), 6 fl. oz. 1
(*Tetley*), 6 fl. oz. 3
black (*Lipton Black Rum*), 8 fl. oz. 2
cinnamon (*Bigelow Cinnamon Stick*), 6 fl. oz. 1
cinnamon (*Lipton*), 8 fl. oz. 2
lemon (*Bigelow Lemon Lift*), 6 fl. oz. 1
lemon and spice (*Lipton*), 8 fl. oz. .2
mint (*Bigelow Peppermint Stick*), 6 fl. oz. 1
mint (*Bigelow Plantation Mint*), 6 fl. oz. 1
mint (*Lipton*), 8 fl. oz. 2
orange and spice (*Lipton*), 8 fl. oz. .2
herbal, loose or bags*:
almond (*Lipton* Herbal Tea), 8 fl. oz. 2
(*Bigelow Feeling Free*), 6 fl. oz. 1
(*Bigelow Mint Medley*), 6 fl. oz. 1
(*Bigelow Sweet Dreams*), 6 fl. oz. .1
(*Bigelow Take-A-Break*), 6 fl. oz. .3

Prepared according to directions on container

   (*Celestial Seasonings Brazilian Breakfast*), 6 fl. oz. 1
   (*Celestial Seasonings Pelican Punch*), 6 fl. oz. 1
   chamomile (*Lipton* Herbal Tea), 8 fl. oz. 4
   chamomile (*Sahadi* Herbal Tea), 6 fl. oz. 0
   cinnamon apple (*Lipton* Herbal Tea), 8 fl. oz. 2
   hibiscus, wild (*Sahadi* Herbal Tea), 6 fl. oz. 2
   mint (*Lipton* Herbal Tea), 8 fl. oz. 2
   mint (*Sahadi* Herbal Tea), 6 fl. oz. 2
   orange (*Lipton* Herbal Tea), 8 fl. oz. 2
   orange (*Sahadi* Herbal Tea), 6 fl. oz. 2
   peppermint (*Sahadi* Herbal Tea), 6 fl. oz. 2
   rosehips (*Sahadi* Herbal Tea), 6 fl. oz. 2
   spearmint (*Sahadi* Herbal Tea), 6 fl. oz. 4
   spice (*Lipton* Herbal Tea), 8 fl. oz. 4
   spicy almond (*Sahadi* Herbal Tea), 6 fl. oz. 2
canned or dairy pack:
   lemon flavor, presweetened (*Hood*), 6 fl. oz. 55
   lemon flavor, presweetened (*Lipton*), 8 fl. oz. 90
   lemon flavor, sugar-free (*Lipton*), 8 fl. oz. 2
instant and mix:
   dry form, 1 oz. 83
   dry form, 1 tsp. 1
   plain (*Lipton*), 6 fl. oz.* 0
   plain (*Nestea*), 6 fl. oz.* 0
   lemon flavored (*Lipton*), 8 fl. oz.* 4
   lemon flavored (*Nestea*), 6 fl. oz.* 2
   lemon flavored (*Wyler's*), 6 fl. oz.* 60
   lemon flavored, presweetened (*Lipton* Iced Tea Mix),
     8 fl. oz.* 60
   lemon flavored, presweetened (*Nestea*), 6 fl. oz.* 70
   orange flavored, presweetened (*Lipton* Iced Tea Mix),
     8 fl. oz.* 60
Tendergreens, see "Mustard spinach"

*Prepared according to directions on container

Tenderizer, meat:
(*French's*), 1 tsp. 2
seasoned (*French's*), 1 tsp. 2
Tequila, see "Liquor, pure distilled"
Tequila sour cocktail:
(*Calvert*—55 proof), 1 fl. oz. 61
Tequila sunrise cocktail mix:
instant (*Holland House*), 1 packet 63
Teriyaki entree:
frozen, beef, with rice and vegetables (*Stouffer's*),
10-oz. pkg. 365
Teriyaki sauce:
(*Chun King*), 1 tbsp. 12
(*Kikkoman*), 1 tbsp. 17
mix* (*French's*), 1 tbsp. 18
Terrapin (diamondback):
raw, in shell, 1 lb. 106
raw, meat only, 4 oz. 126
Thousand Island salad dressing, see "Salad dressings"
Thuringer cervelat, see "Summer sausage"
Thyme:
all brands, 1 tsp. 5
Tilefish:
raw, whole, 1 lb. 183
raw, meat only, 4 oz. 90
baked, meat only, 4 oz. 156
Toaster pastries:
all varieties (*Nabisco Toastettes*), 1.7-oz. pastry 190
apple, Dutch, frosted (*Kellogg's Frosted Pop-Tarts*),
1.8-oz. pastry 210
blueberry (*Kellogg's Pop-Tarts*), 1.8-oz. pastry 210
blueberry, frosted (*Kellogg's Frosted Pop-Tarts*),
1.8-oz. pastry 200
brown sugar-cinnamon (*Kellogg's Pop-Tarts*),
1.8-oz. pastry 210

*Prepared according to directions on container

brown sugar-cinnamon, frosted
  (*Kellogg's Frosted Pop-Tarts*), 1.8-oz. pastry 210
cherry (*Kellogg's Pop-Tarts*), 1.8-oz. pastry 210
cherry, frosted (*Kellogg's Frosted Pop-Tarts*),
  1.8-oz. pastry 200
chocolate chip (*Kellogg's Pop-Tarts*), 1.8-oz. pastry 200
chocolage fudge, frosted (*Kellogg's Frosted Pop-Tarts*),
  1.8-oz. pastry 200
chocolate-vanilla creme, frosted
  (*Kellogg's Frosted Pop-Tarts*), 1.8-oz. pastry 220
grape, Concord (*Kellogg's Pop-Tarts*), 1.8-oz. pastry 210
grape, Concord, frosted (*Kellogg's Frosted Pop-Tarts*),
  1.8-oz. pastry 210
raspberry, frosted (*Kellogg's Frosted Pop-Tarts*),
  1.8-oz. pastry 210
strawberry (*Kellogg's Pop-Tarts*), 1.8-oz. pastry 200
strawberry, frosted (*Kellogg's Frosted Pop-Tarts*),
  1.8-oz. pastry 200
Toffee, see "Candy"
Tofu, see "Soybean curd"
Tom Collins cocktail:
  (*Calvert*—60 proof), 1 fl. oz. 65
Tom Collins cocktail mix:
  bottled (*Holland House*), 1 fl. oz. 67
  instant (*Holland House*), 1 packet 69
Tomato catsup, see "Catsup"
Tomato chili sauce, see "Chili sauce"
Tomato flavor cocktail:
  with beef broth (*Mott's Beefamato*), 6 fl. oz. 70
  with beef broth (*Mott's Nutrimato*), 6 fl. oz. 70
Tomato juice:
  canned or bottled:
    (*Campbell's*), 6 fl. oz. 35
    (*Del Monte*), 6 fl. oz. 35
    (*Heinz*), 6 fl. oz. 39
    (*Libby's*), 6 fl. oz. 33

    (*Musselman's*), 6 fl. oz. 30
    (*Sacramento*), 5½ fl. oz. 35
    (*Stokely-Van Camp*), 6 fl. oz. .40
    (*Welch's*), 6 fl. oz. 35
  dehydrated, crystals, dry form, 1 oz. 86
  dehydrated, crystals, prepared with water, 1 cup 49
Tomato juice cocktail, canned or bottled:
  (*Snap-E-Tom*), 6 fl. oz. 38
Tomato paste:
  (*Contadina*), 6 oz. 150
  (*Del Monte*), 6 oz. 150
  (*Hunt's*), 6 oz. 140
Tomato puree:
  (*Cellu*), 1 cup 80
  heavy (*Contadina*), 6 oz. 75
Tomato sauce, canned:
  (*Contadina*), 4 oz. 40
  (*Del Monte*), ½ cup 40
  (*Hunt's*), 4 oz. 35
  (*Hunt's* Special), 4 oz. 40
  (*Libby's*), ½ cup 45
  (*Stokely-Van Camp*), ½ cup 35
  with bits (*Del Monte*), ½ cup 40
  with bits (*Heinz*), 4 oz. 35
  with cheese (*Hunt's*), 4 oz. 70
  with mushrooms (*Del Monte*), ½ cup 50
  with mushrooms (*Hunt's*), 4 oz. 40
  with onions (*Del Monte*), ½ cup 50
  with onions (*Hunt's*), 4 oz. 45
  with tidbits (*Del Monte*), ½ cup 40
  pizza sauce, see "Pizza sauce"
  spaghetti sauce, see "Spaghetti sauce"
  tomato-herb (*Hunt's*), 4 oz. 80
  tomato paste, see "Tomato paste"
Tomato sauce mix:
  savory mix, dry (*Durkee*), 1¾-oz. pkg. 112

Tomato soup, see "Soup, canned" and "Soup mix"
Tomatoes, green:
  fresh, whole, 1 lb. 99
Tomatoes, pickled:
  (*Claussen* Kosher), 1-oz. piece 5
Tomatoes, ripe:
  fresh:
    raw, whole, 1 lb. 100
    raw, whole, 1 tomato (about 2⅗" in diam.) 27
    raw, whole, 1 tomato (about 2⅖" in diam.) 20
    raw, whole, peeled, 1 tomato (2⅖" in diam.) 19
    raw, sliced, 1 cup 40
    boiled, 1 cup 63
  canned:
    whole, round or pear (*Contadina*), 4 oz. 25
    whole (*Del Monte*), ½ cup 25
    whole (*Hunt's*), 4 oz. 25
    whole (*Libby's*), ½ cup 23
    whole (*Stokely-Van Camp*), ½ cup 25
    crushed (*Red Pack*), ½ cup 45
    sliced, baby (*Contadina*), 4 oz. 35
    stewed (*Contadina*), 4 oz. 35
    stewed (*Del Monte*), ½ cup 35
    stewed (*Hunt's*), 4 oz. 30
    stewed (*Libby's*), ½ cup 32
    stewed (*Stokely-Van Camp*), ½ cup 35
    wedges (*Del Monte*), ½ cup 30
Tomcod, Atlantic:
  raw, whole, 1 lb. 136
  meat only, 4 oz. 88
Tongue:
  fresh:
    beef, medium-fat, braised, 4 oz. 277
    calf, braised, 4 oz. 181
    hog, braised, 4 oz. 287
    lamb, braised, 4 oz. 288

sheep, braised, 4 oz. 366
canned or cured:
  pickled, 4 oz. 303
  potted or deviled, 4 oz. 329
Tonic water, see "Soft drinks and mixers"
Toppings, see individual listings
Tortilla chips:
  (*Doritos*), 1 oz. 140
  (*Pinata*), 1 oz. 140
  (*Tor-Tico*), 1 oz. 160
  (*Tostitos*), 1 oz. 150
  nacho cheese flavor (*Bachman*), 1 oz. 150
  nacho cheese flavor (*Bravos*), 1 oz. 150
  nacho cheese flavor (*Doritos*), 1 oz. 140
  nacho cheese flavor (*Pinata*), 1 oz. 140
  nacho cheese flavor (*Planters*), 1 oz. 130
  nacho cheese flavor (*Wise*), 1 oz. 150
  taco flavor (*Bachman*), 1 oz. 150
  taco flavor (*Doritos*), 1 oz. 140
  taco flavor (*Pinata*), 1 oz. 140
  taco flavor (*Planters*), 1 oz. 130
  taco flavor (*Wise*), 1 oz. 150
Tortillas:
  canned (*Old El Paso*), 5″ diam. tortilla 40
Towel gourd:
  whole, 1 lb. 69
  pared, 4 oz. 20
Tripe, beef:
  4 oz. 113
  canned (*Libby's*), 5 oz. 245
  pickled, 4 oz. 70
Triple sec liqueur:
  (*Bols*), 1 fl. oz. 113
  (*Dolfi*), 1 fl. oz. 107
  (*DuBouchett*), 1 fl. oz. 61
  (*Garnier*), 1 fl. oz. 83

(*Hiram Walker*), 1 fl. oz. 107
(*Leroux*), 1 fl. oz. 105
(*Old Mr. Boston*—60 proof), 1 fl. oz. 105
(*Old Mr. Boston* Connoisseur—42 proof), 1 fl. oz. 97
Trout, brook:
raw, whole, 1 lb. 224
raw, meat only, 4 oz. 115
Trout, lake, see "Lake trout"
Trout, rainbow:
fresh, raw, meat with skin, 4 oz. 221
canned, 4 oz. 237
Tuna:
raw, bluefin, meat only, 4 oz. 165
raw, yellowfin, meat only, 4 oz. 151
canned:
chunk light, in oil (*Bumble Bee*), 1 cup 460
chunk light, in oil (*Chicken of the Sea*), 6½-oz. can 490
chunk light, in oil (*Del Monte*), 6½-oz. can 450
chunk light, in oil (*Icy Point*), 5 oz., drained 278
chunk light, in oil (*Pillar Rock*), 5 oz., drained 278
chunk light, in oil (*Snow Mist*), 5 oz., drained 278
chunk white, in oil (*Chicken of the Sea*), 6½-oz. can ...500
solid light, in oil (*Chicken of the Sea*), 6½-oz. can 460
solid white, in oil (*Bumble Bee*), 1 cup 500
solid white, in oil (*Chicken of the Sea*), 6½-oz. can 490
solid white, in oil (*Icy Point*), 5¼ oz., drained 290
solid white, in oil (*Pillar Rock*), 5¼ oz., drained 290
chunk light, in water (*Bumble Bee*), 1 cup 220
chunk light, in water (*Chicken of the Sea*), 6½-oz. can ...200
solid white, in water (*Bumble Bee*), 1 cup 240
solid white, in water (*Chicken of the Sea*), 6½-oz. can 240
Tuna casserole seasoning mix:
(*McCormick/Schilling*), 1½-oz. packet 104
Tuna, creamed:
frozen, with peas (*Green Giant Toast Toppers*),
5-oz. pkg. 140

Tuna fritters:
  frozen, batter-fried (*Mrs. Paul's*), 7¾-oz. pkg. 540
Tuna noodle casserole:
  frozen (*Stouffer's*), 11½-oz. pkg. 400
Tuna pot pie:
  frozen (*Banquet*), 8-oz. pie 434
  frozen (*Morton*), 8-oz. pie 370
Tuna salad:
  canned (*Longacre*), ½ oz. 24
  canned (*The Spreadables*), ½ oz. 27
Turbot:
  raw, Greenland, whole, 1 lb. 344
  raw, Greenland, meat only, 4 oz. 166
  frozen, fillets (*Taste O' Sea*), 16-oz. pkg. 400
Turmeric:
  ground (all brands), 1 tsp. 7
Turkey, fresh:
  roasted, whole with giblets and skin, 8.6 oz.
    (yield from 1 lb. raw) 644
  roasted, dark meat without skin:
    4 oz. 230
    4 pieces (2½″ × 1⅝″ × ¼″) 173
    chopped or diced, 1 cup 284
    ground, 1 cup 223
  roasted, light meat without skin:
    4 oz. 200
    4 pieces (2½″ × 1⅝″ × ¼″) 150
    chopped or diced, 1 cup 246
    ground, 1 cup 194
  roasted, skin only, 1 oz. 256
Turkey, canned:
  boned:
    (*Hormel Tender Chunk*), 6¾-oz. can 204
    (*Swanson*), 5 oz. 220
    breast, roasted (*Chef's Gourmet Norwestern*), 8 oz. 272
    roll, roasted (*Chef's Gourmet Norwestern*), 8 oz. 288

potted:
  5½-oz. can 387
  1 tbsp. 32
  1 oz. 70
roasted:
  (*Wilson Certified*), 8 oz. 234
  (*Swift Premium Deep Basted Butterball* Young Turkey),
    3½ oz. 220
  dark meat (*Swift Premium Deep Basted Butterball*),
    3½ oz. 210
  light meat (*Swift Premium Deep Basted Butterball*),
    3½ oz. 170

Turkey, frozen:
  (*Morton* Boil-in-Bag), 5-oz. pkg. 120
  (*Swanson Hungry-Man* Entree), 13¼-oz. pkg. 380
  sliced (*Morton Country Table* Entree), 12.3-oz. pkg. 370
  sliced, gravy and (*Banquet Buffet Suppers*), 32-oz. pkg. ...534
  sliced, gravy and (*Banquet Cookin' Bag*), 5-oz. pkg. 133
  sliced, gravy and (*Green Giant Toast Toppers*), 5-oz. pkg. ..100
  sliced, gravy and (*Morton*), 8 oz. 200
  with gravy, dressing, and whipped potatoes
    (*Swanson TV Brand* Entree), 8¾-oz. pkg. 260

Turkey bologna:
  (*Louis Rich*), 1-oz. slice 60
  (*Norbest*), 1-oz. slice 65

Turkey breast, see "Turkey luncheon meat"

Turkey casserole:
  frozen, with gravy and dressing (*Stouffer's*), 9¾-oz. pkg. ...370

Turkey croquette:
  frozen (*Morton*), 8 oz. 440

Turkey dinner, frozen:
  (*Banquet*), 11-oz. pkg. 293
  (*Banquet Man Pleaser*), 19-oz. pkg. 620
  (*Morton*), 11-oz. pkg. 340
  (*Morton Country Table*), 15-oz. pkg. 520
  (*Morton* King Size), 19-oz. pkg. 580

(*Swanson*), 16-oz. pkg. 520
(*Swanson Hungry-Man*), 19-oz. pkg. 740
(*Swanson TV Brand*), 11½-oz. pkg. 360
Turkey drumstick:
  smoked (*Louis Rich*), 1 oz. without bone 40
Turkey frankfurters:
  (*Longacre*), 1 link 128
  (*Louis Rich*), 1½-oz. link 95
  (*Louis Rich*), 2-oz. link 125
Turkey giblet (some gizzard fat):
  raw, 8 oz. 340
  simmered, 4 oz. 264
  simmered, chopped or diced, 1 cup 338
Turkey gravy:
  mix*:
    (*Durkee*), ½ cup 47
    (*French's*), ½ cup 50
    (*McCormick/Schilling*), ½ cup 41
  giblet, canned (*Howard Johnson's*), ½ cup 55
Turkey, ground:
  cooked (*Louis Rich*), 1 oz. 45
Turkey ham:
  (*Longacre*—chub), 1 oz. 37
  (*Longacre*—sliced), 1 slice 20
  (*Louis Rich*), 1-oz. slice 35
  (*Norbest*), 1-oz. slice 40
  chopped (*Louis Rich*), 1-oz. slice 45
Turkey luncheon meat:
  (*Danola* Thin Sliced), 1 oz. 50
  breast (*Hormel*), .8-oz. slice 24
  breast (*Longacre*), 1 slice 25
  breast (*Norbest* Oven Roasted), 1 slice 30
  breast (*Oscar Mayer*), .8-oz. slice 23
  breast, barbecued (*Louis Rich*), 1 oz. 40

Prepared according to directions on container

breast, oven roasted (*Louis Rich*), 1 oz. 30
breast, smoked (*Louis Rich*), 1 oz. 35
breast, smoked (*Norbest* Hickory Smoked), 1-oz. slice 30
loaf (*Louis Rich*), 1-oz. slice 40
smoked (*Louis Rich*), 1-oz. slice 35
Turkey pastrami:
(*Norbest*), 1-oz. slice 40
Turkey pot pie, frozen:
(*Banquet*), 8-oz. pie 415
(*Morton*), 8-oz. pie 340
(*Stouffer's*), 10-oz. pie 460
(*Swanson*), 8-oz. pie 450
(*Swanson Hungry-Man*), 16-oz. pie 790
Turkey salad:
canned (*The Spreadables*), ½ oz. 29
Turkey salami:
(*Louis Rich*), 1-oz. slice 50
(*Norbest*), 1-oz. slice 40
cotto (*Louis Rich*), 1-oz. slice 50
Turkey sausage:
cooked (*Louis Rich*), ¾-oz. link 45
Turkey, smoked, see "Turkey luncheon meat"
Turkey soup, see "Soup, canned"
Turkey summer sausage:
(*Louis Rich*), 1-oz. slice 50
Turkey tetrazzini:
frozen (*Stouffer's*), 12-oz. pkg. 480
Turnip greens:
fresh:
raw, whole, 1 lb. 107
raw, trimmed, 1 lb. 127
boiled in large amount water, long time, drained, 1 cup 28
boiled in small amount water, short time, drained,
1 cup 29
canned:
with liquid, 8 oz. 41

332

with liquid, 1 cup 42
chopped (*Stokely-Van Camp*), ½ cup 18
frozen:
chopped (*Birds Eye*), 3.3 oz. 20
chopped (*Seabrook Farms*), 3.3 oz. 20
chopped (*Southland*), 3.3 oz. 20
with turnip roots (*Southland*), 3.3 oz. 20
with diced turnips (*Birds Eye*), 3.3 oz. 20
Turnip roots:
frozen, diced (*Seabrook Farms*), 3.3 oz. 4
Turnips:
fresh:
raw, without tops, untrimmed, 1 lb. 117
raw, cubed or sliced, 1 cup 39
boiled, drained, 8 oz. 52
boiled, drained, cubed, 1 cup 36
boiled, drained, mashed, 1 cup 53
frozen, chopped (*Southland*), 3.3 oz. 20
Turnovers, see individual listings
Turtle, green:
raw, in shell, 1 lb. 97
raw, meat only, 4 oz. 101
canned, 4 oz. 120
Turtle beans, see "Beans, black"
Turtle soup, see "Soup, canned"

V

Vanilla extract:
  (*Virginia Dare*), 1 tsp. 7
  pure (*Durkee*), 1 tsp. 8
  pure (*Ehlers*), 1 tsp. 13
  imitation (*Durkee*), 1 tsp. 3
  imitation (*Gold Medal*), 1 tsp. ....trace
Vanilla puffs:
  frozen (*Rich's*), 2.17-oz. piece 167
Veal, fresh, retail cuts:
  chuck cuts and boneless for stew, lean with fat:
    stewed, with bone, 8.4 oz. (yield from 1 lb. raw) 564
    stewed, without bone, 10.6 oz. (yield from 1 lb. raw) 703
    stewed, without bone, 4 oz. 267
    stewed, without bone, 1 piece (2½″ × 2½″ × ¾″) 200
    stewed, chopped or diced, 1 cup 329
  loin cuts, lean with fat:
    braised or broiled, with bone, 9.5 oz.
      (yield from 1 lb. raw) 629
    braised or broiled, without bone, 11.4 oz.
      (yield from 1 lb. raw) 758
    braised or broiled, without bone, 4 oz. 245
    braised or broiled, without bone,
      1 piece (2½″ × 2½″ × ¾″) 199
    braised or broiled, chopped or diced, 1 cup 328
  plate (breast of veal), lean with fat:
    braised or stewed, with bone, 8.3 oz.
      (yield from 1 lb. raw) 718

braised or stewed, without bone, 10.6 oz.
(yield from 1 lb. raw) 906
braised or stewed, without bone, 4 oz. 344
rib roast, lean with fat:
roasted, with bone, 8.5 oz. (yield from 1 lb. raw) 648
roasted, without bone, 11 oz. (yield from 1 lb. raw) 842
roasted, without bone, 4 oz. 305
roasted, without bone, 2 pieces (4⅛" × 2¼" × ¼") ...229
roasted, chopped or diced, 1 cup 377
roasted, ground, 1 cup 296
round with rump (roasts and leg cutlets), lean with fat:
braised or broiled, with bone, 8.7 oz. (yield from
1 lb. raw) 534
braised or broiled, without bone, 11.3 oz.
(yield from 1 lb. raw) 693
braised or broiled, without bone, 4 oz. 245
braised or broiled, without bone,
1 piece (4⅛" × 2¼" × ½") 184
braised or broiled, chopped or diced, 1 cup 302
Veal, frozen:
breaded, patties (*Pierre*), 3½ oz. 274
breaded, with Italian sauce and Provolone cheese
(*Pierre Veal Golddiggers*), 3.7 oz. 271
breaded, and spaghetti in tomato sauce
(*Swanson TV Brand* Entree), 8¼-oz. pkg. 290
parmigiana, see "Veal parmigiana"
steaks (*Hormel*), 4 oz. 131
steaks, breaded (*Hormel*), 4 oz. 242
Veal parmigiana, frozen:
(*Banquet Cookin' Bag*), 5-oz. pkg. 228
(*Buitoni*), 19-oz. pkg. 767
(*Green Giant* Baked Entree), 7-oz. pkg. 310
(*Morton*), 8 oz. 300
(*Morton* Boil-in-Bag), 5-oz. pkg. 130
with tomato sauce (*Banquet Buffet Suppers*),
32-oz. pkg. 1,563

335

Veal parmigiana dinner, frozen:
(*Banquet*), 11-oz. pkg. 421
(*Morton*), 11-oz. pkg. 250
(*Morton* King Size), 20-oz. pkg. 600
(*Swanson Hungry-Man*), 20½-oz. pkg. 910
(*Swanson TV Brand*), 12¼-oz. pkg. 520
Vegetable chow mein, see "Chow mein"
Vegetable fat or oil, see "Oils, cooking or salad"
Vegetable gelatin, see "Gelatin"
Vegetable juice cocktail, canned:
(*Sacramento* Tomato Plus), 5½ fl. oz. 35
("*V-8*"), 6 fl. oz. 35
spicy hot ("*V-8*"), 6 fl. oz. 35
Vegetable oyster, see "Salsify"
Vegetable salad:
canned, garden (*Hanover*), 4 oz. 65
canned, sweet and sour (*Hanover*), 4 oz. 83
Vegetable soup, see "Soup"
Vegetable stew:
canned (*Dinty Moore*), 7½-oz. can 162
Vegetables, see individual listings
Vegetables, dehydrated:
flakes (*French's*), 1 tbsp. 12
Vegetables, garden:
mix* (*Lipton Lite-Lunch*), 7 fl. oz. 160
Vegetables, mixed (see also "Chinese style," "Japanese style,"
etc.):
canned:
(*Del Monte*), ½ cup 40
(*Hanover*), 4 oz. 45
(*Libby's*), ½ cup 41
(*Stokely-Van Camp*), ½ cup 40
frozen:
(*Birds Eye Americana* New England Style), 3.3 oz. 70

Prepared according to directions on container

(*Birds Eye Americana* New Orleans Creole Style),
  3.3 oz. 70
(*Birds Eye Americana* Pennsylvania Dutch Style),
  3.3 oz. 45
(*Birds Eye Americana* San Francisco Style), 3.3 oz. 50
(*Birds Eye Americana* Wisconsin Country Style),
  3.3 oz. 45
(*Green Giant*), ½ cup 45
(*Hanover*), 3.2 oz. 45
(*Hanover* Country Mixed Vegetables), 3.2 oz. 75
(*Hanover* Garden Fiesta), 3.2 oz. 47
(*Hanover* Garden Medley), 3.2 oz. 29
(*Hanover* Harvest Vegetables), 3.2 oz. 70
(*Hanover* Summer Vegetables), 3.2 oz. 38
(*Kounty Kist/Lindy*), ½ cup 45
(*Stokely-Van Camp*), 3.3 oz. 60
in butter sauce (*Green Giant*), ½ cup 65
international (*Stokely-Van Camp* Vegetables Del Sol),
  3.2 oz. 25
international (*Stokely-Van Camp* Vegetables Grande),
  3.2 oz. 50
international (*Stokely-Van Camp* Vegetables La Cariba),
  3.2 oz. 20
with onion sauce (*Birds Eye*), 2.6 oz. 110
stew (*Birds Eye*), 3.3 oz. 50
stew (*Ore-Ida*), 1½-lb. pkg. 442
stew (*Stokely-Van Camp*), 4 oz. 60
Vegetarian foods, canned and dry:
  "beef":
    sliced (*Worthington*), 2 oz., or 2 slices 110
    bits (*Loma Linda Tender Bits*), approx. 4 pieces 100
    bits (*Worthington Veja-Bits*), approx. ½ cup 70
  burgers and burger granules:
    (*Loma Linda Redi Burger*), ½" slice 129
    (*Loma Linda VegeBurger*), ½ cup 110
    (*Loma Linda VegeBurger NSA*), ½ cup 120
    (*Worthington Vegetarian Burger*), ⅓ cup 130

337

chunks (*Loma Linda VitaBurger*), ¼ cup 70
granules (*Loma Linda VitaBurger*), 3 tbsp. 70
granules (*Worthington Granburger*), 3 tbsp. 65
"chicken":
　　diced (*Worthington Soyameat*), ¼ cup 120
　　fried (*Worthington Fri-Chik Soyameat*), 2 pieces 190
　　fried, with gravy (*Loma Linda*), 2 pieces 210
　　sliced (*Worthington Soyameat*), 2 slices 130
chili (*Worthington*), ½ cup 190
chops (*Worthington Choplets*), 2 slices 100
cold cuts:
　　(*Loma Linda Nuteena*), ½" slice 162
　　(*Loma Linda Proteena*), ½" slice 144
　　(*Loma Linda Vegelona*), ½" slice 100
　　(*Worthington Numete*), ½" slice 160
　　(*Worthington Protose*), ½" slice 190
cutlets (*Worthington Cutlets*), 1½" slice 94
franks (*Loma Linda Big Franks*), 1 frank 100
franks (*Loma Linda Sizzle Franks*), 2 franks 190
(*Loma Linda Dinner Cuts*), 2 cuts 100
(*Loma Linda Savorex*), 1 tbsp. 32
(*Loma Linda Soyagen,* All Purpose), ¼ cup,
　　or 1 cup reconstituted 140
(*Loma Linda Soyagen,* Carob), ¼ cup, or 1 cup
　　reconstituted 140
(*Loma Linda Soyagen,* No Sucrose), ¼ cup,
　　or 1 cup reconstituted 140
links:
　　(*Loma Linda Linketts*), 2 links 180
　　(*Loma Linda Little Links*), 2 links 90
　　(*Worthington Saucettes*), 2 links 130
　　(*Worthington Super Links*), 1 link 120
　　(*Worthington Veja-Links*), 2 links 140
"meat" balls (*Loma Linda Tender Rounds*), 3 pieces 140
"meat" balls (*Worthington Non-Meat Balls*), 3 pieces 120
sandwich spread (*Loma Linda*), 3 tbsp. 70
sandwich spread (*Worthington*), 2½ oz. 120

"scallops" (*Worthington Vegetable Skallops*),
  ½ cup drained 70
soy milk, see "Soybean 'milk' "
stew (*Loma Linda Stew Pac*), 2 oz. 70
"turkey" (*Worthington 209*), 2 slices 150
Vegetarian foods, frozen:
"bacon" strips (*Worthington Stripples*), 4 pieces 100
"beef":
  corned, see "corned 'beef' roll" or "slices," below
  roast (*Loma Linda*), 2 slices 140
  roll (*Worthington*), 2½ oz. 140
  slices (*Worthington Luncheon Slices*), 2 slices 120
  smoked, roll (*Worthington*), 2½ oz. 170
  smoked, slices (*Worthington Luncheon Slices*), 6 slices ... 130
"beef" pot pie (*Worthington*), 8-oz. pie 470
"bologna" (*Loma Linda*), 2 slices 140
"bologna" (*Worthington Bolono*), 2 slices 70
burger (*Loma Linda Sizzle Burger*), 1 piece 200
burger (*Worthington FriPats*), 1 piece 180
"chicken":
  (*Loma Linda*), 2½ oz. 140
  (*Worthington Chic-Ketts*), ½ cup 180
  fried (*Loma Linda*), 1 piece 190
  roll (*Worthington*), 2½ oz. 170
  slices (*Worthington*), 2 slices 140
"chicken" pot pie (*Worthington*), 8-oz. pie 450
corned "beef," roll (*Worthington*), 2½ oz. 190
corned "beef," slices (*Worthington Luncheon Slices*),
  4 slices 160
croquettes (*Worthington Croquettes*), 2 pieces 150
"fish" fillets (*Worthington Vegetarian Fillets*), 2 pieces ... 215
"ham" roll (*Worthington Wham*), 2½ oz. 140
"ham" slices (*Worthington Wham*), 3 slices 140
"meat" balls (*Loma Linda*), 4 pieces 190
"salami" (*Loma Linda*), 2 slices 140
"salami" (*Worthington*), 2 slices 100

"sausage," breakfast style:
  (*Loma Linda*), 3 oz. 210
  links (*Worthington Prosage*), 3 links 180
  patties (*Worthington Prosage*), 2 pieces 200
  roll (*Worthington Prosage*), ⅜" slice 90
"steak" (*Worthington Stakelets*), 1 piece 180
"tuna" (*Worthington Tuno*), 2 oz. 90
"tuna" pot pie (*Worthington*), 8-oz. pie 460
"turkey":
  (*Loma Linda*), 2 slices 120
  smoked, roll (*Worthington*), 2½ oz. 180
  smoked, slices (*Worthington Luncheon Slices*), 4 slices . . . 200
Venison:
  raw, lean meat only, 4 oz. 143
Vermouth wine:
  dry:
    domestic (*Lejon* Extra Dry), 2 fl. oz. 68
    domestic (*Taylor* Extra Dry), 2 fl. oz. 68
    imported (*C & P* Extra Dry), 2 fl. oz. 74
    imported (*Gancia* Dry), 2 fl. oz. 84
    imported (*Noilly Prat* Extra Dry), 2 fl. oz. 68
  sweet:
    domestic (*Lejon*), 2 fl. oz. 88
    domestic (*Taylor*), 2 fl. oz. 88
    imported (*C & P*), 2 fl. oz. 94
    imported (*Gancia* Bianco), 2 fl. oz. 88
    imported (*Gancia* Rosso), 2 fl. oz. 102
    imported (*Noilly Prat*), 2 fl. oz. 86
Vichyssoise, see "Soup, canned"
Vienna sausage, see "Sausages"
Vinegar:
  cider (*Heinz*), 1 tbsp. 3
  distilled, 1 tbsp. 2
  red wine (*Regina*), 1 tbsp. 2
  red wine, with garlic (*Regina*), 1 tbsp. 2
  white (*Heinz*), 1 tbsp. 3
  white wine (*Regina*), 1 tbsp. 2

Vine spinach:
raw, 4 oz. 22
Vodka, see "Liquor, pure distilled"
Vodka, flavored, see individual listings
Vodka martini, see "Martini"
Vodka sour cocktail mix:
instant (*Holland House*), 1 packet 65

W

shelled, chopped or broken kernels, 1 cup 785
shelled, chopped or broken kernels, 1 tbsp. 50
shelled, finely ground, 1 cup 502
English or Persian:
in shell, 1 lb. 1,329
in shell, 10 large nuts 322
shelled, 4 oz. 738
shelled, 1 oz., or 14 halves 185
shelled, halves, 1 cup 651
shelled, chopped, 1 cup 781
shelled, chopped, 1 tbsp. 52
Walnuts, in syrup:
(*Smucker's*), 1 tbsp. 65
Water chestnuts, Chinese:
raw, whole, 1 lb. 276
raw, whole, 8 oz., or 10–14 corms (1¼″ in diam.) 138
raw, peeled, 4 oz. 90
canned (*Chun King*), 4¼ oz. 70
canned (*La Choy*), 4 oz. 33
Watercress, fresh:
whole, with stems, 1 lb. 79
whole, with stems, 1 cup (about 10 sprigs) 7
finely chopped, 1 cup 24
Watermelon, fresh:
whole, with rind, 1 lb. 54
1 wedge, 4″ × 8″ 111
diced, 8 oz. 59
diced, 1 cup 42
Watermelon rind:
pickled (*Crosse & Blackwell*), 1 tbsp. 38
Wax beans, see "Beans, wax"
Weakfish, fresh:
raw, whole, 1 lb. 263
raw, meat only, 4 oz. 138
broiled with butter, 4 oz. 236
Welsh rarebit:
canned (*Snow's*), ½ cup 180

frozen (*Green Giant Toast Toppers*), 5-oz. pkg. 220
frozen (*Stouffer's*), 10-oz. pkg. 710
Western style dinner, frozen:
   (*Banquet*), 11-oz. pkg. 417
   (*Morton*), 11.8-oz. pkg. 400
   (*Swanson Hungry-Man*), 17¾-oz. pkg. 890
   (*Swanson TV Brand*), 11¾-oz. pkg. 460
West Indian cherries, see "Acerolas"
Whale:
   raw, meat only, 4 oz. 177
Wheat, parboiled, see "Bulgur"
Wheat, whole-grain:
   durum, 4 oz. 376
   hard red spring, 4 oz. 374
   hard red winter, 4 oz. 374
   soft red winter, 4 oz. 370
   white, 4 oz. 380
Wheat bran:
   commercial milled, 4 oz. 242
Wheat bread, see "Bread"
Wheat cereal, see "Cereals, cooked" and "Cereals, ready-to-eat"
Wheat crackers, see "Crackers"
Wheat flour, see "Flour"
Wheat germ, crude:
   commercially milled, 4 oz. 412
Wheat germ cereal, see "Cereals, ready-to-eat"
Wheat "nuts":
   (*Pillsbury Wheat Nuts*), 1 oz. 200
Whey:
   dry, 4 oz. 396
   fluid, 8 oz. 59
   fluid, 1 cup 64
Whipped cream topping, see "Cream" and "Cream, nondairy"
Whipping cream, see "Cream"
Whiskey, see "Liquor, pure distilled"
Whiskey sour cocktail:
   (*Calvert*—60 proof), 1 fl. oz. 65

Whiskey sour cocktail mix:
bottled (*Holland House*), 1 fl. oz. 55
instant (*Holland House*), 1 packet 69
(*White Carousel*) wine:
4 fl. oz. 167
Whitefish, lake:
raw, whole, 1 lb. 330
raw, drawn, 1 lb. 359
raw, meat only, 4 oz. 176
smoked, 4 oz. 176
Whitefish, smoked, see "Chubs"
Whiting, see "Kingfish"
White sauce:
mix* (*Durkee*), ½ cup 119
White Tokay wine:
(*Taylor*), 2 fl. oz. 96
Wine, see individual listings
Wine, cooking:
Marsala (*Holland House*), 1 tbsp. 18
red (*Holland House*), 1 tbsp. 13
sauterne (*Regina*), 1 tbsp. 2
sherry (*Holland House*), 1 tbsp. 20
sherry (*Regina*), 1 tbsp. ....trace
white (*Holland House*), 1 tbsp. 13
Worcestershire sauce:
(*Crosse & Blackwell*), 1 tbsp. 15
(*French's*), 1 tbsp. 10
(*Heinz*), 1 tbsp. 11
(*Lea & Perrins*), 1 tbsp. 12
smoky (*French's*), 1 tbsp. 10
Wontons:
frozen (*Royal Dragon*), ⅓-oz. piece 30
Wreckfish:
raw, meat only, 4 oz. 130

*Prepared according to directions on container

Y

Yam beans, tuber:
raw, whole, with skin, 1 lb. 225
raw, pared, 4 oz. 62
Yams, see "Sweet potatoes"
Yams, tuber:
raw, whole, with skin, 1 lb. 394
raw, pared, 4 oz. 115
Yeast, baker's:
compressed, 1 oz. 24
compressed, 1 cake 19
dry, active (*Fleischmann's*), ¼-oz. pkg. 20
dry, active (*Fleischmann's*—in jars), ¼ oz. 20
fresh, active (*Fleischmann's*), .6-oz. pkg. 15
household (*Fleischmann's*), ½ oz. 15
Yeast, brewer's:
dry, 1 oz. 80
dry, 1 tbsp. 23
Yellow plum liqueur:
(*Dolfi* Mirabelle), 1 fl. oz. 78
(*Dolfi* Cordon d'Or Mirabelle), 1 fl. oz. 83
Yellowtail:
raw, meat only, 4 oz. 157
Yogurt and yogurt drinks:
plain:
(*Breyer's*), 8 fl. oz. 160
(*Colombo*), 8 oz. 150
(*Dannon*), 8 fl. oz. 150

(*Foremost*), 8 fl. oz. 150
(*Friendship*), 8 oz. 150
(*Hood Nuform*), 8 oz. 150
(*Yoplait*), 6 oz. 130
apple:
   (*Colombo* Shake), 6 oz. 150
   (*Yoplait*), 6 oz. 190
   crisp (*New Country*), 8 oz. 240
   Dutch (*Dannon*), 8 fl. oz. 260
   spiced (*Colombo*), 8 oz. 240
   spiced (*Hood* Swiss Style), 8 oz. 240
apricot (*Dannon*), 8 fl. oz. 260
apricot (*Foremost*), 8 fl. oz. 250
banana:
   (*Colombo* Sundae Style), 5 oz. 140
   (*Dannon*), 8 fl. oz. 260
   split (*Hood* Firm 'N Fruity), 5 oz. 140
banana-strawberry (*Colombo*), 8 oz. 235
banana-strawberry (*Colombo* Lite Lowfat), 8 oz. 190
blackberry (*Foremost*), 8 fl. oz. 250
blueberry:
   (*Breyer's*), 8 fl. oz. 270
   (*Colombo*), 8 oz. 250
   (*Colombo* Lite Lowfat), 8 oz. 190
   (*Colombo* Sundae Style), 5 oz. 140
   (*Dannon*), 8 fl. oz. 260
   (*Foremost*), 8 fl. oz. 250
   (*Friendship*), 8 oz. 225
   (*Hood* Firm 'N Fruity), 5 oz. 150
   (*Hood* Swiss Style), 8 oz. 230
   (*Meadow Gold* Swiss Style), 8 oz. 245
   (*Meadow Gold* Western Style), 8 oz. 249
   (*Yoplait*), 6 oz. 190
   ripple (*New Country*), 8 oz. 240
boysenberry:
   (*Dannon*), 8 fl. oz. 260

(*Foremost*), 8 fl. oz. 250
(*Meadow Gold* Swiss Style), 8 oz. 245
cherry:
    (*Colombo* Lite Lowfat), 8 oz. 180
    (*Colombo* Shake), 6 oz. 150
    (*Dannon*), 8 fl. oz. 260
    (*Foremost*), 8 fl. oz. 250
    (*Friendship*), 8 oz. 225
    (*Hood* Swiss Style), 8 oz. 250
    (*Yoplait*), 6 oz. 190
    black (*Breyer's*), 8 fl. oz. 270
    black (*Colombo*), 8 oz. 230
    black (*Hood* Firm 'N Fruity), 5 oz. 140
    red (*Colombo* Sundae Style), 5 oz. 140
    supreme (*New Country*), 8 oz. 240
cherry-vanilla (*Colombo*), 8 oz. 250
coffee (*Dannon*), 8 fl. oz. 200
fruit crunch (*New Country*), 8 oz. 240
Hawaiian delight (*Hood* Firm 'N Fruity), 5 oz. 140
Hawaiian salad (*New Country*), 8 oz. 240
honey (*Dannon*), 8 fl. oz. 260
honey-banana (*Colombo*), 8 oz. 220
honey and berries (*New Country*), 8 oz. 240
honey-vanilla (*Colombo* Lite Lowfat) 8 oz. 160
honey-vanilla (*Colombo* Sundae Style), 5 oz. 138
lemon:
    (*Dannon*), 8 fl. oz. 200
    (*Foremost*), 8 fl. oz. 250
    (*Hood* Swiss Style), 8 oz. 270
    (*Yoplait*), 6 oz. 190
    custard (*Colombo*), 8 oz. 220
    ripple (*New Country*), 8 oz. 240
maple nut (*Hood* Firm 'N Fruity), 5 oz. 140
orange:
    (*Dannon*), 8 fl. oz. 200
    (*Foremost* Mandarin Orange), 8 fl. oz. 250

(*Meadow Gold* Western Style), 8 oz. 249
(*Yoplait*), 6 oz. 190
supreme (*New Country*), 8 oz. 240
peach:
(*Colombo* Lite Lowfat), 8 oz. 190
(*Colombo* Sundae Style), 5 oz. 140
(*Foremost*), 8 fl. oz. 250
(*Friendship*), 8 oz. 225
(*Hood* Firm 'N Fruity), 5 oz. 140
(*Hood* Swiss Style), 8 oz. 230
(*Meadow Gold* Western Style), 8 oz. 249
(*Yoplait*), 6 oz. 190
and cream (*New Country*), 8 oz. 240
melba (*Colombo*), 8 oz. 230
melba (*Hood* Firm 'N Fruity), 5 oz. 150
pineapple:
(*Colombo* Lite Lowfat), 8 oz. 190
(*Colombo* Sundae Style), 5 oz. 130
(*Foremost*), 8 fl. oz. 250
(*Meadow Gold* Western Style), 8 oz. 249
pineapple-orange (*Dannon*), 8 fl. oz. 260
raspberry:
(*Colombo*), 8 oz. 250
(*Colombo* Lite Lowfat), 8 oz. 190
(*Colombo* Sundae Style), 5 oz. 140
(*Foremost*), 8 fl. oz. 250
(*Friendship*), 8 oz. 225
(*Hood* Firm 'N Fruity), 5 oz. 140
(*Hood* Swiss Style), 8 oz. 250
(*Meadow Gold* Swiss Style), 8 oz. 245
(*Meadow Gold* Western Style), 8 oz. 249
red (*Dannon*), 8 fl. oz. 260
ripple (*New Country*), 8 oz. 240
strawberry:
(*Breyer's*), 8 fl. oz. 240
(*Colombo*), 8 oz. 230

(*Colombo* Lite Lowfat), 8 oz. 190
(*Colombo* Shake), 6 oz. 150
(*Colombo* Sundae Style), 5 oz. 140
(*Dannon*), 8 fl. oz. 260
(*Foremost*), 8 fl. oz. 250
(*Friendship*), 8 oz. 225
(*Hood* Firm 'N Fruity), 5 oz. 140
(*Hood* Swiss Style), 8 oz. 250
(*Meadow Gold* Swiss Style), 8 oz. 245
(*Meadow Gold* Western Style), 8 oz. 249
(*Naja*), 8 fl. oz. 240
supreme (*New Country*), 8 oz. 240
vanilla:
  (*Dannon*), 8 fl. oz. 200
  (*Yami*), 8 oz. 220
  bean (*Breyer's*), 8 fl. oz. 230
  French, ripple (*New Country*), 8 oz. 240
vanilla-honey (*Colombo*), 8 oz. 220

Yogurt, frozen:
boysenberry (*Danny In-A-Cup*), 8 fl. oz. 210
boysenberry, bar, carob-coated (*Danny On-A-Stick*),
  2½-fl.-oz. bar 140
cherry (*Danny In-A-Cup*), 8 fl. oz. 210
cherry (*Yami Pushups*), 3 fl. oz. 90
(*Danny Parfait*), 4 fl. oz. 160
(*Danny Sampler*), 3 fl. oz. 70
(*Danny-Yo*), 3½ fl. oz. 110
lemon (*Danny In-A-Cup*), 8 fl. oz. 180
lemon-lime (*Yami Pushups*), 3 fl. oz. 90
orange (*Yami Pushups*), 3 fl. oz. 80
peach (*Danny In-A-Cup*), 8 fl. oz. 210
piña colada (*Danny In-A-Cup*), 8 fl. oz. 230
piña colada, bar (*Danny On-A-Stick*), 2½-fl.-oz. bar 70
pineapple-orange (*Danny In-A-Cup*), 8 fl. oz. 210
raspberry:
  (*Yami Pushups*), 3 fl. oz. 90

red (*Danny In-A-Cup*), 8 fl. oz. 210
red (*Sealtest*), 4 fl. oz. 110
red, bar, chocolate-coated (*Danny On-A-Stick*),
    2½-fl.-oz. bar 130
strawberry:
    (*Danny In-A-Cup*), 8 fl. oz. 210
    (*Sealtest*), 4 fl. oz. 110
    (*Yami Pushups*), 3 fl. oz. 80
    bar (*Danny On-A-Stick*), 2½-fl.-oz. bar 70
    bar, chocolate-coated (*Danny On-A-Stick*),
      2½-fl.-oz. bar 130
    with strawberry topping (*Danny Flip*), 5 fl. oz. 180
vanilla:
    (*Danny In-A-Cup*), 8 fl. oz. 180
    (*Sealtest*), 4 fl. oz. 120
    bar (*Danny On-A-Stick*), 2½-fl.-oz. bar 60
    bar, carob-coated (*Danny On-A-Stick*), 2½-fl.-oz. bar 130
    with raspberry topping (*Danny Flip*), 5 fl. oz. 170
Yogurt chips:
    (*Hain*), 1 oz. 144
Yogurt pie, see "Pies, frozen"
Youngberries, see "Blackberries"

Z

Zinfandel wine:
   (*Italian Swiss Colony* Gold Medal), 4 fl. oz. 86
Ziti, frozen:
   baked, in sauce (*Buitoni*), 10½-oz. pkg. 352
   baked, with ricotta and sauce (*Ronzoni*), 18-oz. pkg. 520
   baked, with ricotta and sauce (*Ronzoni* Single Serving),
      8-oz. pkg. 250
Zucchini, see "Squash, summer," "Squash, canned," and
"Squash, frozen"
Zwieback, see "Crackers"